Thinking well is wise; planning well, wiser; doing well wisest and best of all.

*Persian Proverb*

# EDP COSTS AND CHARGES

Prentice-Hall Series in Data Processing Management

Leonard Kraus, Editor

# Finance, Budgets, and Cost Control in Data Processing

**JAMES W. CORTADA**

Prentice-Hall, Inc., Englewood Cliffs, New Jersey 07632

*Library of Congress Cataloging in Publication Data*

Cortada, James W
    EDP costs and charges.

    (Prentice-Hall series in data processing management)
    Bibliography: p. 277
    Includes index.
    1.  Electronic data processing departments—
Costs.    I.  Title.
HF5548.2.C674      658.1'5      79-13820
ISBN 0-13-235655-4

Editorial/production supervision and interior
    design by Gary Samartino
Cover design by Edsal Enterprises
Manufacturing buyer: Gordon Osbourne

EPD Cost and Charges: Finance, Budgets, and Cost Control
    in Data Processing, by James W. Cortada

Printed in the United States of America
10  9  8  7  6  5  4  3  2  1

PRENTICE-HALL INTERNATIONAL, INC., *London*
PRENTICE-HALL OF AUSTRALIA PTY. LIMITED, *Sydney*
PRENTICE-HALL OF CANADA, LTD., *Toronto*
PRENTICE-HALL OF INDIA PRIVATE LIMITED, *New Delhi*
PRENTICE-HALL OF JAPAN, INC., *Tokyo*
PRENTICE-HALL OF SOUTHEAST ASIA PTE. LTD., *Singapore*
WHITEHALL BOOKS LIMITED, *Wellington, New Zealand*

TO DORA

# Contents

# Preface

Companies are spending billions of dollars each year on data processing while not always understanding why there is such a great cost or how to measure its benefits. The need exists for guidance in justifying the acquisition of more technically competent individuals, developing increasingly complex applications, and purchasing or renting larger numbers of computers and related equipment. This book provides advice for both data processing executives and their financial and general management on making business decisions that involve computer technology.

It is my belief that companies spend too much money for the data processing that they already have and not enough for data processing that they need. This book explains how to spend DP dollars more productively.

It shows executives and management, in both general and specific examples, how to improve DP decision making that is relevant to a company's financial situation. For the data processing manager, it describes basic standards that a controller must consider in regard to data processing. For other types of management, the book reveals ways to measure costs and benefits in data processing and explains how some more expensive alternatives will yield greater, long-term benefits.

Because the material is intended for a varied audience, some of it might seem simplified to certain individuals. However, I have found from my experience that there is an incredible lack of basic knowledge in upper management about data processing and its financial justification, and there would be no service done to this area if the opposite were assumed. In order to help the more knowledgeable individual locate relevant topics, the chapters are subtitled and an index is provided.

The first two chapters (intended mainly for the non-DP executive) discuss the issues of data processing trends in general and the difficult problems of applying those currents to short- and long-term planning. They also speak, in specific terms, of relating those developments to the needs and business concerns of a company. The second chapter is especially directed to the data processing management that is weak in the area of planning. The next two chapters deal with the more specific issues of justifying applications in business terms, acquiring programs and equipment, and measuring costs, risks, trends, payback, and benefits.

It is important that your contract negotiations support the financial strategies that you have developed for your data processing; the chapter on contracts (Chapter Five) shows you how. It tells you how to ensure that your legal arrangements will not eventually cost more than you intended. Many fundamental options and their financial implications are described. Both data processing and financial executives make the greatest number of financial and operating errors in the area of contracts because they fail to consider company plans, data processing needs, and technological changes within the industry. This chapter is intended to help people in all levels of management avoid such errors when making acquisition decisions.

Chapter Six describes service bureaus and facilities management as alternatives to using a data processing department within your own company. This issue is an important one because the number of such organizations, already large, is continually growing in size and offerings. Most companies eventually deal with them, regardless of the industry or volume of sales, and they can vary widely in their financial, contractual, and service arrangements.

Budgets, chargeout systems, controls, and accounting affect all companies in regard to data processing. Only recently have formal procedures and research into this subject area led to management involvement with data processing that is equal to its involvement with other departments within the organization. Yet data processing has its unique characteristics. Developing a good DP budget requires that certain considerations be kept in mind that do not always apply to other departments. Also, many data processing managers find that their budgets are not appreciated by non-DP executives. Chapter Seven shows specifically how to create a budget that will be relevant to upper management.

An entire chapter has been devoted to vendors and consultants and a company's relationship to them, defining what can be expected from them and how their activities and knowledge can be channeled to benefit your company's management. Vendors are professionals in their field and often have useful services to offer; but many managers regard vendors as salesmen only and thus allow valuable sources of information and help to go untapped. This chapter clearly defines how management can use vendors to improve investments and increase productivity in data processing.

The sequence of the chapters, in effect, reflects a cycle common to many companies: knowledge of data processing is applied to the needs of the organization; the desired applications are justified; funds are allocated for services, people, software, hardware, and facilities; contracts are signed; and projects are implemented and maintained. To aid the reader, two glossaries have been included, one for financial and accounting terms and the other for DP terms. And as a further aid for continued study of specific points, there is a bibliography, broken down by chapters for easy reference.

In preparing this book, I relied on the advice and comments of data processing, financial, and general management, specialists in the industry, and my colleagues. Although I received much encouragement from my friends within IBM, this book is the product of my work and should in no way be considered an official statement of my employer.

## ACKNOWLEDGEMENTS

Many individuals have been helpful in offering advice and information, critiquing chapters, and being patient with my work. I appreciate their enthusiasm for the project and especially their help. International Data Corporation, IBM Corporation, Share, Inc., and Booz, Allen & Hamilton, Inc. granted me permission to use their copyrighted material for illustrations. Edwin G. Brohm, Account Manager at International Data Corporation, gave me much useful information about the secondhand computer market. Gus Kane and Celeste Gonzalez, both of IBM, made numerous suggestions for improving the manuscript based on their many years of experience. William Curley, Financial Analyst for Keuffel & Esser Company, proved very helpful in developing the chapters on budgets and capital analysis. Paul Becker, of Prentice-Hall, worked closely with me on the development of the book's original outline, while Gary Samartino efficiently moved the manuscript through production into published form. Prentice-Hall was understanding during the book's production as I battled for time to write, work, and live with my family. I especially want to acknowledge the kind patience of my wife, Dora, who once again must have wondered if my typewriter meant more to me than her company. Despite her help and those of many others, there may be weaknesses found in the book; for these I take sole responsibility.

JAMES W. CORTADA

You can't sit on the lid of
progress. If you do, you will be
blown to pieces.

*Henry Kaiser*

*Chapter 1 shows you how changing technology within DP can significantly impact your costs for data processing in hardware, programs, applications, people, and relates them to your company. This chapter will give you the necessary understanding of the industry so that you can keep costs in line, while taking advantage of all new developments. The potential financial advantages of doing this can run into the hundreds of thousands of dollars in small companies and even more in larger firms. The chapter ends with a section on how to relate DP developments to your specific situation.*

# CHAPTER ONE

# Data Processing
# Technology and Trends

Rapid changes of major significance in data processing technology have always affected the economics of DP. All predictions of things to come within the next five to ten years suggest that the changes will be at least as spectacular as in the past. Already users notice evolution specifically in the areas of resale values of older equipment, lower cost per instruction for newer ones, software packages which eliminate the need to write one's own, or the introduction of such improvements as data base to reduce data maintenance expenses. And more is on the way. The ideal situation, when defining financial considerations, is to take into account possible future technological changes in order best to take advantage of them through specific measures in budgets, systems planning, cost justifications, and application development strategies. In considering likely trends, four areas of DP development will be examined briefly—hardware, software, applications, and people—suggesting how these might evolve between now and the next five to ten years. In each case, implications for management will be explored, providing the considerations one must be aware of in making long-range policy decisions and short-term commitments.

As a topic in itself within companies, data processing is growing in importance because of its size. The DP industry in the United States, for example, represents approximately 3% of the Gross National Product, running now into the tens of billions of dollars. Looking at it from the viewpoint of individual businesses, however, in the early 1960s companies might have devoted approximately 0.05% of their sales dollar to data processing services. Today that average is climbing to between 2 and 3% with predictions for the 1980s suggesting the share will grow even more. Another way of measuring growth is to recall that in the mid-1970s approximately 30% of the American work force depended in some form or another on data processing in order to perform their jobs. Industry analysts expect this percentage to climb as high as 70% by the late 1980s as the economy of the industrialized world becomes more service-oriented and we search for more efficient means to conserve declining supplies of raw materials and possibly energy. Moreover, as data processing technology expands its penetration into new areas of applications, and costs decline per unit of work done, the temptation to rely more on computers will be difficult to resist.

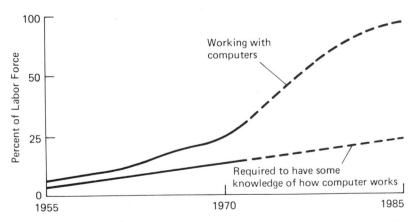

**Figure 1-1**    Growth of dependence on computers. (*Source: Share, Inc.*)

## HARDWARE DEVELOPMENTS

Since the early 1950s, the proportion of a DP budget spent on hardware has steadily declined. The reduction came from approximately 75% of a typical budget down to between 25–45% today and is expected to go down to about 15% by the late 1980s. At the same time, the amount of data processing used rose enormously, accounting for the steady increase in the number of dollars spent on hardware. Looking at it from the point of view of cost per instruction to execute with hardware (leaving expense of software, facilities, and people out), the expenditure dropped dramatically and consistently from the early 1950s to today. As Figure 1–2 indicates, the drop has been impressive. As a dramatic illustration of the change, the retail cost of hand-held calculators dropped approximately 100-fold in the past decade. Yet the number of transitors for storing bits of memory climbed from 500 million in 1960 to approximately one trillion in 1977. And the ones in 1977 are smaller, can handle more, and cost less than earlier examples. The number of components in integrated circuitry usually doubled each year over the past twenty. The cost of direct-access storage during the same period declined 100-fold while the amount available grew by 500 times. What such figures suggest is that the demand for data processing hardware by commercial users has been enormous while simultaneously its cost declined dramatically. All forecasters in the DP industry predict this pattern will continue at a rapid pace well into the 1980s while other observers remind us that traditionally all forecasts of the industry's development and growth have always been far too conservative.

| First Ship New Generation Computer | Cost/Million Instructions |
|---|---|
| 1955 | $40.00 |
| 1961 | 2.00 |
| 1965 | .40 |
| 1971 | .11 |
| 1977 | .08 |
| 1979 | .04 |

**Figure 1–2**   Cost of processing data using IBM hardware. (*Source:* © *IBM Corp.*)

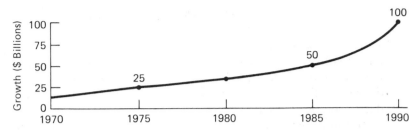

**Figure 1-3**    U.S. DP hardware growth.

## Computers

General-purpose computers, as commonly used in businesses, have enjoyed a continued drop in cost while delivering increased performance
over their history. Measured in a number of different ways, these cost
figures clearly suggest that the trend will continue. In the past twenty
years, the capability of executing a certain number of millions of instructions per second (mip rate) has increased from approximately 20,000
to about five million. Moreover, the speed with which the price of these
instructions per second has declined also increased. Between the early
1950s and the end of 1958, prices fell four-fold per 100,000 instructions
(executions) per second. In the subsequent six years an additional price
reduction of about 20% occurred. From 1964 to 1972, costs fell ten-fold
again. Through the end of 1977, prices dropped an additional three-fold
average across the entire industry for central processing units.

Several technological trends suggest that the steady decline in the
cost of computers will continue throughout the 1980s at a rate similar
to the past, if not even more dramatically. Advances in the development

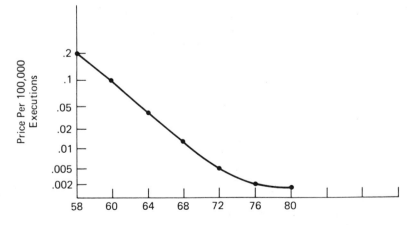

**Figure 1-4**    Computer price performance. (*Source: Adapted from Lecht,
Computer World, Oct. 17, 1977, p. 12.*)

of memory technologies by various firms mean less expensive data storage for computers. Moreover, chip sizes kept growing throughout the 1970s while their prices dropped sharply as supplies increased and manufacturing procedures improved in quality and efficiency. The dramatic inpact of such breakthroughs was clearly reflected in prices. Memory prices dropped by over one third during the 1970s and at present, trends indicate that these kinds of price reductions will continue with current technology during the 1980s, not to mention the added possibilities of follow-on devices. Future storage will include bubble memory with charge-coupled devices and these are expected to drive the cost of computer storage down even further in the early 1980s. Such organizations as the Institute of Computer Science and Technology within the U.S. National Bureau of Standards simply question how dramatic the cost reductions will be rather than whether they are possible.

In recent years, the price/performance benefits visible in large general-purpose computers has been reflected in the rapidly growing mini-computer environment. Throughout the 1970s, prices for such devices and their availability followed a now all-too-familiar pattern. Costs within the last ten years declined nearly 20% in large part because of improved technology of logic circuits and their manufacture. Simultaneously, their speed and quality of performance continued to improve. Higher-density logic chips are now being introduced, which insures that the price for executing instructions will continue its downward trend while providing additional capabilities. These developments are becoming increasingly important, since currently most users of mini-computers are companies with large general-purpose processing computers already installed and thus have the option of selecting the type of computer which is less expensive and more useful for a particular application.

## Disk Storage

Disk storage represents another major source of expenditure for data processing hardware which is also experiencing a dramatic decline in cost with improved speed, capacity, and reliability. Current research is rapidly leading us to the use of fiber optics, lasers, continued refinement of current technologies (especially fixed-pack Winchester devices), and to the production of reliable bubble storage units. Characteristics of the latest generation involve higher density of storage with faster access on both diskettes and disk packs (removable or fixed). Forecasters talk of four-fold increases in capacity per unit of space within a few years. The use of floppy diskettes up to the hundreds concurrently with disk-drive technology will provide increased, inexpensive storage for such peripheral equipment as terminals, printers, and sensing devices while reducing the quantity of cards used. The expanded use of storage will mean greater ability to provide flexible, cost-effective distributive processing away from central host computers for operational levels of a company. Although mass storage devices with 100 to 1000 times greater capacity at large price savings would be consistent with previous historical trends, these would not preclude distributing memory (data) to all parts of a company. In fact, mass storage would provide archival storage capability at central locations which might be too expensive today.

Looking at it in terms of cost per million characters of storage, between 1962 and 1976 the price dropped from about $200 to $2 at a fairly steady rate. Disk capacity per spindle, on the other hand, increased at an even rate during the same period. This provided the benefit of allowing data processing users to increase the amount of online storage at an almost equal rate to cost reductions, experiencing price/performance improvements every several years of three-fold for new or secondhand technology. This went hand in hand with the expansion of online, interactive applications. Industry analysts all suggest that bubble devices, mass storage units, and even faster and more dense tape storage will enjoy substantial price reductions similar to those experienced by computer memory. In fact, since prices have continually dropped each year, justifying many online word processing and office applications will be easier than in the past. In short, the file cabinet as a fixture in the office may become an endangered species going the way of feathered pens and manual typewriters.

Measuring the cost of storage by expense per bit further indicates the kinds of improvement one might expect. Between 1960 and 1980, tape, disk, and fixed-head files dropped in price per bit of storage by approximately ten-fold, which helps account for the great expansion of online and offline (e.g., tape) files now in machine-readable form. The most exciting developments came with disk and diskette storage during the early to mid-1970s. Only computer memory, in the late 1970s, dropped in cost more impressively. Thus where costs of 0.1 cent per bit might have been reasonable to expect at the end of the 1970s, a three-fold decline by the 1980s also seems plausible.

## Printers

The days of the impact printer with their noisy machinery may soon begin to fade into the past. In recent years, impact printing technology has been seriously affected by the introduction of laser printing (such as the IBM 3800 with a rated print speed as high as 13,000 lines per minute) and by ink-jet printing devices. Laser printing effectively incorporates the use of xerographic methods to burn an image at higher speeds than is possible by an impact printer. Ten-fold increases in speed over older devices is normal today as is the expectation that faster units are on the horizon. Ink-jet technology provides better resolution, less noise, faster production and at competitive costs over impact devices. The result is better reliability, less maintenance required, and at reduced costs. Because we are in the early stages of these new generations of devices, industry forecasters are reluctant to suggest what kinds of price reductions one might expect from future printers. However, with the expanded use of online applications using various terminals, the amount of printing may actually decline, particularly as more data is stored on less expensive units rather than in the form of printed reports and files. Such a trend would allow manufacturers to keep the price of printers competitive with impact technology until such time as competition or industry directions dictated otherwise.

## Terminals

A growing part of a data processing department's budget for hardware is for terminals: cathode ray tubes (CRTs), text processing typewriters, sensing devices, data collection units, and remote job entry terminals many with intelligence (programs) and capability of storage. Several trends are clearly visible in this extremely active area.

(1) The variety of specialized terminals will increase (such as devices for retail stores, supermarkets, banks, manufacturing sensing devices, robots) and all at cost-effective prices.

(2) These machines will be more programmable than ever before and have disk or memory available for some data storage, retrieval, and processing away from the host computer.

(3) Many of these devices will have sensing capabilities which will reduce the amount of data input currently done on a keyboard by people. The first signs of the change can be seen in the use of sensing wands and in the application of optics and lasers for data gathering.

(4) CRTs increasingly using gas panel displays will insure higher resolution than is common today, built-in storage and multi-color display of data. Production improvements and the use of less expensive chips will also contribute to substantial cost reductions in the next five years.

The net result: companies can expect a continued demand for terminals from within their organizations which all experts feel shall exceed most forecasts as they double and triple in numbers installed in the industrialized world during the next decade. Currently the number of terminals in technologically advanced countries is growing approximately 25% each year, faster than the DP industry as a whole, and there seems to be no end in sight.

## Telecommunications

Since commercial users have found that by using terminals the power of computers can be placed in any part of the business, much now depends on communication facilities. Yet even here, the cost of doing business is dropping. While computing expenses are declining nearly 25% each year, the cost of communications along telecommunication lines (e.g., telephone lines) is shrinking by an average of about 11% annually. The obvious imbalance caused by having the cost of transporting data become a greater consideration than its usage has led common carriers and leading manufacturers of data processing hardware to compete in this area, to find ways of reducing the cost of transporting information. Several significant developments are well under way as a result.

1. More sophisticated line disciplines are being developed (such as SDLC) which allow a greater amount of data to go down a line at higher baud rates than ever before with fewer control characters. The capability of doubling line speeds has been commercially available for several years and even faster rates are on their way, promising to reduce transmission time and consequently costs. Moreover, the rate of accuracy for transmissions is steadily improving.

2. More efficient use of facilities by multidropping terminals off fewer lines, by means of more sophisticated teleprocessing monitoring software at host and concentrator locations; this reduces the cost of maintaining multiple lines via common carrier. As the capability to support more traffic on a line increases, the number of lines required will drop—unless the demand for telecommunications exceeds performance improvements, which will probably be the case. Also, the cost is declining as the use of optical transmitters becomes more widespread and eliminates the use of metal wires. The long-term effect should be to improve the accuracy of transmissions while reducing costs further.

3. As this book goes to press, commercial telecommunications via satellite are dramatically reducing costs of transporting data while increasing the accuracy of those transmissions. Although the image of a computer having an antenna may seem incongruous, the use of satellite communications is making cost-justifiable applications that call for communicating between continents, across international borders, and around the world. Further, the increased use of teleprocessing, distributed processing, and networks is increasing, all leading to a better use of information among large corporations. Thus applications that, for example, require data transmission from a plant in Germany to a corporate data processing center in the United States become more feasible.

4. As our knowledge about how to develop and evaluate networks

improves with the necessary software monitors, access methods, control units, and simulation packages to help design networks, much of the mystery associated with such projects will go away. This means that executives will find it easier to define more precisely the costs of developing and maintaining networks of increasing complexity and the benefits of such systems. Clearly, much of the application development of the 1980s will require networks using new software and terminals—an area which will profoundly impact the way companies use and accumulate data.

## Post-1985 Technology

Although the further into the future one goes in analyzing technological trends, the less relevant such data becomes for day-to-day business planning, a glance down the road is not unreasonable since much of the post-1985 technology is now in various stages of development in laboratories and will come out at times which the major data processing vendors think appropriate from a marketing and production point of view.

Perhaps the most exciting possibilities come from the Josephson technology which in effect involves the use of memory and logic of incredible speeds operating at the low temperature of liquid helium. Switching speeds are measured in this environment in picoseconds which run 100 times or more faster than contemporary devices. Currently, there are serious considerations for potential manufacturers. We can leave aside the poor field engineer who might get cold repairing such equipment or the operator who has to use it, since technology from the American space program has suggested solutions and ways also to enhance such equipment with proper casing. Marketing considerations suggest that vendors will have to decide if the marketplace is ready for such high-speed technology and when. There is still the problem of developing peripheral devices and software which are compatible with such high-speed computers. Much has yet to be done with lasers and bubble memories in order, for example, to provide balanced systems. Such technologies could also be incorporated in any-size computer or sufficiently advanced device.

A leading analyst of the DP industry, Charles P. Lecht, found after surveying scientists that those familiar with the Josephson technology believe that by the late 1980s, this could provide 10,000 times greater performance than currently is available. Moreover, the cost of a megabyte of storage on a chip might be approximately $30, which is extremely low by today's prices. Eventually we could reach the point where it would take 1000 manhours of programming to give a Josephson computer enough work for less than a second! Obviously, from the viewpoints of cost and performance, data processing hardware has an incredible future ahead.

## Hardware Conclusions

There are approximately nine key factors (trends) which will directly affect DP decisions and their financial ramifications in the very near future, if they are not already doing so now. These considerations grow directly out of current hardware expectations on the part of users and their needs as perceived by manufacturers and industry watchers. Equally important, many of the factors involved are relevant today and have already been identified by executives as having significant implications for budgets and finances. None is inconsistent with the evolution of data processing hardware as outlined above.

1. **Reliability and Availability.** As greater numbers of individuals and more functions of a business become dependent on direct and immediate contact with data processing, management will place greater emphasis on the reliability of the equipment it uses and upon its availability during working hours. To these factors they will be more willing than in the past to assign dollar values. Thus, for example, companies will attempt (as they do now) to answer such questions as how many sales does it cost if the data processing system is out of operation when my entire order entry process is done by way of terminals? How many times each year and for how long can the company afford to tolerate "down time" without losing customers to competition? What does it cost if a bill of material or MRP run is not made and a plant full of workers cannot manufacture a product?

2. **Increased Computer Power.** As we become more dependent on data processing applications, the number of general-purpose and specialized computers which are large, small, or mini will multiply, requiring greater concern for such factors as security, backup, compatibility, communications among computers, consistency of data and applications, auditability, and of course, cost. It is estimated by various analysts that by the mid-1980s there might well exist over 175,000 major general-purpose computer systems such as commercial users have today. Mini-computers are expected to far exceed that number. Such numbers suggest that mini-systems might quickly outnumber general-purpose systems by many times and perhaps provide a 1000-fold increase in the amount of data processing power available over the quantity installed during the late 1970s. Businesses will require that systems talk to each other and serve as backup for inoperative or overworked systems in the future, all in order to provide continued service in an environment more dependent on data processing than ever before.

3. **Improved Cost Performance of Storage.** As we have suggested,

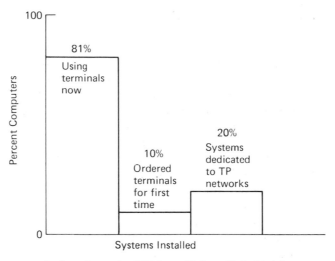

Projected growth:  35% in traffic/year (A.D. Little)

**Figure 1-5**   Computer systems using telecommunications. (*Source:* Guide.)

the cost of storing data and then using it will continue to spiral downward as new technological developments coupled with increased manufacturing efficiencies are introduced. Again, by the mid- to late 1980s, one is talking in terms of a 1000-fold or better increase in price performance. The entire data processing industry is absolutely convinced of this more than on any other subject. The technologies to make this happen are now in the development laboratories and with the larger DP vendors, the issue is now more one of market timing than "can we do it?" Thus, financial questions in the future will turn more on the idea of data being a company's resource to be controlled, expensed, capitalized, and used to provide better, faster, and less costly services. What is often overlooked is the fact that throughout the history of data processing, quantum, not linear, jumps in the demand for data in machine-readable form has been the norm and always in more reliable hardware. That is to say, the amount of data that people have found financially useful has grown stupendously in geometric fashion and not slowly over a long period of time. Thus, for one to consider quantum jumps in the forecasted need for computer or data storage requirements is normal; but, it is a pattern often forgotten by data processing management. With the price per byte of data dropping, this fundamental fact should be remembered when cost-justifying potentially large applications and in developing long-term capacity strategies. Invariably, new levels of payback are always around the corner.

**4.   Increased Use of Microcode.**    As time passes, more manufacturers of computers will package, as part of the hardware, programming which is prewritten at the plant. This will be done in part, no doubt, to discourage competitive hang-on software and hardware, but mainly because of the efficiencies or performance and speed gained on the one hand, and the reduction in user costs of programming on the other. Such capabilities are already visible in wide areas of the economy in such products as microwave ovens with many functions built in, hand-held calculators with more capabilities than mechanical adding machines, self-tuning automobile motors; and, within data processing, virtual-machine-assist capabilities. In years to come, one might expect auditing, job control, operating systems, teleprocessing monitors, and even data base code to be incorporated into microcode which would come with the computer regardless of size. This will mean that there may be a greater number of stand-alone computers for specific applications which are extremely inexpensive (e.g., to control a paper-making machine or to assist in shop floor control in the manufacture of automobiles). From a broad data processing point of view, paging, data editing activities, data access, interrupt functions, and even system control programming will be in microcode, thus reducing the maintenance of such code by a user and providing increased ease of installation and operation. The resulting ease of use (although not necessarily of maintenance for the vendor) will allow for greater concentration of time and resources by a company on application development and less on "household" functions.

5.  **Improved Terminal Cost and Performance.**   As suggested earlier, terminals will come down in cost, be more reliable, varied, useful, and visible in the affairs of business organizations. They will incorporate a greater number of automatic data compression, transmission, and text production features with simultaneous expansion of memory and software. Modems will come more under the covers of terminals and correspondingly have greater error detection and self-correcting features. This will improve performance and availability. All analysts of the DP industry agree that the number of terminals will grow exponentially and in variety. Graphic output along with traditional textual printouts will be more common along with optical character recognition (OCR) devices. We are still too far away from voice input gadgets to take them very seriously although a few are being marketed today. It is the feeling of some specialists that hard-copy terminals will cost about twice as much as typewriters but that CRT devices will be about the same as a home portable color television set. In either instance, it means a dramatic reduction in the cost of hard-copy and CRT terminals over current rental and purchase prices. This in turn will encourage the development of online, interactive applications which might today be marginally justifiable.

6.  **Software Will Increase as Percentage of Cost.**   Cost justification of

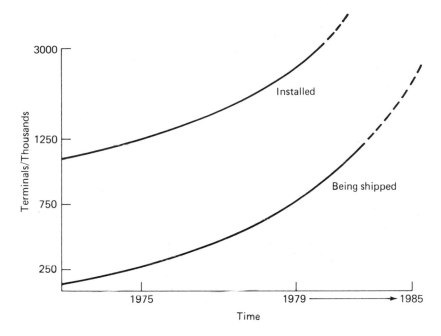

**Figure 1-6**    Demand for terminals (U.S.A.).

applications will tend to concentrate increasingly on the expenses and benefits of application code, software packages, and their maintenance. Increasingly less stress will be placed on the cost/benefits of specific pieces of hardware. More often today, questions are being asked about the quality and quantity of application code and less about terminals, disks, and computers. Thus a greater emphasis has to be placed on the economics of software's expense, capitalization, useful application life and consequently depreciation, benefits, tax implications, and data as a resource and an asset manipulated by various standards, each with its cost/benefit ratios identified. As the next few years go by, DP and financial executives have to develop relevant standards to judge what in many cases is today an unknown area of DP expense and attach values and criteria for performance. In short, software will become a more important topic of conversation among businessmen than it is today.

**7.   Faster, Better, More Complex Teleprocessing.**    Modems, control units, TP controllers, channels, concentrators, lines, satellite stations are becoming more varied, available, accurate, and less expensive. Simultaneously they are being used more, leading to an anticipated greater expenditure in dollars. Better-performing devices and disciplines will mean expanded availability and reliability. Transmission rates will increase, thus making transmissions of vast quantities of data more feasible. Baud rates of 1200 to over 9000 (common today) may readily jump to averages closer to 50,000. Major producers of teleprocessing equipment forecast expense drops of transmissions of ten-fold over the next decade, running parallel to significant cost declines for terminals and modems as well. Those users transmitting large quantities of data from few locations may benefit most since they would require less in the way of editing, line disciplinary controls, and terminals to carry out their operations than those users with larger numbers of small data sets at numerous locations who are competing for access to a telecommunication system. Yet for either environment, the cost of transmitting a byte of data is expected to fall while the facilities to develop more accurate, cost-effective, and available networks will increase. Already, predicting costs and performance of TP networks prior to installation is becoming common. In the next few years the accuracy of these simulations will improve with better modeling packages.

The percentage of transmission errors will continue to decline as increasing numbers of signals carried on telephone and space communications are digitized. Current problems regarding software controls, line disciplines, protocols, networking, and hardware interfacing are being overcome. The DP industry is simply learning more today than ever before about telecommunications and about how to fine-tune existing networks. For a commercial organization, this means the cost and risk of teleprocessing will decline, making interactive applications more attractive than they already are today.

**8.  Increased Online Storage Due to DB/DC.**    Although more will be said about data base and data communication software developments later on, their convenience and improved cost justification mean that increased amounts of online storage will have to be made available for applications requiring interactive communication with direct-access files. Such uses include inquiries, updating of files, and modeling among other functions for vital day-to-day business activities. As technological improvements in storage mediums reduce costs compared to current devices, companies will provide more storage capability for data in machine-readable form. Improved reliability of these devices will help insure the security and viability of data which, because of its cost and relevance, will increasingly be considered as a company asset to be protected with the same accounting and managerial tools as are people, buildings, machines, and trade secrets.

**9.  Hardware Costs Will Increase, But Will Decrease as Percent of DP Budget.**    The consensus of opinion throughout the DP industry is that as a percent of a DP budget, hardware costs will decline. The drop will be between 10% and 20% while the actual expenditure of dollars for more equipment will increase, perhaps even doubling 1977's figures by the mid-1980s. Thus by extrapolation, one could reasonably conclude that total DP budgets would really quadruple by the middle of the 1980s and thereby take a greater chunk of a company's overall budget, possibly doubling over today's percentages. Obviously, the percent of the DP hardware dollar going toward telecommunication costs (terminals, control units, modems) will increase dramatically. Some industry analysts suggest the percentage growing to nearly 40% or more of a DP hardware budget. Put another way, many manufacturers of data processing equipment expect that between 50% and 85% of their revenues in the mid-1980s will be derived from the sale of teleprocessing equipment and are planning their product and marketing strategies accordingly. In turn, the expansion of data base applications, which imply some form of centralized data processing, will encourage teleprocessing until such time as data base conveniences can be effectively, conveniently, and inexpensively dispersed within a network of "distributive processing." This further suggests systems with intelligence and function scattered about the network at operational levels of a company and later at mid-level areas of tactical management—eventualities which still require much fundamental research and development.

The trends already existing when extrapolated into the immediate future suggest that DP and financial executives will have to pay more attention to the costs of software than hardware. Second, they must remember that their center of discussion has to take into account those factors whose costs are growing more rapidly than the number of "boxes" installed. It is therefore to software that we must turn to next for a definition of trends having financial significance.

## SOFTWARE DEVELOPMENTS

In defining software, we find there are basically two types. First are those programs which serve the computer system in general, such as systems control programs (SCPs), teleprocessing monitors, data base control code, sort/merges, and compilers. Second, there are programs which are directly related to some particular application, for example, payroll or accounts receivable. The first are usually purchased packages written by vendors. The second group, although this includes many commercially available packages, contains close to all programs written by commercial users of data processing. Many of the trends regarding application code will be discussed in the next section of this chapter on application developments. The remarks below are primarily aimed at system software because developments in this area, when tied to those in hardware, profoundly influence the nature and cost of applications.

The DP industry as a whole has several general objectives in regard to the evolution of current system software. Improvements are sought in increased function, easier use, and better recovery and error-detection capabilities. These in turn reduce the cost of maintenance of a system's software at a time when the expense of "system" personnel is increasing faster than for any other group of DP personnel. Also, increased automation in the use of system software is coming along with changes designed to reduce the time and cost involved in application development. Simultaneously, a further integration of systems, applications, and data bases to provide more capability for online, interactive transaction driven applications is clearly on the way. Since such software will probably come in pieces and phases over a number of years, increased emulation of currently existing programs will make conversion to newer programs and languages a vital necessity. They will be done easier and less expensively than in the past.

Within the next five to eight years, system code will be enhanced to handle larger volumes of transactions and data, and in an interactive environment. Device independence from system and application code is becoming more common, thus saving on the cost of operations. Protocols for data accessing will decline in complexity, thus making larger amounts of machine-readable information available for increasing numbers of users with appropriate security features a part of these systems. Computer languages for users will become more English-like, less technical, increasingly uniform, and will also be used by programmers in greater numbers than ever before. The net result will be to allow more non-DP personnel to program and use computers without having to go through a data processing department and experience the current bottleneck of not getting more applications than a technical staff can produce. Future data processing professionals will increasingly break away from working with programs at machine-level languages and will instead, write and compile their programs in the language they were written in at a higher level, using such forms as COBOL, PL/1, Basic, or APL. For a company, this means less dependency on programmers.

In the previous section, reference was made to microcode or programs being, in fact, part of the hardware. SCPs and possibly data base code are prime targets for such evolution which means that many data processing personnel would never have to intervene directly with system code. Moreover, application code would deal directly with microcode, suggesting less interfacing with DP. This would reduce the costs of maintenance by shrinking the dollars currently spent working on systems code. The savings, risk of down times and programming failures, not to mention improved operating systems and speed, suggest that application code will reach the level of production much faster than today.

The number of dollars expended on software and hardware in absolute terms will definitely increase. With improvements in software at the same time, the cost of data processing staff will come under greater control since the number of such professionals required to run a computerized system will be contained. Specifically, one would expect to obtain savings in the number of persons needed in the following areas:

- Computer operations
- Data entry
- Application design
- Programming
- System and application maintenance (which may account from 40% to 75% of today's programming activities)
- Personnel dedicated to conversions (related to maintenance and particularly relevant in companies with multiple systems being standardized, e.g., DOS to OS or MVS conversions).

Today, substantial costs of using software are generated from: poor application design, bad coding, unreliability of some expensive packages, requirements that users have detailed knowledge of software, expense of writing programs using programmers, too many software interfaces for file management, languages, recoverability, and, lastly, time that a system is down either because of software or hardware problems thus placing people directly dependent on computers in the frustrating circumstance of not being able to do their jobs. To counteract many of these problems, designers of new software are striving for:

- Reduced operating costs through greater automation of systems
- Increased reliability with backup and fast recovery procedures all automated
- Reduction of cost and time required for conversions which currently threaten to reduce availability of hardware and applications during changeovers
- Easier programming languages and testing of code to encourage non-DP personnel to write their own applications quickly
- More features and capability for data base systems to increase the volume of data usage and make DP operations cost-effective and easy
- Greater system availability by providing more reliable hardware, software, and microcode. SCPs are a prime target since these must work at improved levels to support the better hardware on the way; otherwise, optimal use of new devices will not really be possible.

Closely related to this type of evolution in software are the programs currently written for specific applications. Today system development is predicated on demand for four types of DP activity which have evolved and grown dramatically within the past five years:

(1)   Online applications involving data inquiry, update, and interaction, using data base disciplines which provide faster access to up-to-date information. Airline reservation systems were an early example.

(2)   Online application development involving programming and corrections and alterations via a terminal, thus reducing many of the old bottlenecks associated with batch environments. Increased productivity per programmer and ease of maintenance are the clearly definable benefits of such systems.

(3)   Data telecommunications between terminals and data centers via telephone lines and satellites for batch and online applications. Benefits include reduction in the number of data processing centers, redundancy of hardware and personnel costs, more effective use of integrated data bases, and greater corporate control of operations and information.

(4)   Multiprocessing of online and batch jobs within systems providing for more work being handled simultaneously per unit of time. Users can expect faster turn-around on jobs, reduced requirement for multiple data processing facilities, and currently updated files.

## Data Base Trends

Because the expansion of data base systems represents one of the most important current developments within DP, it deserves special attention. In the past ten years, the number of companies developing online applications has grown enormously. Today, most data processing shops support some sort of an interactive system because, among other reasons, online function provides the capability for:

- Improved customer service, translating into a favorable competitive edge for the company
- Increased productivity of various personnel throughout the organization
- Reduction or elimination of costly and slow manual operations that are expensive because of the personnel required and the errors involved
- Better quality decision making through the availability of relevant data on a timely basis for multiple levels of management.

Managers have clearly seen that the costs of people go up faster than for hardware or software. Moreover, computer technology does not go on vacation, take coffee breaks, or go on strike. The computer's only common feature with people is that it too breaks down and gets sick (although less often), and even then reliability is steadily improving.

In recent years, concern has been evident over the enormous increase in the quantity of data which is tied to specific programs, applications, files, and which may be redundant, never up-to-date, and unwieldy to work with. Thus a customer name and address file, for instance, might exist throughout the company a dozen times over with the odds of all twelve copies being accurate and the same concurrently becoming a problem. Online applications have clearly sold themselves, making the question of data management an important issue in cost control and in preserving the integrity of information—a genuine company asset. Increasingly, therefore, the issue of having a data base management system with its investment of dollars and manpower is one of significant financial concern and worth discussing.

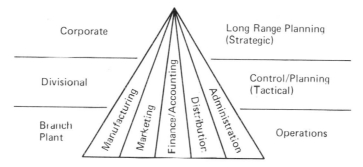

**Figure 1-7**  Data usage requirement.

There is a rapidly increasing demand for computerized data by all groups in a company and at all levels. In response, the growth in the quantity of information in machine-readable form has been so great that an increasing amount of effort is spent maintaining it and the programs to which such data is attached. This "housekeeping" activity has consequently raised the cost of preserving and improving applications. It is widely believed within the data processing community that the cost of maintenance of an application throughout its life is easily twice that of its original development. Therefore, there is a substantial reason to try and reduce the expense of maintenance so that costly labor can be freed for use in other areas. An examination of a pie graph for a typical data processing shop suggests that only about 30% of the budget is available for new application development. An average data processing department easily expends half of that on maintenance, leaving in effect, 15% for new applications. In other words, a large amount of programming

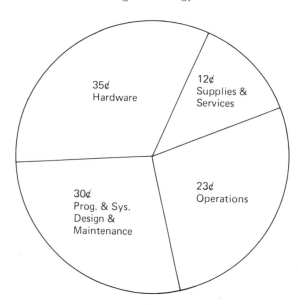

**Figure 1-8**    Data processing dollar.

resources is spent changing files, correcting them, cleaning out "bugs" in programs, and making changes to reflect a company's current needs. This type of activity costs the typical company considerably in lost benefits which cannot be realized from applications that could have been developed if less maintenance were required on existing programs and files. Moreover, working under the handicap of heavy maintenance responsibilities insures that any new project will require a longer period of time for completion, which means that the program will be subject to a greater number of expensive changes during development—all of this costing in man-hours needed and in time lost before a payback is realized. The data processing industry is recognizing that one way to reduce maintenance is to separate the data from the programs which use it. This then allows less highly paid programmers to work on new applications faster since they would not always have to work with file structures. As for maintenance, work may be done either on a file or on a program without disturbing the other—all of which saves time and money.

Programming in a data base environment means that redundant data can be reduced since fewer copies of the same information are needed, less effort is expended to maintain those files, storage capacity is more effectively utilized, and operational and development burdens are lightened. There is the requirement for a data base file manager (a software package), such as DL/1 or Total, illustrating the classic rule that it is less expensive to use software than people. Because of the increasing cost of maintaining existing applications, the growth of data base shops is expected to continue and at an accelerated pace, by most analysts of the DP industry. Moreover, it is consistent with software developments in which integrated files that can be shared by various programs and applications become a prerequisite. Thus the needs of commercial and scientific users on the one hand, and the software strategies of data processing vendors on the other, are jointly continuing the expansion of data bases, especially when they involve online applications.

Discussions regarding cost justification for the initial introduction of data base systems and subsequently a monitoring of costs against anticipated benefits, should include such factors as:

- Improved programmer productivity
- Faster application development
- Reduction of data redundancy along with disk for pre-DB files
- Increased responsiveness to change and maintenance of applications and files.

Data processing vendors and users are increasingly expecting such systems to provide benefits by:

- DB monitors doing increased amounts of routine maintenance previously done by programmers
- Offering facilities which might otherwise have to be developed internally thus duplicating the work done in other shops
- Making growth in the types and quantities of data and applications easier and faster.

Management will continue to find, as it does today, that the establishment of a data base environment takes their data processing one step closer to a fully integrated resource of information, providing the organization with sufficient details needed at each level. Obviously, data base will not solve all problems and bring the ideal environment of all information to all persons, but it is a step in the right direction. Its importance lies in the fact that data can increasingly be made available in greater quantities on a timely basis to operational management. It also allows for rapid and more accurate consolidations of such details into meaningful forms for higher levels of management more concerned with tactical and strategic questions. Thus data can move up and down the organizational structure in relevant forms at costs which are justifiable. In effect then, the fundamental justification for the cost and considerable effort of moving into a data base environment will continue to be the benefits which management feels it gains by having information which is useful to its particular level when it is needed.

## System Control and Audits

Data base environments, with their centralized approach to information storage, clearly raise questions concerning security and auditability. But other factors are also at work. As the number of applications and the amount of dependency on data processing increases, the requirement to monitor data processing constantly in a formal fashion will become more imperative. And, with numerous laws being passed to protect the privacy of individuals and to provide government agencies with various types of data regarding personnel, products, and finances and budgets, there may well be legal requirements to audit packages which have been purchased. Moreover, the same requirements may be imposed on programs and data which are developed within the company. If proper checks and common sense are not used, exposure to loss increases proportionally as activities which could once be verified manually are now checked by other programs reacting to applications and data that have been computerized. Yet there has been less study done on data processing auditing than on controls in other areas of a company's activities. Sufficient thought for backup procedures, should a data processing center be damaged or the data it is responsible for lost, is an issue only now attracting wide attention. Moreover, to improve the quality of new applications and to measure that of application packages, an audit function is essential. Such a function thus does and will continue to find easy financial justification and deserves to be associated either with corporate DP groups or with their steering committees composed of high divisional or corporate management people not necessarily having data processing backgrounds. The important thing to remember is that some form of systematic documentation and control over the flow of data within a company must exist.

We may readily assume that auditing will increase in the areas of computerized application systems and programs, systems development, and computer services. Questions raised will concern the cost of development and maintenance versus other means and solutions, the existence of audit trails throughout an application and the relative costs to protect privacy, improving accuracy, reducing the opportunity for embezzlement, procedures for documentation, backup, recovery, and accounting control. Auditors increasingly have data processing backgrounds and thus are able to participate in the efficient design of applications and in monitoring their growth to measure actual against projected costs. Without such an audit function, cost control would be impossible. Data processing personnel cannot be expected to police fully their area nor should non-DP managers be expected to do more than provide their sincere interest and commitment to controls. Individuals with DP knowledge, reporting to managers outside of data processing, will have to provide the close supervision required to insure that the costs of current and new applications are planned, understood, and adhered to in a reasonable fashion. Increasingly, therefore, such an auditor will contribute to the costing of systems, their control during development, and ultimately the test of their benefits.

## Software Conclusions

In summary, a variety of issues will continue to impact directly on the expenses and benefits of software in years to come, with significant effects on cost controls and justification of applications. Some of the trends are clearly definable and apparent in the business community today, others (e.g., detailed audit trails) are only just now becoming significant for most companies. Such trends in the area of software include:

1. **Shorter Development Time.**    There is a trend toward developing programs quicker and easier through the use of higher-level languages, packaged programs, online maintenance and programming, and pre-generated operating systems supplied by computer vendors. The time it takes to identify potential applications will continue to decrease as the data processing industry collectively gains more experience in automated systems and spreads this knowledge within itself. Thus one could expect to identify and implement packages in a shorter period of time and thus enjoy a return on that benefit earlier.

2. **Costs as a Percentage of DP Budgets Will Rise.**    A recent Diebold study of expenditure patterns for information systems indicated that approximately 30% of a data processing budget was being taken up by new systems development as a national average in the United States. All industry analysts feel that, as the percentage of budget dollars declines for hardware, an increasing proportion will go toward people and software costs. The amount of money for software will increase in gross and percentage amounts with a large part of the application dollar being eaten up by the costs of a personnel. As that factor rises faster than hardware or software costs, companies will attempt to use more software and higher-level languages, particularly by non-DP personnel, in an attempt to hold down the costs of application development.

3. **Better Service and Predictability.**    The quality of commercially acquired software and home-grown code is expected to improve with time for several important reasons. First, an industry-wide attempt is being made to change programming from an art to a science through such methods as modular programming, HIPO, and more detailed documentation and walk-throughs. This reduces dependency on individual

programmers while introducing controls and parameters around the development costs for applications. Second, higher-level languages are being used more today which allows for a nearly English-like coding of applications with further refinement always in development. Third, the competitive nature of commercial software is forcing vendors to produce better packages than ten or fifteen years ago and at a time when more is known about programming. Fourth, predictability of what software can do will simultaneously improve as tools are refined for simulation of applications, teleprocessing networks, and software traffic. Many of these aids are now in wide use and will simply be used by more companies in the years to come. This trend will directly help quantify the costs and benefits of applications, particularly the development expenses involved. Better service and predictability, in short, allow managers to increase the number of nondata processing personnel able to use the computer as a tool while augmenting a company's ability to control some of the unknown or hidden costs previously undefinable.

4. **Maintenance Costs Decline.** It is widely believed, and studies often prove, that twice the amount of money is spent on the maintenance of an application throughout its life than in its original cost of development. Such conventional folk wisdom takes into account inflation, overruns in time required to write the application, the costs of modifying the original to meet the evolving needs of users, and Murphy's Law of Random Perversity which assumes that anything that can go wrong will. Because the data processing industry as a whole is gaining greater control over the development of applications and software along with its maintenance, there is real reason to hope that the cost of maintaining programs will decline as a percentage of overall software expenses. Changes, errors, improvements, and deletions will increasingly be applied by nontechnical individuals or in data processing shops through the use of such tools as online program debug and maintenance software. Thus the hard cash outlays for maintenance saved can then be applied to other projects or be diverted to different parts of a company's budget.

5. **Data Base Expansion.** It is argued by many that the development of data base systems will encourage the centralization of files for purposes of easier access and maintenance until such time as the physical distribution of data through distributive processing is better understood in terms which are financially acceptable to commercial users. The savings in reduced errors, redundancy of files, and separation of programs from data maintenance will simply encourage data processing departments to move into data base environments. This becomes especially important as the amount of information that must be maintained for online systems increases. It is conservatively estimated that within the next five to ten

years, the amount of information preserved in data base environments will expand at least ten-fold, clearly indicating that new application development should take into account the possibility of reduced costs of maintenance if rewritten to a data base mode. The money saved in possible development and maintenance costs should continue to be a welcome trend as the expense of personnel, redundancy of data, and the press for improved customer service through more accurate files increases.

**6. Legal Requirements Increasing.** There is growing speculation that the amount and nature of software documentation will increase directly as a result of governmental regulations and laws. One could expect these rules to grow in number from such agencies as the SEC, IRS, and scientific commissions and regulatory bodies. Close behind these one should expect state laws. From the point of view of auditability, this trend is already evident. As software expenditures rise as a percentage of total cash spent, one might expect costs to be capitalized. Yet this is a subject not really understood. Currently software development costs are met either through operating leases or by outright purchases; thus capitalization would impose stricter standards on measurement, return on investment (ROI), payback, and project management than is currently the case. Such questions as "Do I buy code or write my own?" will increasingly be subject to the same sort of analysis as is a purchase vs. lease study of a piece of hardware today. Even the subject of what constitutes costs (because of tax and balance sheet considerations) will continue to undergo substantial study particularly in charge-back systems, but more on this point in later chapters.

## APPLICATION DEVELOPMENTS

Of the three major areas discussed so far (hardware, software, and now applications) the one most directly affected by commercial users is that of applications. While vendors, industry analysts, and others will urge the development of this or that application, only users of data processing services can and will determine which are worth developing. The variety of possible applications is based on the simple fact that users are at various levels of sophistication, with even more companies than ever beginning to use data processing services. Furthermore, no two companies have the exact same needs or priorities, as would be reflected in their data processing applications. One can expect that in years to come applications will continue to vary widely from batch accounting work designed simply to reduce labor costs to highly complex teleprocessing simulation studies for modeling of companies on a nationwide system. Transference of information from one end of a computer room to the other will exist along with the demand in other organizations that data be available to wide sectors of a company via satellite communications. In short, the variation will be more diverse and unique as more technical options are made available to companies.

If one accepts the consensus among DP industry specialists that the amount of money spent on information systems will more than double between 1975 and 1985 (a pattern borne out by past experience), then clearly, in the future, companies will use data processing in a variety of ways many of which may not be apparent to us today. Thus traditional areas of data processing—accounting, data collection, bill of materials, work in process, inventory, distribution, order entry, payroll, and general ledger—will grow in number and complexity from batch to online interactive, side by side with programs unique to each industry. This may well involve modeling, simulation applications using data bases, distributive processing, interactive teleprocessing, and multiple languages, on a multinational scale. As the cost of data processing changes, one might expect

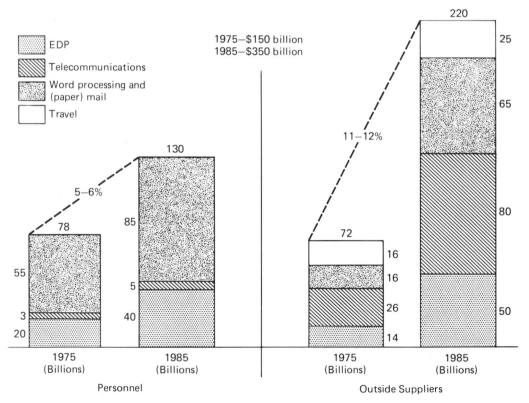

**Figure 1-9** What U.S. organizations spend on information sources. (*Source: Booz, Allen and Hamilton.*)

that applications which were not cost-justifiable in the past might be tomorrow (e.g., where the expense of terminals has to come down or that of a TP monitor shared with multiple applications). Moreover, as hardware costs decline, the use of microprocessors will, in conjunction with rented or purchased accounting packages, become increasingly attractive to companies with annual sales of less than $1 million.

## Centralization versus Decentralization

Perhaps one of the biggest arguments today raging within the data processing industry and simultaneously in the offices of companies that use data processing, is the issue of centralization of DP services versus decentralization. The discussion as an issue has such profound implications for the costs and manner of application development on the one hand, and their use in a company on the other hand, that its financial ramifications must be explored in some detail. Moreover, almost every technical development within data processing in the immediate future takes into account many of the positive factors discussed below. Before reviewing them, let us take as our general definition of the issue the term centralization to mean the processing of information at one or more centers which have large computers and which feed out to remote locations either by mail or terminals. Then, for purposes of discussion, we consider decentralization as the processing of data at remote locations, either by intelligent terminals or smaller computers, and the transmittal of this processed data back to a central site. Obviously the loose definitions just given suggest that even the terms are not fully understood by data processing personnel. Yet these definitions allow the reader to measure the value of the arguments below against the needs in his company and the environment which exists.

## Advantages of Centralization

In discussions of centralization, reference is usually made to the pooling of personnel resources, hardware into one major data center, management of data processing from a single point, and accounting from the same source in any combination of the above. The main advantages cited for centralization include:

- Applications can be developed in a uniform manner for use throughout the company thus forcing standardization and control.
- Design control can be maintained, thus preventing duplicate versions of an application from multiplying through various expenditures of manpower, management, and hardware.
- Larger or wider use of applications often result in cost savings in

centralized shops and made more affordable packages by distributing their costs and justification over a larger portion of a company.

- Greater programming productivity is possible through concentrating a "critical mass" of talent, programming power (people and hardware). Maintenance is simplified by a global approach with much the same justification as with centralized application development.

- Economies of scale are possible with large centralized facilities which reduce the need for multiple DP staffs, space, hardware, and software.

- Management is easier with all major resources at hand for coordinated and productive use, reducing costly inefficiencies.

- Data base developments lend themselves to centralized shops with reduced costs of maintenance, centralized data available to various levels of the organization, and responsiveness to top management's needs and goals.

- Users have access to multiple applications and resources that might otherwise not be available, e.g., greater computer power for modeling and data sharing.

- Users can concentrate on application development and usage and less on hardware and operating software considerations, which are best left to the critical mass of experts at a central site.

- Greater availability is often cited as an advantage because with larger systems, there is often more hardware redundancy for backup, more sophisticated software recovery capabilities, retry techniques, and personnel from both a company and its DP vendors to help insure that systems will be available to all users.

- Physical and software security increasingly is cited as a real benefit of centralization through guarded data centers, passwords, corporate control of access to data and applications, hardware locks, and management controls.

- Long-range planning allows for maximum optimization of hardware, software, and applications for substantial cost-effectivness and benefits to the company as a whole, with evolution of applications and hardware resulting from economies of scale, price/performance changes, and company-wide planning.

- A company's return on investment in a centralized DP shop is often more substantial than from individual data centers, since incremental increases in hardware can be absorbed along with a substantial amount of personnel costs. Without sudden changes in either workload on people or hardware, increased expenses are often less than in smaller-scale shops.

- Politics dictate in some cases that corporate locations will have their own data centers or because there is an empire builder in top management who believes a DP location under his control will help him achieve his personal objectives.

## Advantages of Decentralization

Those who advocate a decentralized approach can marshal an equally impressive array of arguments to justify their position:

- Applications can be developed to meet a specific company's needs, thus allowing local management to compete and operate more wisely.

- Design and implementation can be done without additional layers of management being involved, levels which may be thousands of miles away, unaware of particular situations, and thus not sensitive to local conditions.

- The cost of hardware and software might be lower and hence more manageable locally, rather than going to a centralized data center with its "arbitrary" charge-outs or "monopolistic" cost of services.

- Expenses for local DP sites may be offset by requiring less equipment and providing local control (unless, of course, there are too many such locations).

- It may be easier to manage small groups of people more closely identified with the section of the company which pays their salaries. These local data processing personnel would be expected to have a clearer understanding of their division's mission and could better be utilized to benefit one part of the company and to fulfill more requests of the users in a specialized environment.

- The risk of total loss of DP services company-wide due to some catastrophe is reduced by having multiple sites. Also, local interest in DP security is usually higher than at corporate level because it involves their own data.

- Corporate gives greater independence to those local groups which are profitable parts of the company—"Don't touch them; they must be doing something right, they're making money!"

- Return on investment can be good because the project is smaller, one more quickly developed (due to less management control and red tape argue some), and might be implemented on a smaller (less costly?) system. If multiple locations argue this case, then the question arises, is the ROI better this way than through centralization?

Many industry specialists, increasing numbers of data processing managers, and most executives who have been in a centralization vs. decentralization debate, will argue that there are real merits to both cases, particularly when each is costed out over a period of time and matched against company goals and business conditions. Many data processing experts are suggesting today that the wave of the future (and indeed an increasingly common situation today) is a combination of both environments where, in fact, a centralized control of data processing exists alongside multiple DP shops. Thus the advantages of such an environment should be noted briefly.

## Advantages of a Mixed
## Centralized-Decentralized Environment

A combined environment takes advantage of the best of two worlds: centralized control and planning of applications, and DP developments in general with the best in distributed intelligence and local access to substantial amounts of data and applications. The distribution of data processing power locally has grown out of a need to provide remote sites with more detailed data than might be required or stored at a central locale. These directly address the needs of local operational management, e.g., on a plant floor or in a distribution center specializing in selling part of the product line. Simultaneously, outlying locations complain that central shops are too rigid in procedures, insensitive perhaps to their needs, and have greater priorities than users far away or in other divisions. Therefore, some decentralization appears attractive to operational management.

In recent years many suggestions have been made to the effect that a portion of a company's data base can be resident at remote sites for immediate, and perhaps less expensive, use by operational levels of the company. Such an arrangement would call for summary data to be sent to divisional or corporate headquarters for tactical and strategic use by upper management and planners who are not interested, for example, in the explosion of a bill of material but simply in how many units or a particular product were built at what cost. In combination with significant developments in the price/performance of terminals and telecommunications systems (hardware, lines, and software), such an environment is becoming more appealing than ever before. Subsystems of data and specialized applications complement the concept of a corporate information system by feeding it the details required for every level of the company. Obviously, those that either have plans for such systems or in fact enjoy them today have had a long road to travel.

In each of these cases, many factors have to be considered. Many of the most common, but not the only aspects, are:

- Costs of communications, lines, terminals, and personnel
- What portions of which applications should be available locally
- What controls are established to insure corporate standards remain in force regarding the nature of data, its usage, and protection
- Reliability of multiple systems
- Costs of people and benefits over time in developing such applications from existing centralized or decentralized systems
- Degree of dependency of local sites on centralized data centers
- Offloading central site's computers so that other work can be put on them; e.g., whether intelligent terminals or minis are cheaper than a larger computer with more telecommunications
- The degree of local operational efficiency to be gained by centralization or partial centralization of services
- The need for control over all data processing services to avoid significant costs in redundancy, unjustified applications, modifications to existing files and applications, and simple waste of resources in manpower, supplies, time, and hardware.

In short, one would look for a balance between centralized management of information with the need for local operational control over its use, to the benefit of the company as a whole. Goals include keeping the cost of application development down along with telecommunication costs, minimizing overall operating expenses, and optimizing DP's contribution to user needs. Many companies with distributed processing are suggesting further that their experiences have indicated the following:

- Multiple processing centers (e.g., minis or intelligent terminals) insure that if one site goes down everyone else does not, as would happen with a centralized shop. This benefit should be kept in mind in planning applications.
- A combination of centralization and decentralization means greater responsiveness to user's need at the local level; therefore any centralized planning and control should allow for local participation in decision making to at least some degree. Otherwise, remote sites will find their data processing requirements being met outside the boundaries established by top management.

- Distribution of processing may not be more expensive than remote job entry since a central site's computer and staff may not have to be as big as in a nondistributed environment. Thus the question of who supports and develops applications and has responsibility for their welfare has to be resolved.

On the other side of the argument, in a distributed environment the loss of standardization and accountability is a problem. Top management may find that little empires, with their associated costs, continue to grow unless this tendency is constantly and carefully monitored. This is particularly evident in those companies where distributed processing with terminals having memory also have the ability to compile and link edit programs written at remote locations. Obviously every type of environment has a monetary value and costs associated with it vary from company to company. The bottom line on distributed processing, however, must not be forgotten. It is that there will be more of it in years to come as applications, software, and hardware developments make it more attractive. Moreover, it will impact the way data processing is made more available to users in new and interesting applications.

## Application Conclusions

At the heart of the question regarding the cost and benefits of data processing is what you use it for. All business discussions emanate from this fundamental concern. But some clear directions for the immediate future are already visible and provide a checklist of future applications for all companies. There will be:

(1) Continued elimination of manual repetitive tasks for employees whose salaries and benefits are rising faster than the expenses of data processing.

(2) Traditional accounting, manufacturing, distribution, and inventory control applications will be added where none existed before and today's will be modified to meet new demands.

(3) Greater modeling for problem solving will become common as management searches for better definition of options in decision making.

(4) More energy-saving applications will be evident, e.g., those which control costs of fuel, electricity, air conditioning, and gas.

(5) More interactive, online applications in real time for faster processing of data and better customer service requiring fewer people with increasing amounts of up-to-date data at their fingertips.

(6)    Further integration of data and applications into data base environments to save on costs of storage and to increase central control of DP operations.

(7)    Applications will appear which bring data processing management closer to the decision-making processes of the company as a whole and at all levels, but particularly at the top.

(8)    There is a trend toward declining development of new batch applications in business as online systems continue to expand as a percentage of all development work.

(9)    Further expansion and integration of various timely data and applications at operational levels is evident with more sharply tuned management systems to measure actual performance against planned objectives.

(10)    Further integration of systems simultaneously with data processing moving out into new user areas; e.g., point of sale terminals such as we see in supermarkets and retail stores, are already a reality in the industrialized world with more to come.

(11)    Expanded planning and control systems will be integrated for more levels of management in a serious bid to consolidate these functions. The data processing area offers a greater number of tools for this than any other technology or management philosophy.

(12)    There is an increased use of terminals and optical readers for data input, update, and inquiry.

(13)    Greater amounts of data capture at the source in real time, rather than in transcribed fashion in batch mode at data centers, will also find easy cost justification.

(14)    Increased reliance on telecommunications in applications in "explosive" amounts (according to most authorities) is assumed.

(15)    Further integration of recovery procedures, forgiveness for errors by users and all at less cost per transaction than ever before is a design criterion now being matched by programs and software packages in increasing amounts.

(16)    The restriction of reports and the use of paper to exception reporting is a norm which will be with us in a matter of only a few years.

(17)    Less travel by personnel through improved effectiveness of communication of data will reduce the costs of energy, people, hotel and airline tickets, while improving productivity by way of increased interaction among individuals using terminals.

The list could be expanded to include more controversial topics. It is believed by most DP industry specialists, however, that the above list represents those tendencies which managers will continue to find attractive from the points of view of control of the business and cost/benefits. Hardware and software trends compement the expectations in application developments. None of the above trends is revolutionary or leading-edge today (as of 1979) and they are, in fact, quite common particularly among large companies. The tremendous growth will simply be in smaller organizations while the larger ones will refine and add to their data processing resources. In short, the immediate future will see a continuation of trends and experiences clearly definable and existing today.

## PERSONNEL DEVELOPMENTS

It is argued by all experts on data processing and its economics, that the fastest growing element of a data processing budget, as a percentage of total cost, is people. Moreover, the rate of dollar growth is greater than for any other element. Yet at the same time, the typical roadblock to the development of more beneficial applications is the lack of sufficient people, no matter what size the DP shop. Consequently, current and future trends in personnel are critical to understanding how best to manage data processing costs and investments.

Since no portion of a data processing budget is bigger or growing faster than that dedicated to personnel, much attention has to be paid to it. The demand for additional staff is a frequent problem in most commercial organizations and especially for that portion of a staff which is most highly skilled and consequently most expensive. The challenge managers have is to improve the productivity of the staffs they have, while extending data processing services to those with little or no technical background. Some of the obvious tools available include the use of such techniques as English-like computing with high-level languages, user data input, and better utilization of existing DP resources.

In 1971, a Diebold study indicated that the fastest growing categories of DP personnel included systems analysts, programmers, and systems operators, with data entry personnel last. A report by the American Federation of Information Processing Societies, Inc., suggested that in the mid-1970s, there were over one million and a half individuals in the United States alone in those four categories. Programmers made up approximately 20% of the group, systems analysts about 15% and the rest was divided between data entry and hardware operators. Inevitably, DP executives will look for various ways to control these expensive personnel costs.

But all industry analysts agree that the biggest bottleneck in the

| Year | Computers | Programmers |
|------|-----------|-------------|
| 1955 | 1,000 | 10,000 |
| 1960 | 5,500 | 30,000 |
| 1965 | 22,500 | 80,000 |
| 1970 | 70,000 | 165,000 |
| 1975 | 225,000 | 220,000 |
| 1980 | 700,000 | 275,000 |
| 1985 | 1,100,000 | 330,000 |

**Figure 1-10**    U.S. computers and programmers.

development of beneficial applications is the lack of good, and conse-quently, expensive programmers and analysts. Specifically, more program-mers means more analysts to provide them with the logic for applications, and administrative and clerical personnel. Thus various projections of hardware price increases versus people costs clearly suggest that personnel expenses will have to rise dramatically both in salaries (due to an insuffi-cient supply of skilled individuals) and benefits (ranging from 20% to 40% of salary). Along with the costs of salaries and benefits one must factor in the need to provide increasing amounts of training in new hardware and software products, and in changing DP techniques for application development, languages, software, resource utilization, and project man-agement. It is rapidly a source of concern as to whether education should be by independent study courses, schools established by vendors, or through colleges and consulting firms.

Among the critical issues for the future are how to get nondata processing people to share the load carried by technical staff, and also what should be done to increase programmer productivity. The second question is currently a hot issue and deserves some examination. Tech-niques used successfully in varying degrees to improve productivity include:

- Using software packages whenever possible as opposed to writing your own or at least modifying existing programs. Such packages include data base management, report generators, file management code, statistical and mathematical packages, and modeling sys-tems.

- Reducing the amount of totally new software required for a new application from the average current level of 80–90% to such low figures as 10–25% by finding ways to improve the life and rele-vance of existing programs.

- Simplifying requirements to reduce the need for expensive specialists, which ultimately led to the typical cost overruns of the past. Make systems simple enough so that part or all of a new requirement can be met by users doing development work.

- Increasing the use of interactive programming techniques for maintenance of existing programs and files, and for development of new systems, all resulting in more lines of revised or tested code from existing staff.

- Expanding the use of project management techniques to avoid costly overruns in time and money or in bad design and coding which ultimately need to be redone. Crusty old DP managers jokingly believe that a project poorly planned will take three times as long to develop while a properly controlled one only twice as long. Such folklore is not far from the truth—hence the interest in modular programming, techniques such as HIPO, and walkthroughs with constant auditing to insure quality and quantity of work.

- Encouraging improved communications between users and data processing personnel so that applications are designed to meet the needs of a particular group the first time.

- Increasing the use of system performance analyzers, modeling of applications (e.g., network traffic and DASD requirements) for tuning and project planning.

By using some of the above means, and others that may come along, the single most expensive element in a DP budget can come under greater fiscal control despite rising costs. The history of programmer productivity in the industry suggests the types of gains one might expect. Between 1955 and 1965, productivity, as measured by lines of tested code completed, doubled and from 1965 to 1975, rose an additional 33%. In other words, the industry enjoyed an improvement of about 3% compounded annually. This degree of improvement is expected to continue at about the same rate over the next five to ten years although many see future rates rising to as high as 10% in the best of shops.

With such gains in productivity still lagging far behind those registered for hardware (computers improved by about 60% compounded annually), managers will try to increase users' share in data processing's work. There are some obvious means being used to enlarge the user's role:

- Making available interactive systems and terminals in user areas for simple inquiries, file updates, modeling, and small amounts of programming.

- Educating users about DP so that applications are well thought out for efficiency and ease of development.

- Creating more reliable systems available where users really need them, which implies better hardware and software reliability and maintenance of systems being done in as close to a real-time environment as is possible.

- Expanding the number of users who are inclined toward DP. This group includes scientists, engineers, accounting and financial analysts, budget managers, product development and scheduling people, payroll managers, order entry and commission agents, secretaries using word processing systems, and administrative assistants to executives in need of specific iterative data. These individuals can help insure that existing DP resources are fully used.

The challenge for managers is to create a balance between utilizing people versus computer power to complete a job. Readers, sensors, and other automated data collection systems will relieve much of the burden from people as they are beginning to do today, with favorable cost results. Nevertheless, technical personnel are not expected to disappear. The trend at this time is toward fewer technical people working on applications. These personnel are spending more time supporting systems, which increases the possibility of non-DP people contributing to the development of applications. There is also a trend now toward reducing the cost of hardware operators as systems become easier to operate and evolve toward increased automation. All personnel costs are periodically reported by such publications as *Computerworld, Infosystems, Datamation,* and other trade publications. Thus it is easy to measure your company's personnel expenditures against the industry as a whole and salaries for top performers can be kept competitive. Such data would help in short-term budgetary planning as well as in long-term personnel requirements analysis.

## IMPLICATIONS OF DP TECHNOLOGY

This chapter has identified a number of trends in the development of hardware, software, programs, and use of DP personnel that, if properly correlated to a specific company's plans and policies, would help provide optimum use of computerized facilities. The implications of these can be summarized briefly by reducing them to a few key issues.

1.   Each company should recognize that DP is a useful tool only if it is used wisely and on a timely basis in those applications which offer the greatest return on investment. These applications will vary from company to company but what should not vary is the fact that the tool is used properly.

2.   Optimizing return on dollars invested requires that applications be carefully planned and their development closely supervised and when completed, maintained in the most efficient manner possible. This requires upper-management concern and involvement.

3.   When appropriate, companies should take advantage of leading-edge technologies, which in many cases offer new options for merging new developments with existing DP environments. The ideal situation is to replace older technologies at the exact time that the next generation's equipment or software is deliverable. To be sure, this economic goal is difficult to achieve and must be tempered by the need to verify that the new technology really does what it is supposed to do. Yet coordinating with anticipated developments in DP should be an important part of a company's DP plans. In fact it is essential since the alternative would cost too much.

4.   Closely tied to item three above is the suggestion that a company balance cost against flexibility. This is nowhere better illustrated than with hardware. Figure 1–11 illustrates the point. New technology, for example a computer, may initially price out more to lease or purchase at time of delivery, but probably has either a shorter lease contract or the capability of being resold at a high percentage of original cost than might

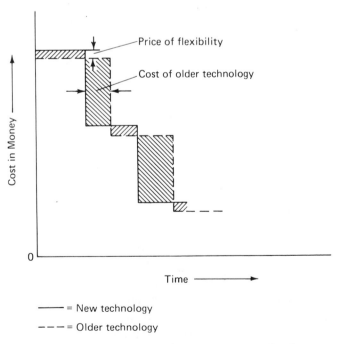

**Figure 1–11**   Cost over time: new vs. old technology.

older technology which is initially acquired for less money but forces a longer lease or purchase commitment on a company. Although more will be said about this issue in subsequent chapters, it is important to realize that how flexible you want to be in changing technologies and what price you wish to pay is a vital issue. As a rule, the greater the flexibility the higher the cost. Conversely the longer the commitment the smaller the expense unless major technological innovations make the price/performance ratio of newer products more attractive (often the case with computers). Thus one company with a serious immediate cash flow problem might opt for older hardware in order to defer the cost of new technology (differences between the vertical solid and dotted lines) while one in better shape might afford new technology knowing that in the long run it would be less expensive and more reliable.

5.    In the development of applications and the writing of programs, there is a cost of lost opportunity associated with that which is put off for a future date. Take for instance, the company which five years ago decided that the cost of developing MRP for manufacturing was too high and today decides to go ahead with it. That organization will find that the inputs are greater in number and complexity, and will definitely discover that programmers are far more expensive. Thus putting off application development has a cost associated with it in terms of benefits not yet realized and the normal inflationary effect on the expense of people and software. Merging the improvements in cost/performance of new technology with the needs of a company today is difficult but helps organizations use DP more productively.

6.    Applications and data are one of a company's assets and must be treated as an investment to be protected. When 1% to 5% of a company's budget is devoted to data processing, no viable alternative perspective exists. Applications cost a great deal and thus must be optimized. Data must be protected from loss, damage, misuse, or criminal activity by giving weight to those techniques, software, and policies which protect them. Also, considerations of reliability of hardware and software on the one hand, and concern for availability of data when you want it on the other, has to take on increasing importance in costing out DP services. Manufacturers of DP products, government regulatory agencies, auditors, and DP executives all agree that protection and proper use of information as a company asset is important. It remains for each organization to insure that at home data has an assigned value and is treated accordingly. Correlating new developments in DP with the needs of a company is extremely helpful.

7.    The first six items above represent actual operational philosophy in many companies but not yet in all. DP in many cases is improperly used and thus remains an expensive, poorly used tool, a burden or neces-

sary evil. In such an environment, management will simply have to realize that it is less expensive to run their business profitably if DP is optimized properly. This may require new thinking and policies, especially where DP is still primarily an accounting function under the control of one executive who knows little about data processing and could care less about learning more. For such an organization, the cost of DP is high.

If data processing is treated as an investment, as opposed to simply an expense, a company will discover more opportunities for increasing their return on DP dollars, time, people, and effort expended. The rest of this book will be devoted to illustrating specifically how to make data processing both cost-effective and an attractive investment.

The genius of good leadership is
to leave behind a situation
which common sense, even without the grace of genius, can
deal with successfully.

*Walter Lippmann*

*Everyone says to plan but very few show you how. This chapter will indicate in very specific terms how to establish long-range plans for data processing, then show ways to control those plans. Next short-term immediate planning is illustrated and related to long-term planning. A summary of general policy guidelines will bring each of these topics into focus. It is important to understand how to relate long- and short-term planning to each other within a department and then to an entire company. The process is logically laid out in the order that it should come: long then short, company-wide then departmental. This will avoid contradictory programs and major cost overruns that cancel out the value of data processing projects.*

# CHAPTER TWO

# Goals, Planning,
# and Data Processing

Experience and analysis of business practices both confirm that a well-run company has a greater chance of being competitive and profitable than one run poorly. This obvious fact grows out of another important observation: well-run companies are those that know their business environment, understand what their objectives are, and have plans for attaining them. Again an obvious fact, but one which is often not applied to data processing. As the amount of a company's budget increasingly is devoted to DP, the pressure to do more short-term and long-term planning to provide operating strategies and directions becomes critical. Planning in this phase of business is essential so that applications can be developed which are relevant and timely, in order that hardware can be ordered and installed when needed, and that costs may be controlled. These activities require the kinds of discipline which exist in other parts of the business, applied now to data processing. This chapter will discuss many of the elements in planning as they apply to data processing. Planning in this environment involves looking at applications, hardware and software acquisitions, services, and people. Company goals at each level of management should be taken into account and measured against overall objectives and standards established by the organization.

## LONG-RANGE PLANNING

A primary step in fitting the use of DP into a company's activities involves making sure that data processing contributes to the organization's mission. Thus step one requires a company to share its general, long-range objectives with data processing management, plans which may go out three, five, and even ten years so that no fundamental decisions in DP are ever made which contradict the primary game plan. Second, at each level of a company's organization, managers from DP must participate in the establishment of long-range and short-range goals in order that their day-to-day decisions do not contradict fundamental directions of any key group in the company. Third, at the operational level of management, data processing should be heavily involved since it is at this juncture that specific decisions regarding the development of applications, changes in old ones, and the acquisition of equipment (based on company financial guidelines) are made.

Because these three requirements are applicable to any organization, the size of the company is irrelevant. While the above three points sound very good in theory and in textbooks, the increased use of data processing today requires that they be followed in practice. Leaving aside the specific political or interpersonal considerations which may make the process of planning easier or harder, the fundamental fact that has to be understood is that data processing must be an integral part of company-wide planning at all stages and levels in order to maximize a company's DP investment and insure quality services.

Planning with DP is no different than with any other group in a company. Long-term objectives are set, strategies developed to carry them out, potential problems to overcome identified, and responsibilities and timetables established. This is followed by a periodic review of results to determine if plans have to be changed or new problems resolved. This same process can be applied within the data processing department. The issues which must be addressed in order to control costs and produce relevant services include the following:

- Memory and computer requirements over the next five years in six-month intervals for at least two years

- Peripheral equipment requirements over the same time frame for:
  terminals
  data entry devices
  disk and tape drives
  printers
- Personnel for coding, application design, maintenance, data entry, clerical work
- Major software directions, for example, data base and TP
- Education to support new applications, software and hardware directions, new coding and management methods
- Applications by priority of importance to the company and DP to take into account:

  (1)   Company's needs
  (2)   Available DP resources
  (3)   Financial guidelines
  (4)   Political considerations
  (5)   DP industry's directions.

Robert E. Linneman and John D. Kennell published in the *Harvard Business Review* (55, no. 2, March–April 1977, 141–151), a list of ten steps one could use for long-range planning in general. As part of a company-wide planning effort, these points are relevant to DP. Moreover, they can also be applied within the data processing organization once DP management understands fully the environment in which the company operates. In developing their list, both authors realistically assumed that one could not devote a great deal of time to planning and that long-range planning at best is risky.

*Step One: Define Your Company's Mission and Policies.* A good definition of what the company does is important. For example, does it sell cars or is it in transportation? Do you sell computers or information systems? This type of questioning should be followed by a definition of what sales should be over the next few years along with profits and investment criteria. Specific goals should be established; for instance, increase profits after taxes from 10% to 12% within the next four years. Policies might be to compete only within the United States and to introduce new products on a bi-annual basis.

*Step Two: Set a Time Limit into the Future for Purposes of Planning.* Should you plan one or two years into the future, or five to ten? Perhaps one should do several sets of planning for various time frames. For example, short-term planning could indicate that sales will grow at 10% per year; therefore the company must plan to have sufficient product available for the market. Yet long-range forecasting might suggest that maturity of the current product line will lead to a 20% drop in sales each year beginning in the fourth year. Thus one view must be balanced against the other. For data processing, planning might indicate that heavy capital investments for the next five years have to be made soon rather than two years into the future. The point to remember is to relate company situations to DP and then time decisions to fit a particular organization's clock of events.

*Step Three: Understand Your Company's Strengths and Weaknesses.* What are the strengths, weaknesses, and directions of your industry and how do these compare to those of your company? By definition, the same applies to DP. If the banking industry, for instance, devotes on the average 5% of its operating budget to DP and your bank only 2% is there a problem; are there applications you should be developing which everyone else has and that make them more competitive than you? Linneman and Kennell warn against accepting as facts myths about a particular industry or your company. This advice is particularly applicable to DP, where the best illustration of this is with the acquisition of computers. Myth: "I have enough horse power for the next five years." Fact: Overwhelmingly, companies that are constantly adding on new applications, run out of computer power long before they planned. Myth: "I guarantee that the online order entry system can be brought up in six months." Fact: Most applications in DP take longer and cost more than is forecasted. Identify your capabilities and the basis for judgments to avoid obvious problems. DP strengths might include such things as a good programming staff with little turnover in personnel. Thus stability and a good knowledge of the company is resident within the department. Or, all applications are fully integrated with a common set of files. This means that maintenance as a percent of all programming activities might be low.

Conversely, weaknesses must be identified realistically and then attacked. In data processing, examples usually include such things as dated software technology, stand-alone card-oriented applications, antiquated hardware, incompetent or just generally unimaginative DP management. These are serious and quite common problems which if allowed to persist will prevent companies from acquiring low-cost data processing services and relevant applications.

*Step Four: Identify Those Factors Which Will Impact Your Plans.* Assumptions about your industry, the nation's economy, or a company within your corporation, are factors which must be considered. Obviously within data processing, factors mentioned in Chapter 1 are worthy of consideration. Specific projections which one can believe in should be defined. Examples include: A company believes that demand for its type of product will increase 11% each year over the next four years.

The same company believes competition will increase 7% each year for the same period. Or, in data processing, a manager might, for instance, believe that computers will cost 25% less in five years and that he reasonably will require 60% more power than is currently used. Another: Salaries for skilled systems analysts will rise 15% each year over the next five and you assume that your analysts will leave your company if their salaries are not competitive with the industry. Thus one would have to plan salary increases for staff to keep up with the DP industry as a whole, in spite of what the personnel department says.

*Step Five: Prepare a Laundry List of Those Variables Which Have Make-or-break Influences on your Company or Department.* What has always helped or hurt your company or department in the past? Try to pick quantifiable elements, such as the growth of the economy, the cost of computers and people. The role of inflation and the power of competition could also be included. For those interested in detailed planning and who can afford it, a consulting firm may be hired to identify those variables which affect a company or department within an industry and to identify what future trends will continue to impact it. Linneman and Kennell suggest that for "shirt-sleeve" planning, the list might include only four or five elements with some ranking for probability. Those that you feel are important you keep and drop the less significant ones. Remember to keep in mind their timeliness, and eliminate unreasonably abnormal major disasters such as World War III. Make each variable independent of all the others, keeping separate dependent variables which might simply be useful for fine-tuning plans.

*Step Six: Assign Values to Each Major Variable.* This exercise, although not easy, allows one to develop a list of priorities. Do not take seriously something which has an extreme value that seems ridiculous, but take seriously even those which appear marginal. Remain objective by having others review your lists. A DP example illustrates the point. Your company has just discussed the possibility of application X which is to provide three benefits: displacement of current costs, increased productivity and efficiency, and improved decisions, performance, and policies. Each has been assigned a dollar value for high, medium, and low probabilities. (See Chapter 3 for an illustration of how this is done.) Now a group of managers wants to quantify their consensus view of the benefits to be obtained from this application by assigning them a rating of 1 through 10 (low numbers suggest little faith, higher increased confidence it will happen).

As the table in Figure 2–1 indicates, these managers believe application X will probably give reasonable chance of benefits in all three categories. Thus an executive might interpret what was forecasted as medium dollar benefits as what he probably will get in exchange for this ap-

Benefit Table for Application "X"                                    Date _____

| Benefit Type | Probabilities (Odds) | | |
| --- | --- | --- | --- |
| | High | Medium | Low |
| Displacement of costs | 1 | 4 | 8 |
| Increased productivity and efficiency | 2 | 6 | 9 |
| Improved decisions, performance and policies | 5 | 8 | 10 |

**Figure 2–1**

plication's expense. Thus if high probability of benefits had a value of $175,000, medium $105,000, and low $35,000, then a manager might safely conclude that he could expect $105,000 in benefits. He can take this dollar amount and compare it against the costs of that application and make a go or no go decision. Or, he could compare this project against possible other ones and select that which has the highest rate of return.

*Step Seven: Develop Various Game Plans to Use.* This step essentially requires you to develop several operating plans which take into account the variables and factors already developed in the first seven steps. Linneman and Kennell suggest that three but not more than four options (scenarios) are ideal and that three is probably the best number. Make each one plausible and real by using those factors in which you have great faith. Write the scenario out with the assumptions that influenced your thinking so that if read five years from now the reasons for your decisions and the environment in which you operated at the time a stance was taken can be understood. Make these descriptions short, that is to say, one or two paragraphs. And while the authors recommend building these with variables that have values assigned to them, the process can be kept quite simple.

Using data processing as an example helps illustrate the point. Your company forecasts 20% increase in sales each year for the next four years. That means your online order entry system is going to have to handle that many more transactions which in turn means more order entry clerks, terminals, and disk capacity for inventory and customer files. Specific values for purposes of the budget can be assigned to the costs of people, terminals, and disk. Scenario number one might simply talk of these elements. Number two may raise the question of converting to a data base environment now before the costs get way out of line, while option three ignores the order entry problem for now since the company may have a bigger one in inventory which will require attention by data processing instead.

*Step Eight: Develop a Strategy for Each Scenario That is Consistent with Your Company's Objectives.* Be flexible, go after the most important issues, and develop plans which will allow you to change should the goals and objectives of the company also evolve. Thus in scenario number one, the DP manager might go for an incremental increase in people and hardware so that he could devote more attention to inventory. In option two, he might plan on converting one application at a time to data base so that he could pay attention to expansion of the current order entry system while in number three, inventory applications might be built but under data base and with hooks so that it could be linked to a revised order entry system sometime in the future.

*Step Nine: Check How Flexible Your Scenarios Are Against Other Options.* How flexible are your plans should the assumptions behind one of the scenarios change, be proven false, or more true than before? Can you switch quickly or slowly toward another without having lost what you did in the currently adopted one? These are common-sense types of issues which are not unique to data processing. Most company departments worry about such questions. DP departments must also be flexible in order not to expend a great deal of effort, dollars, and commitment on something that must be scratched.

*Step Ten: Pick the Best Strategy and Implement It.* Often this step emerges as a compromise between various scenarios and should be one that DP can live with. Thus, using our example again, the DP executive might decide that from now on, all new applications will be developed under data base and that modifications to the online order entry system will be geared toward handling larger volumes of transactions. Furthermore, this manager might decide to acquire more disk storage now for data base development through purchase and plan next year to build up the number of terminals installed. The order entry department might also plan next year on hiring clerks and training them so that it might be ready for the anticipated increase in orders which incidentally they feel will only be 10% rather than 20%.

Finally, Linneman and Kennell echo the same warning that all proponents of planning systems do, namely, planners must be in agreement that their options and plans are realistic and that they must be checked periodically to insure that the assumptions underlying them reflect the true environment existing for the department or company in question.

Reviewing results is a core ingredient in any DP planning. When common sense is applied to this exercise, departments should have an understanding of what they are doing, why, and how to change as conditions dictate.

## PROJECT PLANNING AND CONTROL

Project planning can be for something as small as making a minor change to a program or to the development of a whole series of interrelated applications costing hundreds of thousands of dollars and years to implement. Planning, however, is a way of life that should exist in all DP departments. Thus the principles which apply to all types of data processing projects can be used for each and every activity of a department to insure management control over costs, overruns, security and relevance. The basic cycle of project planning consists of the following steps:

- Identification of a potential project
- Definition of costs and benefits
- Preliminary design of a project
- Approval to continue forward
- Detail design of project
- Management approval to continue
- Writing programs for the application
- Testing of programs (project)
- Putting into production
- Post-installation review.

The key element in project planning is to understand what has been done and what remains to be completed. At each stage, full documentation should be prepared to insure that everyone understands what is happening and that those who must make decisions have in fact made them. Progress and failures can be checked this way through a series of status reports and meetings. In this manner, costs for application changes and developments can be controlled. All seminars, books, and articles on project planning stress these points. In short, it is cheaper and less time-consuming to organize a project than to charge forward without having seen to all the necessary details and commitments. In the pages to come the principles behind any project planning will be applied to data processing to illustrate how discipline in DP can be imposed much as on any other sector of a company.

Since illustrating the various stages of a project to upper management less familiar with its details are Gantt and Pert charts. From the very beginning of a DP project, these can be used as tools to familiarize all with plans and progress. Gantt charts are used in a variety of ways and are common within the DP industry. In its various forms tasks are listed in sequence along the left hand side downward while dates for completion or progress extend toward the horizontal right. Figures 2-2 and 2-3 illustrate two variations of this chart.

Pert or activity network charts show what tasks have to be completed before others may begin and also what activities can be done concurrently with others. This type of graph is particularly useful where there are complex installations being developed involving multiple groups of people who must coordinate their activities. Moving an office from one building to another, establishing a new data processing shop, or setting up a nation-wide network of terminals are prime for using Pert charts. Whether a Gantt or Pert chart is used, each is particularly useful where multiple tasks have to take place because the charts give a quick view of how a project is coming along. They allow dates, tasks, individuals, and costs to be assigned. Moreover, they help clarify what kinds of changes can be made along with the way they might affect other activities and dates for completion.

| Target Dates for Completion  Tasks + Man | January | February | March | April | May | June |
|---|---|---|---|---|---|---|
| Task 1  Man A | XXXX | | | | | |
| Task 2  Man A | | XXXX | | | | |
| Task 3  Man B | | | XXXX | XXXX | | |
| Task 4  Man A | | | XXXX | XXXX | X | |
| Task 5  Man B | | | | | XXX | |
| Task 6  Man A | | | | | | XXX |
| Task 7  Man C | XXXX | XXXX | | | | |
| Task 8  Man D | | | XXXX | XXXX | XXXX | |
| Task 9  Man C | | | | XXXX | X | |
| Task 10 Man C | | | | | XXX | |
| | | | | | | |
| | | | | | | |

X = 1 week of completed work

Figure 2-2    Project "A" Gantt chart (see Figure 2-5 for another version of this report).

| Task | January | February | March | April | May | June |
|------|---------|----------|-------|-------|-----|------|
| Assigned (A) | $100 | $150 | | | | |
| Task "A" Actual | $90 | $162 | | | | |
| Assigned (B) | | $200 | $250 | $210 | | |
| Task "B" Actual | | $210 | $230 | $210 | | |
| Assigned (C) | | | | | $100 | $50 |
| Task "C" Actual | | | | | $95 | $40 |

**Figure 2-3**    Project "A": budget Gantt chart.

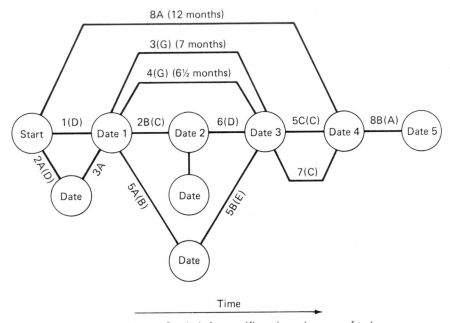

Letters and numbers:  Symbols for specific tasks and groups of tasks.

**Figure 2-4**    PERT chart.

All projects have their costs and these must be managed. This fact can only be properly handled and appreciated through a system of controls that is rigorously applied. Cost control must begin in the initial stages of project planning and must not end until the project is completed. Afterwards, during the post-installation review, the reasons for the project coming below or over budget should be understood so that the next one will come in at assigned budget. There are fundamentally two parts to a financial plan: a budget and a record of what was actually spent. The budget obviously remains an estimate of the cost of personnel, travel, equipment, and facilities over time to complete a project. These numbers should be broken down by line item and for each month into dollars. Although this document should then not always be considered as fixed in concrete, the projected budget remains a benchmark to be measured against throughout the life of project.

The second element involves reporting actual expenditures for each line item throughout the project. Most companies have a formal procedure for this activity but in those that still do not assign budgets to DP departments or projects, one should be established. What is also critical to realize is that every level of management in a project should understand how much they have been allotted in a budget and how much they have spent year-to-date so that they too can monitor and control costs with a sense of being part of a team. Written controls facilitate constant monitoring of costs so that if the project is being delayed or expenses rise at a particular point not previously forecasted, someone will be in a position to identify the problem early and take appropriate remedial action.

## Planning a Project: A Checklist

There are many individuals who believe that all the planning in the world will never replace dumb luck. To be sure this is true. However, it is also true that planning helps a great deal, and yet planning a project may in fact be the most difficult part of executing it. Without careful planning, there is a high risk of all subsequent work going roughly, exceeding budgets, coming in late, and not being of high quality. There are certain characteristics of a good project plan which should become part of your operations:

(1) Understand the system to be built and realize that changes must be controlled.

(2) Prepare a detailed, comprehensive plan in writing.

(3) Let all those involved in the project understand where it stands throughout its development, by using memorandums, reports, and meetings.

(4) Let every person involved have specific areas of responsibility and also understand everyone else's.

(5) Devote considerable attention to the details of defining a system's requirements so that no serious omission is discovered too late.

(6) Plan carefully and be ready to change the plan as events dictate. Always keep the written plan current, to reflect accomplish-

ments, changes, and remaining tasks. Do not forget to incorporate into this document changes in responsibilities, budgets, and dates.

(7)   Put into writing requirements for manpower and machine time, budgeted and actual, since these are usually two key items that undergo a great deal of change.

(8)   Measure all activities against the written plan, line item by line item at each predetermined milestone in the project.

(9)   Prepare a formal report with a rough description of the system's requirements, for use by upper management early in the process.

(10)  Gain necessary commitments for continued work on the project at various key milestones: at inception, after requirements analysis, system design, and system test.

## Basic System Requirement Phase

The objective of this early phase is to define the goals of a particular system, what has to be done in order to realize these goals, and to establish some standard of performance to determine their acceptability. This is a process in which interaction among users and data processing personnel is critical, ultimately leading to a statement of criteria with which both are in agreement. Patient and constant dialogue is essential for the success of a project at this point since the users may not fully be aware of what DP can do for them and, conversely, data processing might not totally realize the problems and concerns of a particular group. Through careful discussions, moreover, the cost justification of a system can emerge early on in the conversations, allowing management to make a first-cut decision on whether or not to continue with the project. This is also the phase where many joint meetings are held, gathering of data takes place (such as will be illustrated in Chapter 3), questionnaires and interviews are carried out, and observations are made. The result of this series of exercises should be a document which can be one page long for a minor change to an existing system or a lengthy report running into dozens of pages for a complex proposal.

## Systems Requirement Checklist

There are approximately ten points to keep in mind at this early stage of project management.

(1)   Spend the time to define requirements now in order to avoid later making changes which are costly due to inappropriately designed and coded work.

(2) Insure that all relevant groups participate in defining a system, not just DP.

(3) Gather data, analyze that information, and document everything.

(4) Design the inputs to be provided for the system and the outputs to be generated in some detail with both users and DP in agreement on these.

(5) Define as many of the operational elements of the system as possible; for example, determine data entry procedures and what a system will do with that data gathered.

(6) Investigate what files, applications, and programs already exist that can be used and what has to be developed from scratch. This will help reduce the time required to implement a project and save on development costs.

(7) Use those data collection techniques which are most practical for the project in question. Factors to consider include cost, what the users are used to, quantity of data to be collected, the nature of available computer and terminal technology.

(8) Take into account possible changes in the future to the proposed system and evolution of DP technology. For example, should the system be able to tie into a planned future application? What about distributing the processing, since that may become less expensive as time goes on? What about using data base file systems now?

(9) Use a workbook process whereby initial requirements can be expanded during the detailed design phase in an almost fill-in-the-blank form. Such a workbook could be designed for the project in question at this early stage, less easily later.

(10) Generate a report which defines clearly the goals of the system as of this time, specify what it should accomplish, and the means for measuring the application's performance and acceptability to the users and DP. In short, document the rules of the game.

## System Design Phase

Once the requirements for an application have been spelled out, the next step involves a conceptual design for the system. This is the detailed outline of the project which, after acceptance, becomes the basis for the actual coding and development of the application. The design phase also provides another opportunity to identify all inputs and outputs while furthering the analysis of potential problems and benefits. Opportunities for future projects, possibly related to the current one, and identification of the scope of the effort can be included at this point. Following this phase, management will have greater detail on which to base a subsequent decision to take the development process even further.

At this point, those who are to develop the application should be picked, hired, or at least identified. This group should have expertise relevant to the project and be as small a group as possible to avoid cumbersome management problems. Obviously, a healthy balance of people between those who are conceptual types and others who enjoy doing detailed work is advisable.

## System Design Checklist

A considerable number of points should be kept in mind during the system design phase. Here is one area where conceptual work, when properly done, will provide the solid basis for detail coding and testing of an application against a predetermined schedule and budget. Therefore it is an important one requiring considerable attention. A checklist of tasks recommended in the design phase could include:

1.   Break up the design process into modules so that concurrent work can take place. A top-down approach is useful. Under this method, the project is divided into smaller pieces of work which become more susceptible to control. The benefits of such design methods are: they establish testing milestones; they insure correct and thorough design of all portions equally; and they identify those areas which need redesign. Make the changes now since it is always far less expensive to modify plans early rather than afterwards during the development or testing stages.

2.   Take a hard look at the question of interfaces between existing applications and the proposed one. Define all interfaces now while the number of people involved is small and the quantity of private arrangements among them can be kept at a minimum. Many interfacing problems can be identified now along with what existing code can be reused or needs to be rewritten. Again, modularity is a useful idea since it allows you to break up the task into manageable pieces. During this phase, interfaces might include the use of existing code, files, house rules, identification of common functions, and the choice of simple solutions over complex ones. It is at this stage also, that one can decide whether it is less expensive to write new code or use the old and to reflect such decisions in the final budget for the project.

3.   Use existing design tools which have already been proven to be useful throughout the data processing industry. These include a detailed structural narrative of the project, diagrams showing the flow of data,

HIPO techniques, modeling and simulation (to estimate response times, traffic on lines).

4.  Begin to determine which programming languages to use for the actual coding of the application. The factors involved in this decision include: how the language handles data; its mathematical capabilities; utilities which support it; availability of trained programmers in a particular language; the ease and speed with which a particular medium can be used to meet the deadlines established for the project.

5.  Insist that storage maps be drawn up in simple form defining where and how much data will be placed on disk and tape along with determining the quantities of data, number and size of tables, and file formats.

6.  Equally important is to determine how much equipment will be needed. Define its configuration, cost, and points in time when it will be required so that physical installation planning can be performed on schedule with the total costs identified for management.

7.  Next compare the output of this phase in the process to the design goals and earlier plans already established and documented in order to eliminate contradictions, misconceptions, and faulty data. The result should be an updated plan complete with a documented list of requirements to build the system. There should also be a written statement on the costs and benefits of the application.

8.  Now establish a test plan to measure the system by and obtain agreement for its use after the coding has been completed. Testing is such a critical issue that it is worth a checklist of its own.


## Test Plan Checklist

This is in effect the agreement between DP and users: "If the system does the following in such a manner as you and I agree to, then it will be accepted and used by my people." All tests should have the following features to insure that key conditions are met by the new application:

(1)  Testing confirms that all logic errors are gone and accuracy exists.

(2)  All design criteria and objectives have been met.

(3)  Processing is done on a timely basis for the user.

(4)  Inputs are acceptable and relevant to DP and users.

(5)  Appropriate outputs are produced on a timely basis for users.

(6)  Company and industry standards and regulations are met.

(7)    Detailed documentation exists for auditing and program maintenance.

(8)    Overflow conditions are satisfactorily accounted for in data management.

(9)    Error conditions are tested for and procedures are available for handling them effectively.

(10)    Interfacing conventions are all adhered to throughout the application.

(11)    Compilations and assemblies are all clean and free of errors.

(12)    The process of testing an application is fully understood by all parties involved.

(13)    Any changes to the application, as a result of testing, should be documented, studied for possible impact on the system, and any details regarding costs for processing, manpower utilization, etc., incorporated into the project's documentation. This will allow management to have that information available at the time it is called upon to authorize the application to go live.

### Project Control Procedures

From the very beginning of any application development, some control of the process must take place and ultimately one individual is responsible for its success or failure. Thus the problem of how to maintain control throughout the process is a continuing one. An example of a project control device actually used by many companies is the Gantt chart shown in Figure 2–5.

Without good project control procedures, unnecessary expenses will be incurred as deadlines are missed, additional manpower is required, and hardware and software expenditures continued without a reasonable return on the investment soon. Many of the techniques mentioned in the preceding pages can be used at every phase of the application's development but others are only useful at certain times.

### Changes in an Application Development Process

It is important to identify those points which need to be kept in mind throughout the entire process and remain relevant from beginning to end. First, all plans are subject to change and thus modifications should be used by management as a tool for controlling the progress of a project. Second, too many project managers deviate from the agreed-to plans as they get deeper into the development of a new application, thereby in-

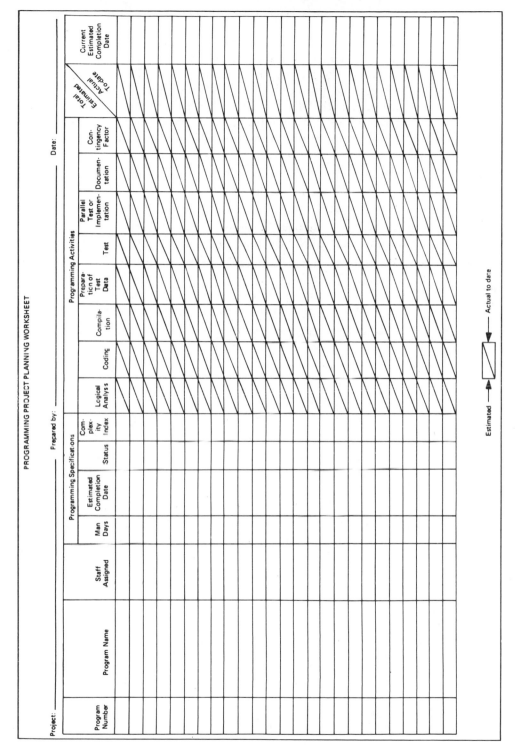

**Figure 2-5** (*Source:* © *IBM Corp.*)

creasing the chances of running late, incurring cost overruns, and not producing an application suitable for his users. Third, project managers must not become bogged down in technical details or concentrate on specific problems to the exclusion of the project as a whole. This is a common problem with DP managers who become interested in technical details and fail to realize that project management requires more of his skills as a manager than as a technician. Thus attention to the whole and not merely to its parts is essential. Plans should be flexible enough to accommodate change as time goes on. To do this, changes should be incorporated into the system providing they have met the following conditions:

(1)   The system changes have evolved out of and eventually will become part of the documented plan of action.

(2)   The changes have been reviewed periodically and management has signed off in some formal manner before their becoming part of the plan, so that they may be considered as understood, cost-justified, and expected to improve the application.

(3)   A formal mechanism exists for discussing change and incorporating that procedure into the project.

(4)   Proposed changes have been fully documented before being accepted. (Figure 2–6 illustrates the initial form that can be used for a change request.)

(5)   Periodic reviews of plans have been held at all levels of involved management to insure full understanding of changes.

These five points as a rule provide several important benefits. First, they provide a means of maintaining tight control over the entire process. Second, they help to insure that considerable attention is given to changes before the modifications become part of the plan. Third, one is forced to document changes to the same level of detail as are all other aspects of the project so that misunderstandings and ill feelings are kept to a minimum. Finally, they force everyone to conform to either original schedules or modified timetables after management has signed off on changes. In advance, everyone involved in a project will understand what is expected of them under the new conditions.

## Reviews

Periodic reviews should be held throughout the project to insure control. These consist of essentially two types. The first involves an examination of the plans and what has been done to date, problems encountered and overcome, weaknesses identified and corrections approved, rejected, or proposed. These reviews usually involve management at the project level and just above, both DP and user. Reviews should be held at least at the end of each phase of the project to review the past and gain approval to continue on with the next step. This is particuarly important after the design phase and just before coding actually takes place, because the development stage is the one requiring the greatest allocation of programmers, acquisition of hardware and software, and consequently costs the most.

The second type of review is of a more technical nature, usually held within the DP group. Its purpose is to walk through the flow charts of each aspect of the application in order to make sure that inputs, logic, and outputs are correctly developed and handled, all of the details and objectives of the new system met, and in fact the appropriate code and files developed. These technical reviews should take place on a periodic basis during each of the phases of project development right down through testing and eventually a post-installation review. On occasion, such reviews might be attended by users to insure that those using the application appreciate what inputs to provide, how to use terminals, and understand the outputs generated. These reviews have as their ultimate objective to catch technical flaws in the logic, programming, hardware configuration, and use of software. They are also the vehicle for developing a strategy for testing the system. All reviews should contain specific objectives, have a predefined time limit, and generate a well-understood document with a follow-up plan.

## Development Phase

With controls in place and armed with a detailed design, one can enter the development phase. This is the most time-consuming and expensive stage of a project because it is the time when the application will be written and tested involving the largest number of people, software packages, and possibly the installation of more hardware. There are basically two measures which have to be taken at this point. First, programmers have to be assembled and given their responsibilities. Second, their output must be checked and tested. The relevant issues in this phase can be cataloged as programming teams, coding methods, communications, tools, and testing.

## Programming Teams

A management technique which is proving most effective in assembling programmers for a project is the chief programmer team concept. In the past a project manager might have had several technical assistants (development programmers) all working independently of each other. Now with chief programming teams (CPTs), one assembles groups to carry on the programming for a portion or all of an application, depending on the size of the project. These teams consist usually of a leader, a chief programmer skilled in the appropriate languages and application, usually other programmers if needed with related skills but with specialties of their own, a librarian responsible for preserving all plans, documentation, computer runs, files, tapes, cards, etc., plus any additional people necessary to carry out a specific part of the project.

With the use of CPTs, the flexibilities found in top-down and modular programming are carried forward into the development and testing phases. With such teams one can take on a portion of the project, assign specific responsibilities to each team member, and coordinate the activities of all. The amount of responsibility which should be assigned and the number of teams that must work on various parts of an application depend on individual experiences, size of the project, its degree of difficulty to code, complexity of the logic, and personal feelings of programmers and managers. However, the DP industry is rapidly approaching the general conclusion that no individual team should be given the responsibility for producing more than 100,000 lines of code. Beyond that, one should consider multiple teams reporting to a project leader who can coordinate the activities of various groups, monitor progress, and shift resources around as needed.

## Coding Methods

Once a CPT has been created, the method by which it will work is as important to a successful project as all previous activities. Preserving the benefits of modular programming by breaking up a project into manageable pieces makes control and development easier. Therefore, a manager should insist that his CPT use:

1. *Top-down Development.* Much like top-down design, this involves the writing of the most important, highest-level logic first, followed by supporting modules, each of which can be tested before the next level or piece of code is written. Although there is much literature on this technique, it is important to understand its benefits in this book. First, the higher-level modules are repeatedly tested against the newest modules, to insure that the most important pieces of code are the most frequently tested and corrected. Second, control over the quality and accuracy of coding is assured. The top-down approach is an ongoing process which allows management to identify and solve problems early before they generate costly revisions to an existing system.

2. *Structured Programming.* This allows a manager to guide his programmers into writing code which all other members of a CPT can understand, eliminating a programmer's fascination with exotic programming

and logic which offers the company no benefit. This technique forces standards of identification, use of predefined commands, macros, and conventions, the elimination of unnecessary branching, and uniformity of coding expression on all members. Benefits include the ability for individuals to manipulate and use larger blocks of code, reduction in the number of errors, and thus shorten the time it takes to produce tested code (an expensive item in all application development), and well-documented programs.

Both techniques provide a considerable amount of flexibility for management to make relevant changes within a minimum amount of either uncertainty (risk) and rewriting of code. When company management philosophies are also applied, these coding techniques and the use of CPTs allow fine-tuning and adjustments throughout the coding process.

## Communications

The methods just described suggest that there has to be substantial attention paid to communications. Every system design assumes having all involved individuals understand the objectives of their mission, their own responsibilities and successes to date, and appreciate what everyone else has done or is doing. Seven simple actions will help satisfy the need for good communications.

(1) Use kick-off meetings at the start of the development phase to review plans, goals, time tables, and have all groups present.

(2) Make available a document defining the general requirements of the system and a statement of each individual's responsibilities and deadlines.

(3) The written plan of action should be available and up-to-date.

(4) Establish a library for the project with one central source for all the machine and human readable documentation, outputs, etc., for easy access by project members.

(5) Insist on frequent discussions within CPTs, among managers above the team, and with users throughout the development phase. Encourage openness of discussion and make key responsible individuals accessible to everyone involved.

(6) Periodic reports detailing progress should be made either orally or in writing to the entire group.

(7) Educate new members of the CPTs effectively so that they have both the technical skills required and understand the scope of the project to which they are assigned.

## DP Tools

No one is an island in such a coordinated environment as is proposed in this chapter. Therefore, data processing personnel should avail themselves of all tools which are relevant to their work. It is less expensive, for instance, to buy a piece of code than to write it yourself; therefore coding aids or packages should be used when possible. Such devices offer cost justification because they improve human productivity, reduce the time it takes to pass through the development stage, and these tools can be used for other projects in the future, thus spreading their cost over more than one application. Useful tools with a good payback worthy of installation in most DP shops include software monitors, automated data or documentation generators or systems, specific application packages, teleprocessing and hardware simulators, diagnostics, special language processors and compilers, analyzers, and relevant operating and programming systems for use in, for example, online program maintenance or coding.

## Testing

While methods for testing applications could easily take a chapter or more to discuss, suffice it to keep in mind several key points. First, the testing should be against standards either already existing within the company or which have been agreed to in advance and in writing for this particular application during the design phases. Second, testing of code should take place within the DP department while application tests should be conducted with the participation of the users to insure acceptability. The following guidelines will help insure a successful test.

(1) Use a documented testing procedure.

(2) Keep the users in mind when testing a system to insure it meets their needs and is convenient for them.

(3) Allow testing to be done whenever possible by individuals not attached to the application development team, in order to remove bias and offer fresh perspectives.

(4) Overlap testing of systems and code during the development phase so that any remaining serious problems can be caught as as early as possible.

(5) Everything must be tested. This includes all code, documentation, and procedures.

(6) Maintain a log of testing results, corrections, and changes, all properly documented and preserved in the project's library.

(7) Attempt to test all code and procedures in a consistent manner throughout the entire process.

(8) All problems should be reported in writing on a uniform document, preferably a form. This will allow for easier identification of trends in problems, preservation of problem reports, and their corrections.

(9) Scheduling of tests in advance so that appropriate people, software, and hardware are available will reduce wasted effort and time while insuring a smooth flow of events. This need for scheduling is particularly important in small DP shops where testing might interfere with normal production work.

## Installation and Acceptance Test Phases

Following all design, coding, and testing comes the actual installation of the application and its final acceptance by users. Although these phases are fairly simple and short, considerable care must be taken to make sure they are executed properly, because by now the company has invested a great deal in the development of the new application. If not properly handled, costly delays in implementation of the new system may occur. The application will appear to be ineffective and before it is really given a chance, bad press will keep it from being properly exploited.

Several points should be kept in mind to help the transition from DP's testing to actual productive use by another department.

1. Establish a schedule for the actual transition which includes such items as hours when the application in question will be available to users and designate specific hardware and personnel for the move. These same people should later be assigned the routine task of supporting the application and doing maintenance on it. Insure the availability of necessary terminals, cabling, telephones, user personnel, etc., to be in place by the time you go operational.

2. Train the users. Practice sessions run by DP and later by users are essential. New forms and procedures should be reviewed and practiced with. Also prepare a written guide to the new procedures to replace previous pages in an already existing handbook or as the first of what should be an ongoing process of documenting company policies and practices.

3. At this stage in application development, review sessions between DP and users should take place constantly to insure that the transition to the new set of procedures is carried out smoothly. Invariably, un-

anticipated problems arise, but with continued follow-up they can be identified quickly and usually solved without much difficulty.

## Maintenance Procedures

Shortly after an application has been put into use it undergoes a period of great danger to its existence, because at this point most of the criticisms that will ever be raised against it come up. Users, straddled with the new procedures, will compare their tasks against time-worn habits and traditions within their department. Inevitably they will complain about something, despite all the planning and discussions between them and DP held over a long period of time. Some of the criticisms, to be sure, are unreasonable since they grow out of a normal resistance to change, but others may be quite real and serious enough to warrant examination. Therefore, management should make it their policy to review periodically how well the application is being received, and to provide procedures for changing it as the needs of the company evolve.

By program maintenance we mean the alteration of an existing system or file to account for new conditions (for example, a new formula for calculating a cost), or to add new procedures, functions, or data to an existing application. Maintenance also includes correcting problems in logic, improving inputs and outputs while attacking new problems generated by software and hardware changes. Most DP managers would claim that between 50% and 70% of their staff's time is spent on maintenance of existing applications. Therefore, maintenance is an expensive activity that must be managed. To improve the effectiveness of the maintenance effort without tying up even more considerable resources, I suggest the following procedures.

1.  Create a form which must be used to document every request for a change and then use it every time (see Figure 2–6 for a sample form). Dozens of variations of this form can be found in DP publications and auditing guides. Essentially all alike, they include information on what changes are being requested, the benefits of such changes, and quantifiable improvements and savings must be accounted for. DP should add the cost of these fixes, and signoffs by users' management and responsible authorities within DP in writing must take place. Some statement must also be made whether or not the request was acted upon. This document will allow changes to take place which are cost-effective while preserving a record should a disagreement among departments take place later.

2.  All changes must be documented, flowcharted, tested, and accepted by users before they go live. This will prevent costly errors on the part of either DP or user departments. Treating a change like a new

Title _____

Originator _____ Date ___/___/___

Location _____ Phone No. _____

Request: _____
_____
_____
_____
_____
_____
_____
_____
_____
_____
_____
_____
_____
_____
_____

Justification                          Recommendation

System Development Cost    _____    _____
System Operating Cost      _____    _____
User Savings               _____    _____
                                          _____
Qualitative Benefits _____     _____
_____             _____
_____             _____
                                          _____
Name _____ Date ___/___/___    Name _____ Date ___/___/___

Disposition:   ☐ Approved    ☐ Cancelled,    Authority _____ Date ___/___/___

**Figure 2-6**    Sample of change request. (*Source: IBM Corp.* © *1975.*)

application is often considered a nuisance but, in the long run, is less expensive and safer. Too often one hears stories about a small change to an application taking place by way of a telephone call or a casual visit to a programmer which results in hundreds of thousands of dollars worth of losses because some calculation variable was incorrectly put into the system. It is to avoid this kind of inexcusable, costly, and sadly frequent error that formal procedures should exist.

3.    If an application is expected to require considerable efforts for maintenance, for example, programmers or analysts, then their expense should be accounted for either in cost justification of the application or in the current DP budget. Some DP departments even charge users for maintenance.

## Post-Installation Review

With a set of procedures having been established to maintain a system, one simple task remains to complete the process: the post-installation review. The purpose of such a review is primarily to determine what one did well or poorly so that the experiences gained now can be effectively applied to the next project. Equally important, one should also take time out to determine if the application in question is operating to everyone's satisfaction. If not, then changes should be discussed in order to increase the usefulness of the new system. A checklist to guide a post-installation review includes the following points.

1.    The review should be between users and DP with high-level management involved to insure sufficient support and participation.

2.    About one month after completing the project and again around three, six, and twelve months later, similar reviews should be held. An effective tool is the survey form which many companies send out to users (particularly if there is a large number of them and scattered all over the country) much like a Gallup poll. If you use such a form, include space for comments since users may come up with suggestions and complaints not anticipated by your questions.

3.    Document all discussions, results of surveys, and action plans. Moreover, users should be told what were the general results of such surveys and meetings and what has been done to improve the system. It is imperative that users be part of the solution so that they identify with the application and will use it. Otherwise, an expensive investment becomes a costly white elephant.

4.    Most important, all parties to periodic post-installation reviews should be allowed to be open, honest, and candid in expressing their views about the new system.

## Summary of Project Management

Figure 2-7 offers an illustration of the various phases of a well-controlled project, reflecting the stages described in the previous pages. What a manager should note from the figure is the relative time required for each phase. Some can be quite short while others (for example, development) may run well over a year. It is worth reviewing some of the key elements behind project management which cause companies to structure formal procedures for all application development.

1. Applications are becoming increasingly complex, time-consuming to develop, and expensive. They interrelate with existing procedures, data bases, and reflect company policies. And increasingly, large numbers of a company's personnel depend on DP systems to do their jobs. Therefore, if applications are not handled in an organized fashion they may never be completed, rarely reflect the true needs of a company, and usually prove far more expensive than originally thought.

2. Since management authorizes the development of applications, which ultimately impacts the profitability of the organization, there is constant concern as to whether they make the company competitive, and provide good and fast customer service. Thus a well-thought-out appli-

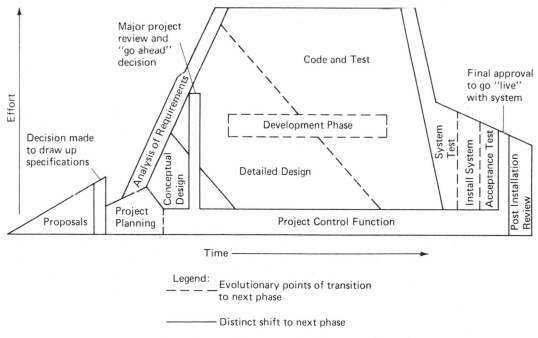

**Figure 2-7** Life cycle of a new system.

71

cation is essential since it may mirror an organization's weaknesses to the outside world. (One thinks of a good versus a bad order entry or billing system as examples.)

3.    The development of an application on  a timely basis may often have a profound impact on the ability of a company to maintain its profitability at certain levels. For example, the establishment of an inventory control system so that it would be in use at a time when management anticipates their product line to be mature or increase in size, may be vital to the survival of the organization. Thus, projects in DP must be coordinated to contribute to a company's game plan in much the same fashion as other departments.

4.    Controls help management at every step of the way to determine if the costs and benefits of a particular application are still justified given the current business environment. This last feature is ultimately the most important reason for introducing a disciplined approach to the development of applications.

## SHORT-TERM DP PLANNING

In part one of this chapter, it was suggested that long-range planning by DP and their companies as a whole provide the fundamental advantage of allowing all activities to be coordinated for maximum benefit. In the previous section on project planning, the emphasis was on achievement of long-range goals through specific application development. These two activities have one common characteristic: they take place over a long period of time and involve various parts of a company. There is another form of planning, namely, short-term planning within the data processing department for specific items over a smaller period of time. Such planning is essential if DP is to anticipate its needs and have them reflected in annual budgets. Moreover, without such short-term plans, top management will not fully understand what long-range goals might cost. Therefore, it is mutually advantageous both to DP and higher management to insist that a departmental list of needs be established, prioritized, and quantified by cost. At least this way, management can fight for certain allocations or reject demands deemed unreasonable.

For data processing, short-term planning involves understanding what kinds of hardware and software will be needed now, next year, and in the subsequent two to five years with their associated costs. Second, a definition of personnel requirements is also important. While it would be difficult to determine specific costs for people and products three to five years out, it is not unreasonable to come within a few percentage points in forecasting expenses for the next eighteen to twenty-four months and have that kind of data reflected in a DP plan.

## Hardware

Perhaps no question causes more arguments and discussions on a continual basis than hardware. The demand for hardware comes not only from DP management, but also from operations, vendors with new products, and users demanding more terminals and better response times. Hardware is usually a large line item in a budget and thus a tempting target for a controller wishing to cut down expenses, who might forget that the equipment was cost-justified. As hardware products evolve and the needs of a company change, the pressure to discuss equipment continues, causing more conversations. A convenient way to approach the problem is to think in terms of function. How much computer power do I need for processing? Of what level of reliability must it be for me to do my work and support the company's users? How much data storage capability do I need for all the files and what kind of devices should be used? If data entry functions are changing along with the need and timeliness of data, how best do I support this? Translate these functional and volume requirements into specific products (hardware) with their associated costs over a given period of time. As demands and hardware costs and capabilities evolve, a written hardware plan can be updated.

Before developing such a plan, let us understand the computer requirements. There are basically two issues always to be resolved. First, how many cycles (horsepower) do I need and when? Second, how much memory must I have and when? Both these questions should be answered the best way possible in order to determine how much computer power to plan for next year, the year after, etc. This activity also impacts the kinds of hardware strategy and financing (which will be discussed in Chapter 4). The way to define your needs is, first, periodically measure the computer cycle, memory, and channel usage. In virtual storage type devices, also examine your paging rates. There are innumerable packages on the market today that will provide this kind of data at a relatively small cost. Many operating systems also provide such information (for example, IBM's OS/VS system control programs). In fact, when considering which major operating system to go to, one should give careful attention to such features. Second, this output should be compared against previous experience with cycle and core demands. Invariably, DP managers underestimate the amount of computer power that they need. They may also not be using what resources they have in the most effective manner. Thus if you look back over the past ten years within your own company, and plot that track record (particularly after the addition of some major application), you may find that the DP managers contracted for computers for five or six years, yet later found themselves severely constrained after four or less. This happens frequently enough for top management to insist on detailed and constant monitoring of computer usage especially when long-term contracts extending beyond four years are being considered.

Since the history of the industry as a whole suggests that quantum jumps in computer power demand are the norm every several years, a DP manager might reasonably assume that this pattern would be reflected in his shop, especially if the volume of business is growing or if the number of applications increases. Thus it is essential that a company understand the history of computer power requirements within its own organization and compare that against more current data on its computer usage. The outputs of various computer monitors might be graphed and the impact of putting new applications onto the system evaluated. This kind of exercise allows one to have a better understanding of what new applications and increased volumes of transactions will do to a computer system.

Figure 2-8 illustrates a hypothetical situation that can serve as a model. In this instance, by 1979, the company will have to acquire more horsepower and should plan much earlier on how to obtain it. Early warning signs would include decreased response time on the terminals, outputs on usage from software monitors, and the planned addition of new applications. Figure 2-9 plots a hypothetical pattern of memory growth for the same company—a pattern which in this case is relatively close to the DP industry's record in reality. When the question of computer usage is looked at this way, a case can be established for feeling comfortable with the current system or to begin planning for another. Such graphs can also be drawn to track the history of response times, paging, and channel utilization in order to determine requirements for other hardware, such as peripheral devices.

Along with an analysis of computer usage, data processing should take a hard look at how much data the department must have in machine-

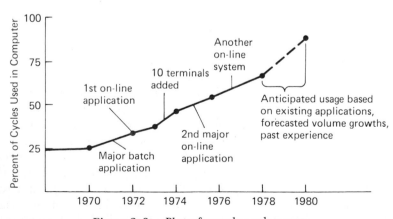

**Figure 2-8**    Plot of sample cycle usage.

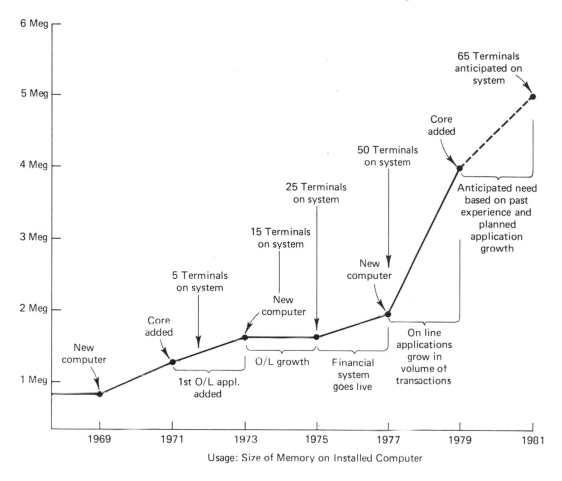

**Figure 2-9** Sample history of memory (core).

readable form and online over a period of at least one to two years. Techniques similar to those used for computers can help again. A combination of software monitors and a history of demand for storage for specific applications and types will allow the development of a forecast to take place that is believable to various levels of management. This kind of data can then easily be compared against the types of disk and tape devices in the market place. Thus, for example, say a company determines that the number of files (at roughly a certain size each) grew between 200% and 215% each year over the period 1965–1975, and at 250% over the next five years with the introduction of numerous online systems. It could take that information and compare it against what new applications were going to be developed and what quantities of data would have to be provided to support existing batch and online systems. This would then allow a DP manager to conclude that he needed certain types of storage devices with specific capabilities over a period of time. The same exercise can be conducted for terminals since they tend to proliferate like rabbits. Their demand should be based on existing applications (with their history of growth in numbers by application) and against anticipated new systems. Figure 2-10 illustrates a hypothetical situation where terminals are viewed both in terms of numbers and by application. Such an exercise can be extended to examine terminals by device types and by cost.

Armed with such supporting data, management can now document a hardware requirements plan for the immediate future and reflect that in the annual budgets. Moreover, by understanding what is needed, management will be in a better position to either reduce the rate of hardware growth, or stabilize it by such means as controlling its usage and regulating application development. And if more is needed, the quantity will be appreciated and can be ordered in time for delivery when needed. By doing the detailed homework for each type of device or software, management at the DP level will find it easier to put together a case for more equipment, much in the same manner as do managers in other departments requiring additional machinery, or people. Figure 2-11 illustrates what a general hardware plan might look like.

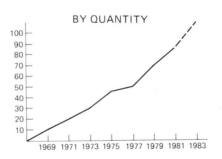

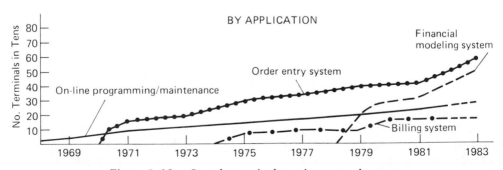

**Figure 2-10**    Sample terminal requirements charts.

**Figure 2-11** Sample equipment requirement plan.

| | Jan. 1980 | March | June | Sept. | Jan. 1981 | March | June | Sept. | Jan. 1982 |
|---|---|---|---|---|---|---|---|---|---|
| Disk storage | 2 spindles disk — Order entry appl. | | | 2 spindles disk — Program on-line | | | 2 spindle disk + control unit | | |
| Tape storage | | | | | 1 tape drive + control unit | | | | |
| CRTs | Order entry 5 | Financial 7 | Programmers order entry 2 | Billing order entry 3 | Finance order entry 10 | Manufactur. billing 5 | Programming 3 | Order entry 10 | |
| Computer memory | | | | 1 Meg. | | | | | |
| Computer | | | | | | | | | 3-4 meg + 2X current cycles |
| Lease increment in thousands $/month | $1.5 | $.7 | $1.2 | $3.3 | $1.6 | $.5 | $1.3-5 | $5-6 | |

A document of a similar type should be part of a general overall planning record which is kept up-to-date for immediate reference.

## Software

A similar exercise should be done for software products. This would include application products, testers, monitors, telecommunication programs, analyzers, and other productivity analysis tools. This is especially important since many packages are expensive and come in a variety of costs: continuous leases, term rents, and purchase only. Often their acquisition must be coordinated with the development of new applications and as a result of overall DP plans, for instance, development of all future applications under data base or programming online. Figure 2-12 illustrates how this planning might be done with software. The two figures on hardware and software plans are commonly used in various forms by a large segment of the data processing industry today. Your company needs only to develop one which appeals to the particular managers involved and is of sufficient detail to cover the issues relevant for the company.

## People

The elements which go into a plan for personnel can also be charted to include the following considerations:

- Number of programmers, systems analysts, operations and data entry personnel needed and when
- Necessary managers for additional staff
- Salaries, bonuses, and benefits for each
- Facilities for each (telephones, offices, desks, etc.)

Such information, blocked out over a one- to two-year period with inflation factored in, gives management an input to the data processing budget that can be varied depending on what new applications are added, and to take into account normal turnover in personnel and inflation. Figure 2-13 illustrates a simple method of keeping track of a personnel plan, including what budget account to charge. As individuals go through their training, line items can be checked off. A similar chart for individuals undergoing a great deal of education might also be useful.

Periodically, management should analyze the rise in cost of personnel, hardware, and software within the DP budget and for the company as a whole in order to understand the relationship among all three groups of expenses. That kind of perspective will influence planning. Thus, for example, if personnel costs rise 200% faster every three years than any

| Application | 1st Qrt 1980 | 2nd Qrt 1980 | 3rd Qrt 1980 | 4th Qrt 1980 | 1st Qrt 1981 | 2nd Qrt 1981 |
|---|---|---|---|---|---|---|
| Programmer Productivity | | | | APL compiler $100/month | On-line lib. $75/month-2yr | |
| Data Base | | DB language $300/month | DB dictionary $100/month | | | |
| Financial Model | | | | XYZ package $15K one time | | |
| Billing System | | Report gen. $300 one time | | | | |
| Analyzers | Disk file anal. $100/mo.-1 yr | | | | | |
| TP System | | | | | | Network simul. $500/month |
| Additional Cost/Month | $100/month | $300/month $300 one time | $100/month | $100/month $15K one time | $75/month | $500/month |
| Total Cost/QRT | $300 | $1,500 | $1,800 | $17,100* | $2,325 | $3,825 |

*Amortize over longer period?

**Figure 2-12**   Sample software requirement plan.

79

| People | 1st QRT 1980 | 2nd QRT 1980 | 3rd QRT 1980 | 4th QRT 1980 | 1st QRT 1981 |
|---|---|---|---|---|---|
| Programmers | 2 @ $18K [5]<br>Billing system | | | 1 @ $18.5K [5]<br>Manufact. sys | |
| Analysts | | | 1 @ $22K [5]<br>Manufact. sys | | |
| Data Entry | 2 @ $8K [2] | 1 @ $8K [2] | | 1 @ $8K [2] | 3 @ $8.5K [2] |
| Education<br>—TP<br>—Data Base<br>—Management<br>—Travel | $1,500 [8]<br>$500 [711]<br>$300 [714]<br>$800 [711] | $300 [714]<br>$400 [711] | $500 [8]<br>$1,500 [714]<br>$450 [711] | $500 [8]<br>$250 [711]<br>$475 [711] | $350 [714] |
| Facilities | $450 [4] | $150 [4] | $150 [4] | $150 [4] | $100 [4] |

All figures are annual expenditures/QRT.
Accounts to be charged are in inserts.

**Figure 2-13**   Sample DP personnel plan.

80

other segment of a budget, management has to determine whether this is due to new application development, lazy programmers, or inefficient use of productivity tools and techniques. Do the current staff merely need to be updated through schooling or are they poorly managed? Is over-staffing the problem, or overwork? Without going through the effort of examining personnel trends from a number of viewpoints, the magnitude of personnel costs will not be fully appreciated. It is not enough to know that DP personnel costs are rising faster than any other segment of a budget or that they account for approximately two thirds of the expense. A company gains the opportunity to address what seems like an inevitable expense as a manageable expense only by looking beyond the numbers to determine how they grew. This in turn will make for better short- and long-term planning.

## SUMMARY

The overall objective of DP planning is to define where you are and where you are going. In most companies, planning future data processing entails the following criteria:

- Match DP industry developments against company needs
- Reflect company goals in DP plans
- Quantify the costs and time for each DP action

Instinctively many managers observe the first two elements, if they keep up with developments within the DP industry and their company. Often the third criterion is poorly handled, resulting in cost overruns, sloppy financial and budgetary management, and delayed receipt of benefits from DP services. Managers frequently complain that planning takes too much time. Yet the best managers and executives are those who do plan and time their actions well. The objection to planning can easily be overcome by reminding such individuals who complain that without planning, the costs of DP would be too high. Once a set of basic plans is in place, keeping them up-to-date is fairly simple anyway. Documenting as you go along makes change easier. Equally important, written strategies give managers a considerable amount of ammunition to use in arguing a case. In short, the well-organized DP plan will stand a better chance of being understood and accepted by a higher management with little or no data processing experience. For such executives a well-thought-out plan would incorporate:

- Costs
- Quantified benefits

- Time tables
- A recommended strategy

For management, disciplined data processing plans and well-defined goals provide two additional benefits. First, the data processing department can be more effectively audited and therefore controlled by higher executives. Second, the accounting standards of the entire company can be imposed on data processing through budgets, projected expense reports, and analyses of proposed applications written for the decision maker who probably knows little about data processing. Increasingly, these two benefits are becoming more important because data processing expenses as a percentage of a company's total budget, generally are growing—a fact one has to assume will continue true for a given company until proven otherwise.

The three sections described in this chapter (long-range planning, project planning, and short-term DP planning) will allow a company to take into account developments in the data processing industry, a company's immediate and long-range goals, and provide the necessary discipline to insure cost-effective performance. The next chapter will take this discipline one step further by illustrating how to cost-justify specific data processing services.

I like fighting successful people,
attacking them, rousing them,
trying their mettle, kicking down
their sand castles so as to make
them build stone ones and so on.

*George Bernard Shaw*

*Knowing why and how you use computerized technology is the basis for determining all costs in data processing. Chapter 3 helps you define why and when to use computers, shows how to justify in business terms the use of computerized technology, and illustrates through specific case studies the process of justifying new applications. In each instance business considerations and business terms are related to technology. Unique situations within data processing that affect justification and ultimately business decisions are defined carefully. By the end of this chapter you will be able to justify an application and compare its desirability to other non-DP projects within a company.*

# CHAPTER THREE

# Applications
# and Their Justification

The reason any company spends money on data processing is to derive benefits from the use of applications. What a company uses computerized technology for provides the justification of all its expenses. Everything stems from this fact. All hardware, software, people, and space in data processing are an outgrowth of applications required by the business. For the vendor, it determines his sales. For the management of a company it governs data processing policies, costs, and usage. In the following pages, we will illustrate how to analyze applications to determine and justify their costs. There are as many ways to justify applications as there are companies and the variables in each case differ significantly. However, justification for new applications generally come from several simple sources.

## REASONS FOR APPLICATIONS

1. *Cost Savings.* Those tasks which are repetitive and require a substantial amount of human resources which could be performed less expensively and more accurately by a computer provide a tremendous source of justification. This, for example, might include clerical accounting functions and simple inventory control.

2. *Improved Service.* When certain functions grow to such large proportions that service to customers or major groups of users degrades, data processing becomes a viable tool to remedy the problem. Examples include inquiry of customer files on terminals to satisfy requests for information on ordered products, rapid inquiry about stock availability, or status of A/R files. Being able to process orders on a timely or competitive basis often provides system justification.

3. *Accuracy and Timeliness of Information.* As the volume of data being processed by a company increases, the need to have access to that information quickly and to have it accurate becomes critical. For instance, being able to determine at any given time the amount of inventory on hand might influence service to customers. Being able to make an immediate credit check might prevent an order entry clerk from accepting business from customers with a poor payment record. Being able to discipline the flow of information into a company quickly could allow management to know how much cash it has on hand so that a decision can be made on how to invest it quickly.

4. *Control of the Business.* This is perhaps the most important reason given by managers for using data processing and yet it is one of the most difficult to define and cost-justify. Managers all agree that understanding what is going on in the business as early as possible allows them to make better quality decisions and to react to growing problems. Thus, for example, a manufacturing manager would want to know how many parts he had on hand and be able to plan his orders for more in order to keep the production flow continuous. Understanding that back orders are increasing faster than orders in general would clearly indicate that production is insufficient and perhaps, if known early enough, the problem could be resolved before customers began doing business with a competitor. Being able to handle the sheer growth in the amount of data in a manageable fashion with timely reporting to management is an essential contribution that can be made by data processing.

5. *Better Quality Decision Making.* Closely related to control of the business is the need to define in detail various options for a decision. The more information which is available for that decision the better a manager can plan and decide a course of action. The convenience and speed of

computer technology lends itself to this activity. For example, a purchase vs. lease analysis on a particular piece of equipment taking into account taxes, resale values, depreciation, purchase, maintenance, and insurance if undertaken in a manual fashion would discourage all but the most enthusiastic financial officer from defining more than two rough options. With data processing it is possible in a relatively short time to come up with numerous options each with a set of detailed supporting numbers. Now a more informed purchase vs. lease decision can be made.

Although the list could be expanded to take into account politics, budget considerations, etc., most properly justified applications incorporate some if not all of the five characteristics listed above. Justification involves defining two sets of numbers and variables: costs and benefits of a proposed application. The costs can be expensed, capitalized, guessed at or defined in detail. Costs can be considered as an investment or as a necessary evil. Benefits are of two types: tangible, which lend themselves to definition in money, and intangible which are factors perceived to have value for the organization but for which quantification is not possible or desirable. Costs include people, hardware, programs, development, space, files, and forms. Tangible benefits might include savings in personnel salaries and benefits, improved inventory turnover, a percentage reduction in bad debt, or any other advantage which lends itself to quantification. Intangible benefits include the ability to have more accurate information, better control of the business, happier customers, and improved morale within the company. Most applications will include definable and undefinable costs and benefits, some of which might not be realized during the stages of justfication, design, and development but which become clear months and years later.

## HOW TO START AN APPLICATION JUSTIFICATION

There are certain characteristics observable in companies that properly study the possibility of adding on an application. This pattern allows management to assess the value of investing effort and money in a given project as opposed to another and to compare DP proposals to non-DP money requests (e.g., plant expansions, additional sales personnel, or in equipment) in similar terms.

1. *Justification Is a Joint DP-User Activity.* Dialogue between the two groups will allow DP to understand a user's problems, concerns, and wants while in return data processing personnel can define the kinds of things they can do to satisfy other departments.

2. *Initiative to Explore an Idea Is Taken by Both Groups.* Through normal daily interaction, various application ideas will occur to both DP

and user departments. This exchange of ideas should be encouraged with initial discussions by both to determine what basis, if any, exists for conducting a justification study.

3.   *All Studies Are Documented.* Following the guidelines developed in Chapter 2 for any project, potential costs and benefits must be put down on paper and shared among the various involved groups so that they can be expanded upon, defined, and understood by all with no misconceptions or understandings.

4.   *Users Take Primary Responsibility for Defining Objectives and Characteristics of a New Application.* No data processing specialist will understand a particular user's job as well as the user unless he devotes considerable time to the study. Thus to avoid a lengthy period being devoted to studying a possible application, the bulk of the work in the initial stages of defining a system's objectives and its inputs and outputs should be done by users. This should be done with the advice of data processing so that the results are usable for more detailed design and coding later. Using HIPO, top-down design, and other techniques allows a company to develop an internal proposal quickly.

5.   *Once an Idea Looks Good, Higher Levels of Management Become Involved.* After an initial study suggests that an application might pay good dividends, then both user and DP management must become involved so that the proposed application can be measured against company-wide objectives and be molded to guidelines established by DP and user departments. Thus, for instance, DP management may advise that for all new online applications include a data base format, which would influence the costs and benefits of a new system. Upper management might wish to impose cost ceilings for a particular year. The important thing to remember is that with upper management involvement, to the degree that the application has high or low costs and benefits, insures that its acceptance or rejection will be made after consideration of many factors and not just those growing out of two departments.

6.   *Management is Flexible in Accepting Cost and Benefit Data.* Cost and benefit studies may not actually represent what the true figures ultimately might be, despite all good intentions, risk analysis, and hard work. Management therefore should require as good a survey as possible but be prepared for the numbers to change as detailed study, design, and implementation continue. By not holding departments to a strict set of numbers in an almost contractual manner, users and DP are encouraged to reveal possible risks and additional sources of benefit that they might otherwise not share with their management.

# A CASE STUDY ON COST JUSTIFICATION:
## DEFINING BENEFITS

The best way to describe how an application is cost-justified is to illustrate the process. It should be kept in mind that the factors involved vary by company and application. However, the kind of exercise done below can be adapted to virtually any application. In our simple case study a company decides that it wants to install online systems. The company knows that the possible application candidates include inventory control, A/R, A/P, billing, and order entry—all to speed up processing. Areas of tangible benefits would also include cost avoidance now and in the future, displacement of people, and tax credits.

In discussing inventory problems, management determines that the objective is to reduce the cost of inventory by maintaining less available stock but not to the point where customer service degrades. To meet this dual objective they conclude that their inventory control system would have to help:

- Reduce obsolete products
- Improve forecast of demand to establish minimum levels of safety stock
- Provide various types of exception reporting
- Improve the way ordering and receiving are done to speed up service and avoid outages and delays.

It was generally agreed that a more precise system for ordering economical quantities should be employed and that warehouses must be stocked depending on item activity throughout the country. DP also suggested that a procedure for automatic generation of purchase orders would be possible to generate.

Upon further examination, it was discovered that receiving documentation took one day to get to the computer before inventory reports could be updated. Through the use of a terminal, instantaneous updating would be possible. Thus inventory stock could be cut by one day's sales. If gross inventory were forty million dollars and there were 250 working days in a year, dividing the sales by the days and taking the percentage of inventory carrying cost gives us the savings. Thus $40,000,000 divided by 250 yields $160,000 plus carrying cost (e.g., 20% in our case which equals 20% of $160,000 or $30,200) means $160,000 plus $30,200 for a total savings of around $190,000.

Looking at the accounts receivable area, the accounting department defined as possible areas of savings:

- Reduction of bad debt write-offs
- Reduction of unearned discounts being taken by customers
- Credit checking at order entry time to avoid credit overruns.

Further study led to the conclusion that a shorter collection period could be established by: speeding up customer payments, going to exception reporting, and automated generation of dunning letters. Current procedures would be reviewed carefully to determine how the accounting department handled follow-up on delinquent accounts and applied payments. After consultation with the user department it is agreed that processing through terminals instantaneously might reduce the collection period by one day, providing that the three procedures listed above were utilized. A look at the annual A/R shows $20,000,000 outstanding. Divided by 250 days yields $80,000 in possible savings just in this area alone.

Next, analysis of the cost of goods sold (accounts payable portion of the expense) was conducted. Personnel in A/P thought potential areas of savings would come from:

- Taking vendor discounts (not always done now)
- Improving freight and volume discount benefits by consolidating orders to smaller number of vendors
- Ordering additional supplies, inventory, etc., when vendors had special prices, providing carrying costs were less than the special discount prices
- Generating statistics on money spent this year versus last year by vendor, vendor location, and by product or item.

In moving on, similar discussions with the order entry and billing personnel suggested that converting to prebilling from post-billing would offer several advantages. Time from receipt of order to mailing of invoices should be reduced. Second, picking slips for warehouses could be printed at the same time as invoices. Third, picking slips could have items listed in sequence in which they were stored at the warehouse to speed up the work there. Overall benefit involved reduction of time from when the order was placed to the time the invoice was sent to the customer.

In the course of this study, it was discovered that there were twenty order entry clerks and ten keypunch/verifiers working full time. Currently it takes one and a half days from order entry to invoice printing. With an online system DP says half a day in the cycle would be cut. Since the controller and his staff agreed that customers would pay sooner if they received their invoices earlier, the area of potential savings was defined. In this case, an additional half day's worth of A/R would be realized or half of $80,000 which yields a $40,000 one-time benefit by prebilling.

In the course of this survey, it appeared that another area of savings would be in labor costs. In each application area, numerous individuals were carrying on functions that might be partially carried out by computerized means. The areas of personnel savings included:

- Automating repetitive manual operations
- Increasing the productivity of personnel already employed
- Reducing the need to hire additional people
- Displacing persons for use elsewhere in the organization.

Determining people displacement savings is a simple calculation. Once it is agreed by users that a certain number of individuals could be removed from a certain function by a computerized application, their salaries and benefits are added up. Cost avoidance for anticipated future personnel also are taken into account. Thus for example, four people at $10,000 each can be saved in our case for a savings of $40,000 in the first year. For each year of the analysis the four salaries are tabulated with (in our case) a 6% annual inflation factor. Therefore, in year two the savings is $42,400, year three $44,900, etc. This kind of exercise can be done for as many years of the analysis as necessary. Future savings in people who did not have to be hired once the new application is operational should be done in the same manner. There still continues the myth that computers will displace people. In reality, one rarely hears of anyone being fired because they were replaced by a computer. What really happens is that the displaced individuals are used in other parts of the company that have a need for additional help. What is often overlooked is the fact that moving people around within the organization is often far more desirable than firing them and hiring new people for other departments. By firing individuals, managers would be losing people who have a certain knowledge of the company and of its activities—experience and information which in itself is an asset to the company. At most, the change of people simply results in shifting personnel costs to other budgets, to areas where they can be productive, and into positions that help keep down the cost of adding people to the payroll.

After an analysis of people in various functional areas, the DP department moved into its own operations to determine what old equipment savings it could obtain by changing devices to accommodate online systems supporting inventory control, A/R, A/P, billing, etc. It determined that certain currently installed devices would no longer be needed and others could be slower and consequently less expensive models.

In the online environment it was decided that order entry should be handled by the order entry department, thereby eliminating the need for ten keypunch machines currently used to punch order entry cards. With fewer cards being punched, slower card and punch readers could be used for other processing. The DP analysis looked like this:

> 10 keypunch machines at $100/month = $1,000/month
>   × 12 months yielded. . . . . . . . . . . . . . . . . . . . . . . . .      $12,000
> Downgrade card punch from 300 to 100 cards per minute
>   yielded $200/month savings × 12 months yielded. . . . . .      $2,400
> Downgrade card reader from 1200 cps to 600 cps led to
>   $150/month × 12 months yielded . . . . . . . . . . . . . . .      $1,800
> Monthly card cost reduction of $300 × 12 months yielded. .      $3,600
>
> *Total savings by displacement* . . . . . . . . . . . . . . . . . . . . . .      *$19,800*

Finally, the question of profit improvement came up. With a new online receivables system, the marketing staff determined they could avoid a repetition of last year's loss of $5,000,000 in cancelled orders because of out-of-stock conditions and back orders. The vice-president for sales said he would believe the new system would save him one million dollars in lost sales with the same level of inventory as now and thus committed to the smaller number for profit calculations. The calculation is performed in the following manner:

$$\text{Current profit before taxes (\%)} = \frac{\text{PBT}}{\text{Net sales}}$$

$$\text{In our case:} = \frac{\$100,000,000 \text{ (from annual report)}}{\$300,000,000 \text{ (from annual report)}}$$

$$= 33.3\%$$

Sales increases            = $1,000,000

PBT increases            = Sales increase × current PBT%

In our case:            = $1,000,000 × 0.333

            = $330,000

These, then, were the various means for establishing areas of savings and benefits. At this point one must consolidate all of the savings which have been quantified and agreed to by the users, into a simple document that can be used to work against when comparing costs against savings. For our case, Figure 3–1 serves this purpose. Another sample format for showing benefits and costs is illustrated in Figure 3–2. In both instances, note that the benefits should be defined for the anticipated life of the new change or at least for the minimum period of time required for any project within your company.

| Area of Savings | Potential Last Year | Years | | | | | Totals |
|---|---|---|---|---|---|---|---|
| | | 1 | 2 | 3 | 4 | 5 | |
| Inventory reduction | 190,000 | -0- | 100,000 | 190,000 | 220,000 | 250,000 | 760,000 |
| Sales increase | 1,000,000 | -0- | 500,000 | 1,000,000 | 1,150,000 | 1,300,000 | 3,950,000 |
| A/R reduction | 80,000 | -0- | 10,000 | 90,000 | 180,000 | 200,000 | 480,000 |
| O/Entry cycle reduction | 100,000 | -0- | 50,000 | 100,000 | 130,000 | 160,000 | 440,000 |
| Displace warehouse personnel | — | -0- | 8,800 | 18,400 | 29,800 | 42,800 | 99,800 |
| O/entry personnel displacement | 40,000 | -0- | 40,000 | 42,400 | 44,900 | 48,000 | 175,300 |
| DP hardware displacement | 19,800 | -0- | 21,000 | 22,200 | 24,600 | 27,000 | 94,800 |
| Total annual savings (in cash) | 1,429,800 | | 721,000 | 1,463,000 | 1,779,300 | 1,979,800 | 5,999,900 |

Assumption by users in this case is 15% annual growth in sales and slightly less for expenses in current environment. (Chart does not include costs of on-line applications.)

**Figure 3-1**   Summary of savings.

Following any attempt to define the tangible, quantifiable benefits, the soft or intangible benefits should also be accounted for in any project assessment. Typically there are at least seven general areas of benefit one might find: improved customer service, better management, more positive company image, better financial ratios, a higher level of customer satisfaction, improved employee morale, and more efficient operations. Perhaps the question of improved asset ratios is the easiest one to quantify of the group and the one most often ignored. Each company must determine for itself how such ratios might be measured. One example can be illustrated using inventory ratios to illustrate the kind of exercise one might perform.

| | *Old* | *New* |
|---|---|---|
| Cost of Goods Sold (COGS) | $250,000,000 | $250,000,000 |
| Inventory Value | $65,000,000 | $60,000,000 |

Given the costs of goods sold and their value before implementation of a better inventory control system and the new values after such a system is installed, a determination can be made about the impact of the new application on both inventory turns and shelf life.

# SYSTEMS DEVELOPMENT
## PROJECT CASH FLOW SUMMARY

Request No.: _____

Project Name: _____

User: _____

Prepared By: _____

| Year | 19____ | 19____ | 19____ | 19____ | 19____ | 19____ | Total |
|---|---|---|---|---|---|---|---|
| Present And Projected Operating Costs: | | | | | | | |
| | | | | | | | |
| | | | | | | | |
| | | | | | | | |
| Total Present Operating Costs | | | | | | | |
| Less: Operating Costs Under Proposed System (Use Present Costs Until Time Of Implementation): | | | | | | | |
| | | | | | | | |
| | | | | | | | |
| | | | | | | | |
| Total New Operating Costs | | | | | | | |
| Net Savings In Operating Costs | | | | | | | |
| Plus: Other Intangible Benefits (Give Details Of How These Additional Savings Are To Be Realized): | | | | | | | |
| | | | | | | | |
| | | | | | | | |
| | | | | | | | |
| Total Benefits | | | | | | | |
| Less: Development And Implementation Costs And Staffing Level | Cost / Staff | Cost / Staff | Cost / Staff | Cost / Staff | Cost / Staff | Cost / Staff | |
| System Design _____ | | | | | | | |
| Program Specifications _____ | | | | | | | |
| Program Coding And Unit Test _____ | | | | | | | |
| System Test _____ | | | | | | | |
| Parallel Test _____ | | | | | | | |
| Conversion _____ | | | | | | | |
| Total Development And Implementation Costs | | | | | | | |
| Net Benefit (Cost) | | | | | | | |
| Present Value Factors (At ___%) | | | | | | | |
| Yearly Present Value Of Net Cost (Benefit) | | | | | | | |
| Cumulative Present Value Of Net Cost (Benefit) | | | | | | | |

**Figure 3-2**   (*Source: IBM Corp. © 1975.*)

|  | | Old | | New | |
|---|---|---|---|---|---|
| Inventory turns = | $\dfrac{\text{COGS}}{\text{Inventory}}$ | $\dfrac{\$250,000,000}{\$65,000,000}$ = 3.85 | | $\dfrac{\$250,000,000}{\$60,000,000}$ = 4.16 | |
| Shelf life | = $\dfrac{360 \text{ days}}{\text{Turns}}$ | $\dfrac{360}{3.85}$ = 93.5 days | | $\dfrac{360}{4.16}$ = 86.5 days | |

These figures in turn can be given monetary values by dividing the dollar amount of inventory by the days and then applying that against the above calculations.

## Tips on Making an Accurate Forecast of Benefits

The process just described in the case study is a fairly common one in practice although not always an easy procedure. The biggest problem one faces is obtaining agreement on the quantifiable benefits. Usually users are reluctant to sign off on certain benefits which will result in their obtaining a smaller budget or reduced head count. DP often hesitates as well to make promises that it might not be able to honor. Yet one cannot stress strongly enough the need to develop quantification that both parties can live with. If need be, upper management must use its authority to obtain the numbers. Otherwise the process of justification becomes an unmeasurable and meaningless exercise, particularly when, after a new application has been developed, management wants to look back and determine the accuracy of its projected benefits.

In order to build the level of confidence of both user and data processing management in its forecasts of benefits there are several proven techniques that can be used. Without them, forecasting benefits will be an ultraconservative event, managers will be too cautious, and consequently all will be unrealistic. The net result would be a hard uphill fight in finding justification. Nothing could kill a potentially good application faster than the unwillingness to develop sound cost justification and even to take a few risks in accounting for benefits. A healthy, open-minded recognition by upper management that, despite careful work and risk analysis, actual benefits might not always match forecasted numbers is essential. To help build accuracy into the benefits and for that matter into costs, consider doing the following.

1.  Discuss a proposed application with other companies that already have it installed, interviewing both users and data processing personnel. Good applications are usually looked upon with pride by a company and its personnel are often willing to discuss its details, benefits, and

costs. Computer and software vendors are excellent sources for such references as are the various data processing and professional business associations.

2.   There is a growing amount of literature on computerized applications in just about every business journal and for every industry. Consult these since many give detailed case studies of particular applications already installed.

3.   There is no substitute for detailed study of the current operations and how they might be computerized. Issues to consider during the study include:

- Number of repetitive functions of the same kind performed in an hour or day
- Number of individuals (or man-hours) performing a particular function, their salaries and then breakdown of cost per activity or person
- Cost of materials, forms, furniture, devices, etc., used for a particular service
- Size and quantity of files of data and forms needed for specific activities
- Determination of the cost of lost opportunity by not being able to do more now in a particular area; for example, take more orders
- The cost of doing and using anything this year, next year (grown for inflation by a percentage), and the year afterwards.

In short, examine the detailed functions needed or being used now and gain agreement from all parties on the numbers obtained. By building forecasted benefits on a solid basis of detailed homework, confidence in the estimated benefits will rise. Moreover, objections to committing to numbers will diminish. Long-term, forecasted benefits should be compared against actual attainments to determine what the pattern of behavior is in your company. Do your users traditionally understate benefits and overstate costs? Are benefits of a new application less than forecasted by DP? Why? Such information will help the justification of future applications to be more realistic and acceptable.

## A CASE STUDY ON COST JUSTIFICATION: DEFINING COSTS

The next step in the justification process is to define all the costs of a possible new application. There are essentially two types of expenses involved: recurring and one-time. Examples of recurring costs include the monthly rental or purchase charge for computer equipment, salaries for additional personnel, utilities, rental of software packages, supplies, in short, any expense which is faced throughout the life of the application. Examples of one-time costs include the expense of software conversion, freight charges for delivery of new equipment, the electrician's bill for additional power for computers, air conditioning, education of programmers, and parallel operations during the testing period.

Using our case study the following recurring costs were identified for the online system:

**Additional computer equipment:**

CRT Terminals

| | | | |
|---|---|---|---|
| Order entry dept. | 24 | Sales | 1 |
| Receiving | 3 | Controller | 1 |
| Buying | 3 | A/R dept. | 5 |
| Warehouse | 1 | DP | 2 |

*Total cost of 40, each at $100/month* . . . . . . . . . . . *$4,000/month*

Terminal Printers

| | | | |
|---|---|---|---|
| Order entry dept. | 2 | A/R dept. | 3 |
| Buying | 1 | DP | 1 |
| Receiving | 1 | | |

*Total cost of 8, each at $150/month* . . . . . . . . . . . . . *$1,200/month*

Terminal control unit . . . . . . . . . . . . . . . . . . . . . . $1,000/month

Computer memory upgrade (500K bytes) . . . . . . . . . $500/month

Disk storage (4 spindles) . . . . . . . . . . . . . . . . . . . . $1,000/month

*Total equipment cost* . . . . . . . . . . . . . . . . . . . . . . *$7,700/month*

**Additional software (monthly charge):**

Teleprocessing monitor . . . . . . . . . . . . . . . . . . . . . $400/month

Data base monitor . . . . . . . . . . . . . . . . . . . . . . . . $500/month

Software aids . . . . . . . . . . . . . . . . . . . . . . . . . . . . $200/month

*Total software cost* . . . . . . . . . . . . . . . . . . . . . . . *$1,100/month*

**Additional personnel:**

2 teleprocessing programmers ($2,000/month each) . . . $4,000/month

1 data base administrator/programmer . . . . . . . . . . . $2,200/month

*Total personnel cost* . . . . . . . . . . . . . . . . . . . . . . . *$4,200/month*

**Additional utilities (annual):**

*Electricity for air conditioning* . . . . . . . . . . . . . . . . *$1,500*

**Salary increases for order entry personnel:**

*24 people at $1,200 per year each* . . . . . . . . . . . . . *$28,800*

All this data should then be annualized so that recurring costs can be measured more clearly against annual benefits and be incorporated into a budget. In our case the numbers might look like the following:

**Annual recurring costs for online system:**

| | |
|---|---:|
| Additional computer equipment | $92,400 |
| Additional software | $13,200 |
| Additional people. | $50,400 |
| Additional utilities | $1,500 |
| Salary increases for order entry personnel | $28,800 |
| *Total annual recurring costs* | *$186,300* |

Note that every recurring cost possible was included, even a small one such as utilities. The same thoroughness must next be exercised with one-time costs. In our example they might look like the following:

**Site preparation:**

| | |
|---|---:|
| Cables for CRTs and printers | $2,320 |
| Cost of installing cables | $5,300 |
| Electrical wiring. | $3,000 |
| Furniture | $5,000 |
| Air conditioning addition. | $18,000 |
| *Total site preparation cost* | *$33,620* |

**Education:**

DP staff

| | |
|---|---:|
| Tuition | $10,000 |
| Travel | $3,000 |
| Expenses | $6,000 |
| Salaries | $15,000 |

Terminal operators

| | |
|---|---:|
| Training package development | $1,000 |
| Operator salaries | $15,000 |
| *Total education cost* | *$16,000* |

**Conversion:**

| | |
|---|---:|
| Systems analysts (15 man months at $1,500/month each). | $22,500 |
| Application programming (55 man months at $1,200/month each). | $66,000 |
| Systems programming (4 man months at $1,800/month each). | $7,200 |
| Keypunching (10 man months at $1,000/month each). | $10,000 |

User dept. management and people . . . . . . . . . . . . . . .   $42,000

*Total conversion costs over 27 months. . . . . . . . . . . . . . $147,700*

**Freight charges for computer equipment and furniture . . . . . . .    $2,000**

**Parallel operations . . . . . . . . . . . . . . . . . . . . . . . . . . .   $26,000**

**Vendor services. . . . . . . . . . . . . . . . . . . . . . . . . . . . .   $20,000**

As with recurring expenses, one-time expenses should now be summarized. Taking the above numbers the summary would look like this:

**One-time cost for online system**

Site preparation . . . . . . . . . . . . . . . . . . . . . . . . . . .   $33,620

Education. . . . . . . . . . . . . . . . . . . . . . . . . . . . . . . .   $16,000

Conversion . . . . . . . . . . . . . . . . . . . . . . . . . . . . . . . $147,700

Freight. . . . . . . . . . . . . . . . . . . . . . . . . . . . . . . . .    $2,000

Parallel operations . . . . . . . . . . . . . . . . . . . . . . . . .   $26,000

Vendor services . . . . . . . . . . . . . . . . . . . . . . . . . . .   $20,000

*Total one-time costs . . . . . . . . . . . . . . . . . . . . . . . . . $245,320*

Figure 3-3 illustrates how the costs would be broken out for the case above over a five year period. Here each of the costs defined above is distributed by year for each line item so that both detail and gross num-

| Area of Cost | Years | | | | | Totals |
|---|---|---|---|---|---|---|
| | 1 | 2 | 3 | 4 | 5 | |
| Equipment | 50,000 | 92,400 | 92,400 | 93,000 | 93,500 | 420,900 |
| Software | 6,000 | 13,200 | 13,200 | 13,500 | 13,800 | 59,700 |
| Additional People | 20,000 | 50,400 | 54,000 | 59,000 | 63,000 | 246,400 |
| Utilities | —0— | 1,500 | 1,700 | 1,900 | 2,150 | 7,250 |
| Salary Increases O/E Clerks | —0— | 28,800 | 30,000 | 32,000 | 34,500 | 125,300 |
| Site Preparation | 33,620 | —0— | —0— | —0— | —0— | 33,620 |
| Education | 35,000 | 15,000 | 500 | 550 | 600 | 51,650 |
| Conversion | 110,000 | 37,700 | —0— | —0— | —0— | 147,700 |
| Freight | 1,500 | 500 | —0— | —0— | —0— | 2,000 |
| Parallel Oper. | 10,000 | 16,000 | —0— | —0— | —0— | 26,000 |
| Vendor Services | 15,000 | 5,000 | —0— | —0— | —0— | 20,000 |
| Total Annual Cost (in cash) | 281,120 | 260,500 | 191,800 | 199,950 | 207,550 | 1,140,920 |

Figures are grown for inflation where appropriate. (Chart does not include savings of on-line applications.)

**Figure 3-3**    Summary of Costs.

bers can be displayed by year and by grand totals. This summary chart in effect can then be compared to the benefits chart. Note that the cost and benefit amounts are carried out for an equal number of years in order to reflect their true relationship for the period of interest to management. If capitalization of application development and its depreciation become more common, such a disciplined approach must be used.

Several additional factors enter into our projections. First, issues surrounding how each of the costs was developed have not been discussed in our case study simply because they vary too much from company to company. However, those involving hardware acquisition, i.e., purchase vs. lease with its tax and cash flow implications will be treated in more detail in the next chapter. Such issues should be resolved with financial and DP management prior to appearing on the cost summary chart. Another slight variation to the pattern of cost and benefit analysis illustrated so far is to develop a benefit table and a cost table with high, medium, and low probabilities as illustrated in Chapter 2. Such a set of tables would allow management to determine what the probability would be of gaining certain types of benefits and what the smallest and largest quantity of expense might be. For a major project such as our online case study, probability tables should be developed and the numbers agreed to by those involved with the new system before going to top management for approval.

## RISK ANALYSIS

Risk matrices are becoming more popular as both a shirtsleeve and detailed quantification of risks in financial analysis in general. Risk matrices can be used for data processing projects just as easily and they help provide an apples-to-apples comparison of risk to other non-DP proposals within a company. Essentially, one assigns the probability of certain events taking place to a low, moderate, or high risk category. Second, the unit of measurement are numbers, for example, 1 through 9 (a number for each square in the matrix). Lower numbers imply lower risk, higher numbers the opposite. The development of such a table should be a joint effort on the part of DP and the users so that management can believe that each of the statements made in any risk matrix is realistic. The development of a risk analysis requires two steps. Step one involves determining what the actual cash flow would be in each category. Step two requires that they be put into a chart showing their relationship. Figure 3-4 illustrates such a matrix. In this example, everyone is very confident that there will be a $2000 displaced expense but feel that it would be a long shot to obtain $10,000 in increased revenue over and above the $20,000 and $15,000 listed. The long shot in our example

| Category | (Odds) Probability in Dollars | | | |
| --- | --- | --- | --- | --- |
| | Low | Moderate | High | Total |
| Displaced Expense | 2,000 | | | 2,000 |
| Avoidable Expense | 1,000 | 1,000 | | 2,000 |
| Increased Revenue | 20,000 | 15,000 | 10,000 | 45,000 |
| Total | 23,000 | 16,000 | 10,000 | 49,000 |

**Figure 3-4**     Benefit matrix in dollars.

| Category | (Odds) Probability in Dollars | | | |
| --- | --- | --- | --- | --- |
| | High | Moderate | Low | Total |
| People | 2,000 | 1,000 | 500 | 2,500 |
| DP Equipment/ Software | 100 | 50 | 10 | 160 |
| Other | 50 | 30 | 10 | 90 |
| Total | 2,150 | 1,080 | 520 | 3,750 |

**Figure 3-5**     Cost matrix in dollars.

was included in the matrix since a sufficient number of individuals felt the company might be able to realize that additional benefit.

A cost matrix in dollars again provides some measurement of possible exposure to expenses. In the cost matrix, everyone seems very certain that the company will have to spend $2000 on people but that at the other extreme, the chance of only having to spend an additional $500 is low. Figures 3-6 and 3-7 transform the same dollar relationship for the benefit and cost matrices into a measurement of 1 through 9 (in this case). Thus in Figure 3-6, everyone feels that there is a low risk in displacing $2000 in expenses—hence the rating of one—but since they feel that additional savings in displacement are less probable, they assigned the numbers 3 and 6. The arrows simply suggest that what happens at the start of the arrow determines what the probability is to its right. Thus the reason for assigning a 2 to avoidable expense is because of the nature of the displaced expense being anticipated. A rating of 4 in increased revenue influenced giving avoidable expenses in the medium

| Category | Low | Moderate | High |
|---|---|---|---|
| Displaced Expense | 1 | 3 | 6 |
| Avoidable Expense | 2 | 5 | 8 |
| Increased Revenue | 4 | 7 | 9 |

1-Low to 5-Moderate to 9-High Risk (Odds)

**Figure 3-6**　　Benefit matrix by points.

| Category | High | Moderate | Low |
|---|---|---|---|
| People | 9 | 3 | 1 |
| DP Equipment/ Software | 8 | 5 | 2 |
| Other | 6 | 7 | 4 |

1-Low to 5-Moderate to 9-High Risk (Odds)

**Figure 3-7**　　Cost matrix by points.

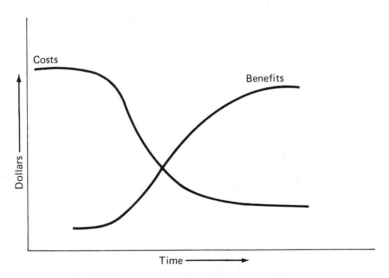

**Figure 3-8**　　Relationship of costs to benefits.

category a rating of 5. In Figure 3-7, a similar numbering system suggests that there is a high possibility that $2000 will be spent on people.

The relationship of the numbers (1-9 in our case) is an important one in trying to quantify risk. The possibility of a particular event occurring increases with the smaller the number. Thus in our matrices, the items numbered 1 will have a better chance of happening than those labeled 5 or even 9. Displaced expenses, being within the control of a company, naturally have much lower numbers than increased revenue which is an activity less under the control of the organization. Avoidable expenses, since they are a function of displaced costs and increased revenue, fall somewhere in the middle and consequently are assigned dollar and number ratings in the middle.

The pattern shown by both the risk matrices and the tables listing dollar values for costs and benefits of the online case study above suggest a common pattern of costs and benefits in any application development cycle. Management should be aware that the high development costs are always at the front end of time and the benefits later. As Figure 3-8 suggests, financial commitment has to be treated more as an investment than as a cost much in the same fashion as that for a new plant or branch office. The tables simply document the details of the expenses and benefits over a period of time so that they can be compared to other candidate projects within the company in common terms.

## FINANCIAL MEASUREMENTS

After documentation of costs and benefits, and possibly using risk matrices to determine probability of costs and benefits, most DP projects are not further analyzed unless they are major in size. They simply come up for decision by top management. However, a further step can be taken to apply the costs and benefits of a DP project to terms financially measurable and thus comparable to other proposals within the company. Specifically, some measurement should be made of profit impact of an application, its payback, return on investment, yield, and tax implications for cashflow. Although it is not the purpose of this chapter to teach the reader how to determine these variables in detail (a subject that could easily fill up a book on its own), it is worth noting that such measurements can be applied to data processing proposals. Today, many companies have computer programs which will generate the necessary calculations for a solid financial analysis of a proposed project.

Upper management will often be requested to pass judgment on a proposed data processing project that has had its costs and benefits defined and for which alternative plans or options are put forth, each with its costs and benefits defined. Two fundamental questions will usually come up. First, what part of the costs require capital outlays which have to appear on the balance sheet, and second, which costs are expensed and consequently have a direct bearing on the company's taxes for a given period of time? Essentially, there are three groups of measurements which can take place now that do not involve budgets specifically: First, executive intuition that one project is better than another; second, a rough cut on benefits to a company by measuring payback periods and average return on investment; and third, there are economic measurements which can be applied such as time value of money, present value, and yield. The bigger the commitment, the more detailed should be the financial analysis. And the degree to which financial analysis is done thoroughly on DP projects, determines the chances of having them approved.

## Payback Analysis

The most common financial analysis on DP projects is payback. In effect, given two alternative investment opportunities which one will return my investment the quickest? A company has $1000 to invest and data processing comes up with a proposal which suggests that $500 will be retrieved in the first year, $400 in the second, $300 in the third, and $100 in the fourth. Manufacturing, requesting some equipment of its own, also wants $1000 and has determined that the company will recover $100 in year one, $200 in year two, $300 in year three, $400 the next year, $500 in the fifth, and $600 in the sixth year. A quick analysis would show that the shortest payback would be the DP proposal and therefore the most tempting by the payback measurement:

$$\$500 + \$400 + \frac{\$100}{\$300} = 2.33 \text{ years to } \$100 + \$200 + \$300 + \$400$$
$$= 4 \text{ years}$$

Yet this particular analysis did not take into consideration very many variables, such as the time value of money or the impact on profits. Payback as a method is usually a useful tool for determining quickly, for example, whether a DP department should purchase some terminals as opposed to renting them to see after what period the purchase would have been cheaper. In the situation above with 2.33 years, this analysis would suggest that after 27 months, the DP investment would generate profits, making purchase an attractive alternative to rent.

## Return on Investment Analysis

There are almost as many formulas for return on investment as there are companies. However, most formulas have a similar basis:

$$\text{ROI} = \frac{\text{Total return on investment}}{\text{Investment}} \times \frac{1}{\text{Life of project}}$$

Using our payback example illustrates the procedure. The DP proposal suggested a return of $1300 for a cost of $1000 over four years or

$$\frac{1300-1000}{1000} \times \frac{100}{4} = 7.5\% \text{ average return for each of those four years}$$

The manufacturing proposal suggested a return of $2100 for a $1000 cost but over six years or

$$\frac{2100-1000}{1000} \times \frac{100}{6} = 18.3\% \text{ average return on investment}$$

In short, by this method of measuring investment, DP loses and the manufacturing proposal wins.

ROI is a popular measurement because of its ease, its answer is a percentage, and it is generally impressive. Yet it has its critics who would argue that it ignores the time value of money in our era of inflation, the sequence of cash flow since the answer is an average percentage, the impact on a company's profits which it does not consider, and also it has too many variations in formula. Most important of all, it allows for no weighted values being given to a proposal because of its control or business attractiveness.

## Time Value of Money Analysis

Given the problems posed by inflation, many companies require that a time value of money analysis be performed on projects of a certain minimum size. Simply put, if you could spend $1000 now, a year later, or two years from the present, which time is the most advantageous for the investment? And by implication, what percent of return must that money obtain to overcome the negative effect on purchasing power by inflation? A company picks an interest rate at which the value of that money must grow in order to keep its purchasing power of $1000 as of today. There are tables commonly available in which you select the year of investment and the percentage of interest (say for inflation) that you feel reflects what will take place and that tells the value of the money. Thus, looking at a present value table, one can determine what the $1000 investment in DP or manufacturing's proposals will provide. By this form of measurement, manufacturing's proposal looks very attractive because there is a greater return on the dollar after a 10%

| | | | Returns on Investment | |
| Years | 10% Factor | (Table Data) | DP Proposal | Manufacturing Proposal |
|---|---|---|---|---|
| 1 | 0.909 | times | $500=$455 | $100=$91 |
| 2 | 0.826 | times | $400=$330 | $200=$165 |
| 3 | 0.751 | times | $300=$225 | $300=$225 |
| 4 | 0.683 | times | $100=$68 | $400=$273 |
| 5 | 0.621 | times | | $500=$316 |
| 6 | 0.564 | times | | $600=$338 |

At present value the return is. . . . . . . . . . . . $1078    and    $1408

Subtract the original investment . . . . . . . . . . $1000    and    $1000

Net present value. . . . . . . . . . . . . .    $78                $408

inflation factor is allowed for. If measured solely on the basis of the first four years, the DP project becomes more attractive. Thus in analyzing alternative proposals, DP management should attempt to evaluate the time differences if net present value (NPV) analysis is to be performed by financial executives in order to make their proposal more attractive or at least to understand the handicap. By itself, NPV again only measures one element: in this case inflation. NPV varies and does not take into account taxes, competitive environment, short payback, or the elements of business control which a DP application might offer over the manufacturing option. As with other financial tools, NPV has its benefits and weaknesses. It is often popular since the answer has the advantage of being expressed in money amounts and anything over zero is profit. It thus takes into account profits and the time value of cash. Its two major drawbacks are that it does not consider the original investment in a project, and it assumes reinvestment at the interest you originally se-lected—hardly realistic these days.

## Yield (Internal Rate of Return)

More popular with financial management than NPV is an internal rate of return measurement (IRR). With DP it is often used in measuring hardware acquisitions. However, increasingly this measurement is being used to evaluate the whole cost and benefits of a data processing project, including in the analysis the expense for equipment, software, develop-ment, people, etc. Yield is the effective rate of annual return on a given investment and thus is a more comprehensive form of measurement that can be used with DP. It is usually based on the actual cost of a project which is discounted by a percentage over time to take into account in-flation. IRR is also a means of measuring the value of transactions, income and outflow, at various times (for example, during the whole life of a project). Most companies have established a hurdle rate or percentage of IRR which a proposal must meet as a minimum. That is, a project will not be considered if it does not meet a minmum internal rate of return. Usually the IRR target will range from 10% to 22% with the average in the past few years being set between 12% and 18%. This figure is often arrived at by taking into account the company's cost of capital at the bank, what it considers it should receive as a fair investment of the money borrowed, and its handling costs within accounting departments. Most computerized financial packages provide IRR analyses which also incorporate tax considerations. (More will be said about tax effects on DP financing in Chapter 4). Curiously, many DP proposals have an IRR which is far above the 12% to 22% hurdle. Take as an example the online case study presented in this chapter. By two different computerized financial packages computing the IRR using 9% cost of capital, the results were IRRs of 230.4% and 251.95%. Either way, the IRR result is impressive.

Keep in mind, however, that IRR by itself is still a popular tool although it should be used along with other measurements. In data processing, its use with hardware decisions of any consequence is common because the answer (a percentage) can be directly related to capital, and thus helps forecast a return on investment as compared to other projects (or a savings account at a bank for instance). Its critics point out that it assumes reinvestment is at the same rate of interest but, more relevant to DP, cash flow is evenly smoothed throughout the period of analysis which in reality may not be the case.

## SUMMARY OF STAGES IN THE COST
## JUSTIFICATION PROCESS

Each phase of the process of cost justification, as described in this chapter, is becoming more essential for data processing proposals. The amount of money being requested by DP management for projects is increasing and systems are becoming more complex, forcing top management to insist that DP proposals be thoroughly documented in terms that are comparable to other projects. Furthermore, management is increasingly insisting on means for measuring actual performance during implementation. Ultimately a formal justification provides a guide for measuring the benefits received and the costs incurred.

There are seven clearly identifiable stages of cost justification:

(1)  Determination that an application might be cost-effective.

(2)  Definition of the proposed application or acquisition.

(3)   Detailed quantification of tangible benefits.

(4)   Identification of intangible benefits.

(5)   Detailed quantification of costs.

(6)   Probability analysis of attaining benefits and coming in at costs.

(7)   Financial analysis of ROI, payback, NPV, etc., to meet generally established company guidelines, commonly called "hurdles."

The seven major steps listed above do not take into account political considerations or individual idiosyncracies. Yet even with the use of matrices for probability, these hidden influences can be taken into account.

## SPECIAL DP JUSTIFICATION ISSUES

There are many DP managers who feel their area of concern has unique problems which do not lend themselves to normal means of cost justification. Often the comments concern the justification of data communications, data base, and contracting software development. And undoubtedly as time goes on, other issues will be added to the list. The point to remember is that they all involve business decisions and not just DP concerns and thus lend themselves to measurement in terms acceptable to non-DP management of a company. Taking our three examples—data communications, data base, and software contracting we illustrate how those areas become business decisions with their benefits and their weaknesses defined.

### Data Communications Justification

Since the bulk of all computers have some form of data communications on them today with even mini-computers and now some microsystems also acquiring terminals for local and remote work, the question of cost justification becomes a common one. Essentially the same tangible and intangible concerns expressed in this chapter apply to data communications no matter what size system or application is involved. However, in looking for cost justification in data communications, several factors usually are worth looking at. First, an examination of how certain pieces of data are handled within an organization may in fact show redundancy of effort and hence redundancy of cost to operate the system (people expense) and store (disk and tape) data. If this can be reduced or eliminated at a cost less than that of a data communications system, justification exists.

Take for example an application where source data is prepared twice, once by an order entry clerk in a sales branch office on a form and then again by a keypunch clerk at a data processing center putting the information on cards. With a data communications approach, the order entry clerk at the branch office would enter the data on a terminal, avoiding the keypunching step. The quantification of benefits includes elimination of the keypunching cost, reduced error rate on data input since it would be entered once and by the people who knew most about the particular transaction, and also up-to-date information on orders. Benefits include the speed with which orders could be processed and inquiries made, as well as the reduced costs associated with the application.

## Data Base Justification

Since the question of justifying data base implementation is rapidly becoming a real issue in many companies with more than $20,000,000 in sales and with indications that even smaller ones may also express concern later, justification in this area also takes on importance. The issues, much as for other applications apply here as well. Furthermore, the key things to look at for justification are:

- Lower cost of file maintenance with data base
- Improved speed of programming since file development may be less costly
- Reduction of errors in files due to elimination of redundancy
- Reduction of disk and tape capacity requirements due to reduction in redundant data
- Increased speed in processing data base applications.

Soft or intangible areas of justification include:

- Improved service to users due to increased speed of programming new requests
- Improved customer service because of fewer errors
- Improved DP morale caused by increased ease of maintenance and development.

One must also net the costs of a data base system against the benefits as well. These development expenses might include:

- Transition costs to a data base environment
- Time and effort required to get to a data base environment
- Complexity of conversion
- Possible need for greater computer power and memory.

## Contracting Software Development

Invariably when a major proposal comes up for consideration, DP may argue that it has insufficient personnel to code the new application and might require that additional people be part of the overall justification. There is an alternative to programming a particular application inhouse, and that is to go to a service bureau or a software house and contract the services. More will be said about service bureaus in a later chapter devoted to the subject; however, some considerations should be kept in mind for contract services in general while developing cost justification for an application. Obviously a design objectives list should be written by the customer with or without the help of a software house. Next, a formal written proposal must be insisted upon detailing the services to be rendered, the inputs and outputs requested, and a deadline for project completion. This document also has to have some price schedule, possibly penalties for late delivery, and always a statement on measuring the quality of the finished application.

There are a number of reasons why a company might want to contract out the programming for an application and some problems also to be faced. The benefits include:

- Cost avoidance in making permanent additions to a DP staff. In effect you are hiring the number of people you need only for as long as they are required.

- If a contract is given to a firm with experience in the particular application involved, the speed with which it could be written might be faster than if done internally.

- The responsibility for managing the development of the application is partially shifted to the software writer.

There are some negative considerations as well to keep in mind.

- The cost of writing an application usually will be higher than if done inhouse since the software firm must make a profit over and above its personnel salaries and cost of computer test time.

- The application may not fully reflect the wishes of your organization since partial control over its development is out of your hands.

- Changes in the application during its development may result in significant cost overruns.

- Management of the project becomes more difficult since it involves two or more organizations.

- Documentation may not always be to your satisfaction.

Whether or not a contract is let on an application, there are some things one should do to insure that the work is done properly, on a timely basis, and within the constraints of a predetermined budget.

## Checklist of Things to Do for a Software Contract

1.   Provide the contract firm with a detailed written document spelling out the objectives of the proposed application, its inputs and outputs, and the extent of the work you wish it to do. This document should be similar to the reports described early in Chapter 2.

2.   Insure that the software firm provides you with a written proposal which becomes the basis of a contract. In order for that company to make an accurate proposal, allow it to interview whomever it feels it should within your company. This will also help the management of the company in question put together a more accurate proposal and contract.

3.   Insist on specific prices for the work and agree in writing on various target dates for the project.

4.   Devote considerable attention to the degree of documentation to be provided by the software firm and on such items as programming languages to be used, file sizes and formats, and packages to be purchased or rented.

5.   Quality of control is essential. Therefore, insist on a period after completion of the application for purposes of testing it, understanding its documentation, and acceptability by the users. You must have clauses describing penalty provisions for poorly written applications and a test period of thirty to ninety days before final payment for the application takes place.

6.   Before actually signing an agreement, ask for references to check. To be sure the software company will probably provide names of other customers who are happy with their work. From these customers you should determine what they did in order to obtain satisfactory work and their advice on how to deal with the particular software firm in question.

7.   Prior to signing the contract, at least make a rough determination on how much it would cost to do the work yourself and then weigh the pros and cons for the last time.

8.   Since all applications require maintenance, make a determination in advance as to who does this. If your people are responsible then make sure that they have access to the software firm for consultation in the future. Costs and obligations for this must be detailed in writing. If maintenance is to be done by the software firm (not usually recom-

mended since you become dependent on someone else) then define responsibilities in advance. Determine if the company reasonably might be expected to stay in business for the near future or the life of the application so that support will be constantly there.

9.   Do not let DP management be the only group in your company to negotiate the contract. Insist that either an accountant, auditor, or ideally a company lawyer participate in the details of the negotiations. Remember software houses and computer vendors negotiate contracts for a living, DP and financial managers usually do not. (More will be said about this important subject in Chapter 5.)

## Points to Consider with Prewritten Packages

Another source of code are prewritten packages sold by vendors or applications written by other companies that are willing to sell copies. These are always attractive options to consider for a number of reasons.

1.   The cost of developing them is spread over many companies and not just yours, thereby bringing the expense of such codes down substantially.

2.   Many of the considerations, inputs, outputs, and quality have been thought out by others and may provide some excellent ideas or features that you overlooked when defining your system.

3.   Sad but true, packages from outside are often better documented than your own internal code. They have to be in order to be marketable. This feature is important since it can save you the cost and effort of documentation.

4.   Packages often have flexible payment plans which allow your company some control over cash flow. Usually they are either rented for as long as you use the code, leased for a period of time and then you own it, or are purchased outright. Typically such code has a 30-to-90-day acceptance period once installed, as a test allowance before you are committed to its acquisition. Some packages even extend this period to as much as six months with or without support.

Many of the precautions listed above for contract software houses apply to prewritten packages as well. Note particularly that you will have to conform to the package more often than to your unique needs. So there is a tradeoff that must be considered. Modifying a particular package may be expensive and could result in limiting the amount of support or guarantee for workmanship on the part of the vendor. These issues must be addressed prior to accepting a package. A simple A/R product does not pose any real problem but an MRP package might. Contracting for software is generally most effective with small companies or firms that have little data processing inhouse. For example, the $5,000,000 wholesale food distributor who leases a mini-computer to do basic accounting would be a typical customer for a collection of packages, probably sold or leased by the mini-computer vendor himself. Another typical customer might be a company that has one specific application to be developed for which an existing package already exists, such as financial modeling. A third case would be an online distribution system for which many software packages exist. An obvious illustration is the DP manager buying a package to do sort/merges, TP monitoring, analyzing, and compiling. In fact it would be a safe thing to say that every DP department in existence has some purchased or leased packages, if for nothing else than for its operating system.

## DP VERSUS FINANCIAL BUSINESS DECISION MAKING

All data processing managers and executives complain at one time or another that they are being forced into making a good financial decision which at the same time is a bad DP decision. Vendors are often quoted saying the same when, for example, a DP manager wants a four-year lease on a computer which he feels will not last him much beyond that point but his financial management pressures him into amortizing the cost over a longer period of time. Financial management traditionally complains that data processing managers do not want to make any long term commitments and stand by them. Moreover, they argue that when DP does make a long term commitment, for example on a computer, they do not always honor their obligation but instead come back asking for a bigger or different machine before the first one has been amortized completely. The fact of the matter is that both groups are correct in their criticisms of each other. On the one hand, DP management wants to keep its flexibility to take advantage of rapidly improving data processing technology and to satisfy the growing demand for their services within the company. On the other hand, the financial executive, concerned with the rising cost of data processing, wants to smooth the cash flow involved and maximize his tax advantages in some controllable fashion. There is no simple solution other than to say that there has to be a balance between flexibility and fiscal responsiblity and that in each company the situation is different. However, some of the details involved can be discussed in general terms.

### Problem of Long-Term DP Commitments

In Chapter 1, some of the patterns in data processing economics were mentioned—quantum jumps in system power with incremental rises in costs and demand for services also growing in quantum fashion. Much of the argument hovers around hardware to be sure, but because of the enormous investment in software and applications, the same concerns are now being felt outside the realm of equipment decisions. The issue with software is exactly the same as with hardware. Financial officials want to establish a period of time for which the software will be useful—and preferably a long one—while DP wants to use it now until something better comes along. Financial considerations dictate that programs have their cost amortized and depreciated over a fixed period of time governed by the accounting practices and tax laws of the nation. Thus major pieces of software such as TP monitors and data base language packages are being settled on for periods of four to seven years as an average.

Besides amortization, payback, and return on investment, there is the possibility that investment tax credit regulations may be broadened at some point to include software, since programs also generate jobs for people—the original objective of the ITC. Already in France and Germany, some tax laws are beginning to treat software much like equipment. Thus it makes good financial sense to treat software in the same fashion and have DP commit to keeping a major piece of software for a predetermined period of time. Less expensive packages can be charged against expenses but significant code should be capitalized.

A second issue of growing importance, and one that also leads to a tug of war within departments, is the issue of an application's useful life. Given the considerations raised in Chapter 1 and the enormous effort one goes through to create an application, companies are beginning to establish a life cycle for applications. This then allows them to define the cost of support for that project, depreciate it in a fashion most advantageous to the company, and decide what portions of the cost will be expensed and which shall be capitalized. In order to establish a useful life for payback, etc., DP and users should be the primary sources of opinion about an application within the company and not just finance or accounting. DP and user departments should agree on a life and then negotiate with financial analysts to determine the financial life of an application and the accounting methods to be used in defining costs and benefits over time. The decisions regarding amortization, depreciation, etc., should best be left in the hands of finance and not data processing since this remains an accounting function. In other words, DP and users should provide the driving force for justification, with finance setting the ground rules for accounting, not the other way around.

## Expense versus Capitalization

The specific issue of expensing versus capitalizing data processing costs is one that must be worked out. In regard to software, there is a genuine need to allow DP flexibility to change packages when new ones become available of greater use to the organization. Yet major pieces should have a commitment of some sort attached to them. Thus, for example, productivity tools should be expensed since they are constantly being changed and the amount of cost involved is usually small in comparison to other DP expenditures. Major application code might be capitalized since its expense will result in usable code for five, seven, perhaps even ten years. Modifications to that application, if small, could be expensed in much the same fashion as buying new parts for a capitalized piece of equipment. By capitalizing major costs, however, the investment in an application can be spread over many annual budgets to the benefit of the DP department's budget (by keeping costs down) while not dramatically reducing the profitability of the company during the period when the costs were actually incurred. Capitalization, in other words, can make large applications more attractive by expanding the possible ways of determining justification. Also, capitalization reminds us that budget considerations are only part of the financial story behind data processing.

## Software Depreciation

DP management people notoriously fail to realize the significance of various methods of depreciation in cost-justifying hardware and software expenditures. This situation is probably caused by the fact that only in the last few years has any consideration been given to the issue of software justification in financial terms in the more industrialized countries. There has always been attention paid to hardware finances but less to software and applications in general; yet today the situation is rapidly changing. To a greater extent, management needs to understand depreciation not only for hardware (more on this in Chapter 4), but also with respect to software. A brief discussion of the major depreciation methods as they might relate to software can be of use when DP is attempting to acquire more code. Simply put, depreciation is the amount of value of a given asset which is deducted each year because of the decline in the worth of that item over a period of time. It is an accounting procedure for spreading the expense in a noncash charge as the value of the asset expires. Since expenses are tax deductible, the temptation to expense everything is great. Governments, however, require that major investments and expenses in cash outlays for property, equipment, etc., be depreciated over a longer period of time for tax purposes. Thus all capital purchases are candidates for depreciation.

1. *Straight-line Depreciation.* The simplest method used, it takes the total cost of an item, freight, setup expenses for hardware, etc., divides this amount by the number of years to be depreciated less the salvage (final) value, and evenly takes the depreciation each year. If an asset has an eight-year life, then under this method one would deduct

12.5% of its value each year less its salvage value. Straight-line is used when financial managers want to minimize the cost of an item in their financial reporting, thereby maximizing profits on paper.

2. *Double-declining Balance Depreciation.* This is a method for accelerating the depreciation of an asset, that is, depreciating a greater portion of it earlier in the life of the asset rather than later. The amount to be depreciated is subtracted from the cost of the item in question before tabulating next year's depreciation. Thus each year the same depreciation rate works on a smaller amount left to be depreciated. For example, in the first year a company could deduct 25% of an asset's value, the next year 25% of the undepreciated balance or in effect 18.75% of the original cost. In the third year the percentage would drop even further. This method will often be used when finance wants to maximize the expense for financial reporting. A company making a great deal of money must constantly be seeking deductible expenses and would look to double-declining as an aid. It is also useful if the item to be depreciated has a relatively short life. In the future a piece of software with a useful life of three years or less might be a candidate for double-declining depreciation.

3. *Sum-of-the-digits Depreciation.* Depreciation is determined by using a different fraction each year for the life of an asset less salvage value. Thus, if an application were to be depreciated (assuming tax laws allow it), then the denominator would be the numbers totaled for the years of useful life. For example, an eight-year life total would be 1 + 2 + 3 + 4 + 5 + 6 + 7 + 8 = 36 as a denominator. The numerator changes each year to reflect the remaining number of years of useful life at the start of this year. In year one, this would equal 8/36 or 22.2%, year two would be a 7/36, or 19.5% etc., for all eight years. This method helps minimize the expense of financial reporting and thereby maximizes profits. DP should be aware that this becomes a useful method for justification of a cash outlay during a year when the company's business is not so good.

## Some Software Depreciation Considerations
## for the Future

In the years to come, applications may become subject to more formal procedures for depreciation, much like hardware is today. It is important to note that in accounting, various depreciation methods can be used, and once in the life of an asset, the method can be changed. Therefore one finds various types of depreciation being used such as double-declining or straight-line. Moreover, two sets of books are always kept: one for public reporting in which the company tries to show the maximum amount of profit and another for tax reporting in which the firm declares the smallest profit. Taxable income is the excess of cash intake over expenses for tax reporting purposes. So it is easy to see that, just as in our own personal income taxes, a company will look for every deduction possible.

Timing becomes a major consideration in selecting a depreciation method, along with the current needs of the company. Do you want to pay the most taxes now on an asset's worth, or pay them later? A growing company may want to defer paying taxes so that management can invest in plants, equipment, inventory, people, etc., to foster growth with its money. Straight-line depreciation is often employed for public reporting (keeps profits attractive), while for tax purposes a company may use an accelerated method of depreciation. With accelerated depreciation the finance department might even use a shorter tax life (e.g., five years instead of seven). This will also depend on the asset. If it has a short useful life you obviously need to depreciate it faster. Thus a computer which one feels might have to be replaced in a few years because of growth requirements or new technology would use an accelerated depreciation. A company that acquires an application for seven years might select a slower depreciation. Thus a combination of factors is always considered including:

- Financial strategy of a company
- Accounting policies
- Tax and profit pressures
- Expense of an asset.

From a DP point of view, the larger an expense or capital expenditure required, the more important it is to be aware of the financial pressures on top management and to take them into account when offering cost justification. The same comment holds true for user departments. Both groups can gain approval for major projects which cannot be absorbed by their budgets only when financial considerations are taken into account. Thus to think, for example, of data and applications as an investment (especially if they are to be kept for a long time) is essential. Laws and accounting practices are leaning in the direction of treating them much as equipment. Therefore the issues discussed and illustrated in this chapter and particularly in the next, suggest how to capitalize and depreciate software purchases and application costs.

There are some other elements to consider. Software developments are coming quickly and the life of a package is shorter today in many instances than in the past. However, major applications, because of their cost, will be planned for long useful lives. Thus in future accounting of costs, management will want to expense short-lived software and capitalize major pieces of code which are integral parts of an application. In practice this would mean that parts of an application might be expensed and others capitalized, making the cost-justification process more complex.

There are a number of unresolved issues, however. Teleprocessing monitors provide an example. Each time the manufacturer of a package brings out a new edition and changes the cost of that product, while dropping support for earlier editions, he forces a user to the latest code. What does this do to the depreciation of the older code? Is it to be considered as a replacement product or a continuation of the old TP monitor? In equipment when you remove one box and replace it with another you start your accounting from ground zero again. With software you may have to have the vendor assign it a serial number which does not change from one edition to another for tax purposes. The problem presented by various editions of code might discourage companies from moving to new versions of a package which have better support from a vendor or simply offer more attractive features. The point is, software accounting is in its infant stages simply because it has only been in the last few years that the cost of packages and inhouse written code has become significant. By the same token, tax laws on software and applications are only just beginning to emerge along with various accounting regulations and standards for security and privacy. It is fairly common today for a state sales tax to be imposed on the purchase or lease prices of software, but applications which have value to a company are only now being considered in theory at least as taxable property.

Ah what a stroke of genius!
A miracle of the mind!
Brilliant in conception,
Flawless in design.
But it has one annoying quirk—
Each time you throw the
   switch on
It never seems to work.

*Anonymous*

*People are trapped into poor financial strategies in data processing hardware more often than in any other sector of the DP industry. This chapter will show you how possibly to save your organization millions of dollars by using some simple common-sense tactics that take into account your needs as well as changes in technology. First we show you how to determine when you need more or different equipment. Next we explain how to determine whether you should lease or purchase it, with all the pros and cons defined. Case studies illustrate how this is done both for computers and peripheral hardware. Finally some very useful time-tested management advice is collected here to guide you in future hardware acquisition decisions.*

# CHAPTER FOUR

# Hardware Costs
# and Their Justification

Today, financial decisions regarding data processing hardware account for a good third of a DP department's budget. Although this percentage is expected to decline in the years to come as the costs of software and personnel rise faster than for hardware, the subject of equipment expenses will remain an important one. The financing of such hardware is also closely tied to the overall objectives of a company and to its data processing department since a key factor in any decision is the length of time the equipment is to be kept. Thus for these reasons, the subject of the acquisition of hardware and its financing must be treated with considerable care. A decision in this area must reflect an understanding of the options available and relate these to application development and software requirements.

In discussing hardware one is really dealing with three groups of equipment: computers, peripheral boxes for computers (input/output devices such as tape and disk drives), and terminals with their hang-on units. The bigger the device in cost and importance, the more serious is the acquisition decision. Computers attract the greatest amount of concern because of the length of commitments often required for them, followed next by I/O devices, and last, terminal systems.

For purposes of discussion, a computer is defined as the central processing unit (CPU) which manipulates the numbers in a system, and its memory. Often the term CPU is used to refer to the entire computer and it will be used that way in the following pages to refer either to memory or the processor. Any consideration of the acquisition of a computer obviously involves such issues as the capacity required over time for both cycles and memory, lease vs. purchase, vendor maintenance, reliability and quality of the computer, whether to have centralized processing (for example, all in one computer) or spread it out among smaller processors, minis, and microcomputers. In today's environment, once a company understands its functional requirements for computer power, a considerable amount of attention is paid to the financial options surrounding the acquisition.

## DETERMINING COMPUTER CAPACITY REQUIREMENTS

The first step in deciding what size machine (or machines) one needs is to define the capacity required. That is to say, how much cycle power and memory will be needed over a period of time? This first determination is the most difficult one to make. Specialists will argue that there is no proven scientific, precise method for doing this. A great deal depends on the nature of the applications being run, their size, quantity, future plans, computer architecture, and speed of computing, among many other variables. However difficult this task can be, there are some steps that may be taken to help management reach some conclusions upon which to base decisions.

1.   Since computer cycle size and speed are quantifiable by the vendor and the size of one device versus another easily compared, one can begin by determining what the past historical pattern of growth in cycle and memory demand was like in the company. Invariably management will find that every time they brought in a new computer, the memory jumped 50% to 100% in size while the cycles increased 25% to 200%. In large part this was due to cost of cycles dropping dramatically with each new generation of equipment and also to the fact that most computer vendors produced computers in sequential sizes which ascended dramatically as the CPU became bigger. Thus, for example, at the low end of a

family of computers one's option might be a 256,000-byte-size memory machine while the next size CPU might begin at 500,000 bytes with no alternative in between. The cycles in the second machine might well be 100% greater than the smaller computer's. Since prices for a 500,000-byte device would not be 100% greater than for a 256,00-byte product, migration upward in quantum fashion was never financially prohibitive. So understanding the pattern of growth in your company would indicate in one way what size your next machine might be. This next size could thus be defined in terms of relative internal performance, cycle speeds, memory size, and number of channels required for I/O and communication devices.

Closely related to this exercise is a determination of how much the computer was used over a period of time. For years there have been software analyzers which have measured such things as the amount of memory being used at any given time of the day (against known applications), response time for terminals, channel utilization, cycle utilization, paging rate, I/O calls, and partition size, usage, and rate of transactions being brought to partitions. Most operating systems have reporting capabilities to provide some of that kind of information while vendors will sell other more comprehensive packages to do the same. If this has never been done in the past and usage is suspected to be high, run such a package in the machine to understand current usage. Computer vendors will invariably supply data on what is considered high, medium, and low utilization of their products for all phases of usage (memory, cycles, and channels) and can help to let you know if in fact your machine is "running out of gas." One analogy is to compare high utilization to the lawn mower designed to cut one-inch-high grass now being used to cut three-inch-high grass—here utilization is sufficiently high enough to warrant consideration of a large lawn mower or "tuning" the yard so that it is cut before it ever reaches more than an inch in height. The same kind of exercise applies to a CPU.

The data gathered from these various exercises can then be grafted to indicate a pattern of usage either by cycles, memory, paging, or channel utilization over time. Figure 4–1 illustrates the actual growth in usage of a medium-size computer over four years during which a major online application was developed each year. In this particular case, DP management could prove that in four years it had strained the machine to full cycle utilization and came very close to doing the same with its memory. Channel utilization was also quite high. In this instance, the usual fine tuning to balance the load of memory, cycle, and channel utilization had been done throughout the four years to improve throughput. Yet this pattern of activity clearly suggested that more cycles were needed (perhaps a 100% more for the next four years if in fact application growth and volumes of transactions were expected to be the same

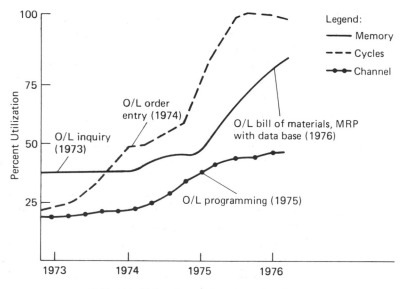

**Figure 4-1**    Capacity history.

as in the past). Channel increases were also needed. Notice that specific applications could be identified as the cause of increased usage, particularly the manufacturing system under data base which pushed up cycle usage more than channel usage. One simply had to recall when a particular application went live on the system and to measure the differences in utilization before and after. Order entry, in this example, could thus be accused of forcing up channel utilization more than any other application.

2.   If a major new software package or application is expected to be put on a system, consult with the vendor, and with companies that have already installed the particular application or package, and also with data processing user groups (SHARE and GUIDE are two excellent ones) to determine how much computer power should be available. This kind of experience and iterative data, although never precise, is reasonable enough upon which to begin to make a computer selection and allows one to help quantify the size of machine needed. Using an example from the IBM product line illustrates the point. A company with a well-utilized IBM model 138 with a half a meg of memory decided it wanted to convert its files to data base format. In talking to vendors of data base language packages and to several users who had similar file sizes and applications, it was determined that a computer upgrade to an IBM system model 148 or a 3031 would be required simply because the memory requirements

might increase approximately 300,000 bytes (forcing a onc-meg expansion since the 148 and 3031 did not come in smaller sizes) and that cycle needs would jump approximately 1.5 times over the 138's capability. Thus the issue then revolved around the question: Would it be a 148 or a 3031 and should it be from IBM by lease or purchase, or from a third party? Then the cost could be factored into the justification for moving to data base. In short, the issue finally became a financial one.

3.    There appcar on occasion in various DP publications, such as *Computerworld* (the DP industry's leading weekly newspaper), charts of relative performance of one piece of equipment against another, which can be used as a measurement of utilization. This suggests that if utilization were to increase by a certain percent each year, then over a period of "x" years one would need "y" amount of power and that this could be obtained with specific computers over a predetermined period of time. One recent table, for example, suggested that a company with an IBM 158 model 1 at full capacity with a growth rate in utilization for the next four years expectcd to be about 10% would have the option of going to an AP system followed by a 158 model 3 or could just move directly to a 3033. Again at this point the decision on which strategy to employ becomes a financial one. In each individual instance, DP management must be required to state what its anticipated computer requirements are for a given number of years and to define a number of options such as using a bigger computer, two or more, or a scrics of minis—either stand-alone or integrated into comprehensive systems. These are technical considerations which must be presented before any financial analysis can take place.

In defining options for management, some of the most important information which DP should supply to financial management includes:

- Availability of particular products
- Contractual options
- Sources for the equipment (for example, vendors or leasing companies
- Realistic resale values of particular pieces of equipment
- Number of years they would be willing to commit to a particular option
- Age of the specific computer generation (Is a particular option on the verge of being made unattractive due to an anticipated availability of a new generation of equipment?)
- Second-hand market for older technology which might be financially attractive
- Impact on ability to provide specific services to the company (Is a particular online application's availability so great that newer

technology must be used because of its increased reliability over older ones?).

Armed with these kinds of data, financial issues can next be considered.

## THE PURCHASE VERSUS LEASE ISSUE AND COMPUTERS

Invariably once a particular computer has been identified as meeting an organization's requirements for capacity over a predefined period of time, the question arises: Should it be rented, leased, or purchased? Renting in data processing usually means paying a monthly fee for a particular piece of equipment with a very short commitment to a vendor, usually 30 to 180 days. A lease requires a commitment of anywhere from one to ten years in exchange for a lower monthly charge than would be paid if renting. The average computer lease from a manufacturer is four years, from a leasing company four to seven years. Then there is purchase which can be done directly by a user, financed through a bank with title being held by either party, or through a buy-out lease from a third party.

### Advantages of Rental

- Least amount of commitment, greatest degree of flexibility to change equipment.
- Useful in dynamic environment where future cannot reasonably be determined (not usually the case).

### Disadvantages of Rental

- Most expensive option available.
- More difficult to find vendors or third parties willing to enter into such arrangements.
- Provides little security to the DP operations (equipment might be removed).

More realistic as an option is leasing a computer for a period of time.

### Advantages of a Lease

- Less expensive than rental.
- Commitment is shorter than purchase (4-6 years as an average).
- Little risk of obsolescence.
- Payments are level and predetermined.
- Reduces risk of being oversold by a vendor.
- Does not require working capital.

- Assures better servicing by a vendor who owns the machine.
- Reduces risk in relying on residual values.

### Disadvantages of a Lease

- Not always the least expensive way to have a computer.
- Cash flow is expensible, therefore cannot take advantage of borrowing or use of capital.
- Might allow DP management to adopt too small a machine knowing that it will eventually go away (but maybe not soon enough).

Then there is the option of ownership which becomes increasingly popular as the price of rental, lease, and purchase of a computer rises in actual dollar amounts spent.

### Advantages of Purchase

- Least cost over long term in comparison to rental or leases.
- Residual value goes to the owner.
- No extra shift rental or lease charges, thus cash overflow is controlled.
- Solid investment (safe, understood, high return).
- Flexible acquisition cost (depends on terms).
- Can be capitalized and amortized over time.
- Can take full Investment Tax Credit (ITC).
- Pride of ownership.

### Disadvantages of Purchase

- Commitment is usually the greatest (longest).
- Requires a solid understanding of your company's future DP needs.
- A certain amount of risk in residual values (for resale purposes).

Various conditions apply to different situations which makes one option seem more attractive at a particular time than at another. But there are some general reasons why companies look at one option over another. The following lists, although not complete by any means, illustrate conditions commonly found.

### Why Lease?

- No capital investment is required.
- The obligation is short.

- Cost is controllable.
- Service leverage against the manufacturer exists but not if acquired from a third party.
- Reduces need for long-term planning.

In short, leases are usually attractive for companies that do not understand their DP needs, or have hardly any major plans worked out, or who cannot make long-term financial commitments because they have borrowed too much or need to put their capital into other, more critical projects. It is also a viable option for a company wishing to keep its DP hardware always at or near current generation.

### Why Purchase?

- Offers a profitable outlet for investment funds, thus lowering possible operating costs in future years.
- Long-term use expected from a particular computer.
- Takes advantage of high residual values (in comparison to non-DP equipment in general).
- Provides a more favorable cash flow.
- Conforms to some company policies on equipment acquisitions.
- It is an investment.

Companies which purchase data processing equipment usually are confident about how long they will need the hardware in question (usually four or more years) and have access to capital which can be invested in this project. This will include small and large companies and those in good and poor financial condition. With leases, those in poor financial shape will tend to stay away from purchases because of restrictions imposed on them by creditors and banks.

## Characteristics of a Lease

There are basically two types of leases common in data processing: the traditional lease and a conditional sales lease, with the differences defined by the U.S. Internal Revenue Service for tax purposes. A true lease has the following characteristics:

- Term is for less than 30 years, otherwise it is considered a conditional sales lease.
- Lessor must obtain reasonable return on investment from rent (6% to 10% considered reasonable).
- Renewal option must be real (gives lessee first option to meet an equal genuine outside offer).

- No repurchase option provision in the contract exists, thus parity between a lessee and an outside offer remains.

Financially the implications are important. If it is a real or "true" lease then the company leasing the equipment takes the depreciation deduction and not the vendor's customer. Your company can, however, deduct the expense of the lease. Investment tax credits can pass to either party depending on the contractual arrangement made by both. If the lease is a "conditional sales contract" then the company that leases the equipment takes title and holds title on the equipment from its date of installation and not the vendor or the third-party leasing or broker firm. If you hold title, then your company can claim the depreciation and the ITC. However, you may only deduct the interest portion of your payments from taxes.

In an operating or service lease the charges for finances and maintenance are included in a single monthly lease fee and this amount is not usually amortized. The lease is usually written for a period shorter than the life of the computer. The lessee usually has cancellation rights as well. In a sale or lease-back contract (financial lease) the lease will not include maintenance charges which would be a separate arrangement. Nor would it provide for sales or lease taxes; these additional cash flows are on top of any contractual monthly payments. There are few or no cancellation clauses without you the user paying heavy penalties to cover the debt on the computer. This form of a lease is the most common used by brokers and third-party leasing companies. These third-party leases usually run for longer periods of time than leases from a manufacturer (but not always so) and are for smaller amounts of monthly charges since the leasing company will be amortizing the cost of the equipment over a longer period of time than a manufacturer. The increased length of a third-party lease protects the leasing company from obsolescence should manufacturers announce new products. Moreover, with shorter depreciation periods being used today (5–7 years), more flexible arrangements are possible. Another trend is that of leasing companies playing the role of a broker, thereby passing title on to the user and with it the risk of obsolescence. (More will be said about leases in Chapter 5.)

## THE FINANCIAL DECISION ON COMPUTERS

Discussing leases and purchases is important but the basic question is still how to make a decision. The issue is no different than for any other acquisition in business. The key to the question is how long does one need a computer? The factors to consider include the following:

- Impact of it being a budget or investment issue.

- Requirement for looking at specific evaluation points:
  - (1) Alternative technical solutions
  - (2) Business environment
  - (3) Financial environment
  - (4) DP environment and needs
- Need to balance factors in an iterative manner.

There are some points to consider besides the above, including specific financial concerns such as whether to invest or treat an acquisition as a budget item. Along with these are business and DP points to address. The following list contains several of the issues.

| Financial Factors to Consider | Investment (purchase) | Expense (lease) |
|---|---|---|
| (1) Does the decision involve a great deal of money? (If yes then it is an investment issue.) | Yes | No |
| (2) Can you afford a major capitalization of a project today? | Yes | No |
| (3) Are there any policies in place today which restrict methods of acquisition to short-term decisions (too much debt now)? | No | Yes |
| (4) Are there other factors influencing a decision financially today? | | |

| Business Factors to Consider | Investment (purchase) | Expense (lease) |
|---|---|---|
| (1) Can you reasonably predict your rate of growth? | Yes | No |
| (2) Is the business subject to large swings in volume of sales? | No | Yes |
| (3) Is there a long-range business plan in place? | Yes | No |
| (4) Are your services or products going to remain the same? | Yes | No |
| (5) Do external business factors highly influence your operations? | No | Yes |
| (6) Are there any other business factors influencing a decision today? | | |

| DP Factors to Consider | Investment (purchase) | Expense (lease) |
|---|---|---|
| (1) Do you have a 4-to-6-year plan? | Yes | No |
| (2) Does the proposed computer support your long range plan (memory, function)? | Yes | No |
| (3) Are you independent of technological changes? | Yes | No |
| (4) Do you believe computer costs will fluctuate during the course of your commitment? | No | Yes |
| (5) Are there any other DP factors which will influence a decision? | | |

## PURCHASE VERSUS LEASE: STRATEGIC CONSIDERATIONS FOR COMPUTERS

The number of variables discussed in the pages above suggests that many issues help determine whether to upgrade, downgrade, go to the latest technology, or older generations, to single computers or multiple units, to distribute the function through minis and intelligent terminals or centralize them. It is also possible to acquire equipment from both manufacturers and third-party leasing companies and brokers. Financing can be internal, from a bank, or a leasing company. As a rule of thumb, management should try to reduce the hardware decision to two to four possible options and then do the necessary financial analysis. More than four alternatives will simply confuse the decision and make it difficult to resolve while only one provides no options.

Next, in order to identify the costs of a particular alternative one should define the following variables:

- Depreciation method to be used
- Life of the computer in the company
- Lease and purchase price of the computer
- Who gets the ITC, how much, and when
- When would the computer be resold and by whom
- Cost of local, state, and federal taxes
- Be prepared to include the impact of maintenance and physical site preparation expenses
- Whether sales taxes will be carried on the books as expenses,

capitalized outlays, or be passed on to a leasing company or broker through a lease

- Quantify termination charges for early-out of a contract
- Establish a salvage value closely related to what the computer will sell for when it is finally replaced.

## Computer Resale Patterns

The last suggestion is one of the more sensitive variables in any financial analysis and, therefore, requires considerable attention. The higher the resale value of a particular computer, as a percent of the original purchase price, the lower the actual cost will be over the life of the machine in your company. Placing too high a value on resale is risky, foolish, and badly throws off a financial analysis; while pegging it too low will also make the analysis unreal, inaccurate, and possibly make a justifiable acquisition unjustifiable for no good business reason. Resale, as a factor in any analysis, is becoming increasingly evident to users and more attention is being paid to it. A computer which is fully depreciated at one location may be sold or transferred to another. Resale percentages help users determine whether to buy an older generation's computer or a new one and to predetermine its useful life within their company. Moreover, someone renting or leasing a computer who is aware of resale values may purchase his installed CPU using any accruals earned and sell it immediately on the open market (usually with the help of a broker), thereby realizing a profit.

There are several factors which influence resale value. First, there is the marketing life of a computer; that is, the period in time when the manufacturer actively sells his product before announcing a new generation of CPUs. In the past this has been about five years but seems to be coming down closer to four or less now. Purchase options and inflation play significant roles in influencing the lease, purchase, and resale prices at this point. Second, is the critical replacement time. Historically this usually has been five to seven years after a product first appears on the market. Today that period is shrinking to something approaching four or less years. Early replacement cycles force residual values to drop faster, longer cycles keep residual values higher longer. Third, late life (usually eight to eleven years from first availability) represents one-generation-old products when the current line is easily reaching its active marketing peak or maturity. Currently, for example, the IBM 370/138 computer fits this pattern. Equipment of this age still has considerable residual value and will compete in some circumstances quite favorably with current generation computers. Last is residual life of equipment typically more than ten years old. These are often two generations old and have very low resale values (5-15% of original purchase price). Software support for these pieces of equipment is rarely available from manufacturers and perhaps not cost-effective anymore.

There are thus many variables regarding age and generation influencing resale. Another which has become a general rule among brokers is that the larger the CPU the higher the resale percentage for the longer a period of time. The smaller the unit the faster the resale value drops and also the percentage of original purchase price. Add to these considerations the following checklist of variables influencing resale values:

- Relative internal performance of one CPU as against another
- Supply and demand
- Maintenance costs
- Power usage
- Size and number of physical boxes in a system
- Secondary placement support (Will the manufacturer maintain the computer when at its second home?)
- Investment Tax Credit
- Availability of maintenance over a long period of time
- Performance and function as compared to more modern computers/software
- I/O compatibility.

Currently, the largest number of computers of all generations in the industrialized world is IBM's. Consequently, much of the second-hand computer market and residual values are determined by actions taken by IBM with its pricing of new CPUs. Moreover, residual values are usually discussed in connection with IBM products since they make up a large share of the second-hand computer inventory. Other major computer manufacturers in the United States, Europe, and Japan are beginning to see their older products in the second-hand marketplace along with non-IBM memory but as of this date, resale patterns are not clearly discernible. Most third-party dealers are reluctant to forecast resale values for IBM and other manufacturer's CPUs too far into the future, other than to say that IBM products are in greater demand as a rule. Therefore, much of what is said, written, and argued about in regard to residual patterns concerns IBM products.

Recently International Data Corporation, which tracks resale patterns accurately for all data processing products, described the pattern of residual values for IBM computers in the 370 product line. Figure 4–2 illustrates the pattern for the older 370s and Figure 4–3 for the more recent 138 and 148 computers. What is interesting to note about these charts is that IDC's forecasts of resale values are traditionally quite accurate. Moreover, what is illustrated in these tables is in line with what

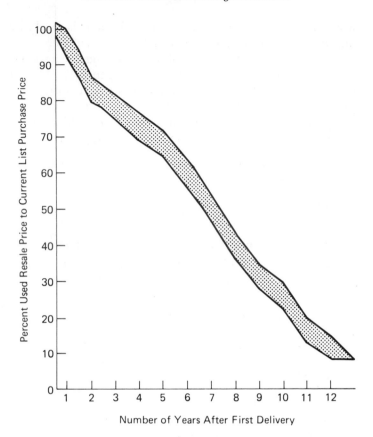

**Figure 4-2**    IBM 370/ 158, 168 (*Source: Adapted from IDC © 1976*).

third-party leasing companies and brokers use for planning purposes. This is an important fact to remember because usually in the data processing industry, third-party brokers and leasing companies are more aware of resale values than any other element in the marketplace and their prices do not vary widely from each other. The other point to keep in mind is that Figures 4-2 and 4-3 indicate the kind of life a price has had in the past and this suggests what might continue at least for the near future.

A closer look at IDC's two charts suggests an interesting pattern. The second chart says that the resale value of equipment drops more rapidly nowadays than it has in the past. This correctly reflects the shorter life cycle of computers as the major vendors introduce new products more rapidly than ever before. Thus, using their example of the 138 and 148, the announcement of the 3031 CPU obviously would cause the prices for 148s to decline since the 3031 was introduced two years after the announcement of the 148. In the previous generation, or half-generation,

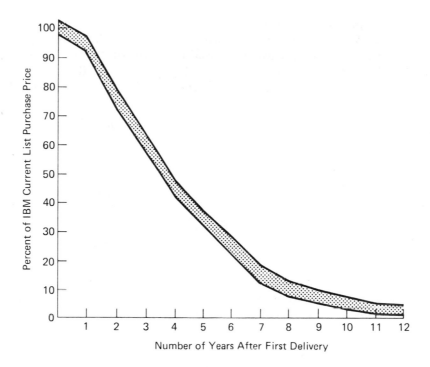

**Figure 4-3** IBM 370/ 138, 148 (*Source: Adapted from IDC © 1978*).

the 148 was announced many years after the 145, which kept 145 values higher for a longer period of time. So the pattern becomes obvious. IDC also suggests that plug-compatible CPUs will reflect a similar pattern because price has always been closely related to performance as well as availability. And with more used computers available in the marketplace (along with more users demanding CPUs), the sell and install cycle for used hardware will speed up. Thus in determining a resale value for any financial analysis one should be conservative (for example, 3–5% lower than what experts suggest) in selecting a resale value. Also, it would be a good idea to discuss with several brokers possible percentages for two, three, five, and six years out for purposes of your analysis. In conjunction with your own experience, a realistic and usable percentage can be arrived at for calculations.

## Impact of Cost of Capital on Financial Analysis for Computers

After residual values, the cost of capital impacts a financial analysis considerably. Thus a higher cost of capital will trip upward the cost of a particular option while a lower one will drop it dramatically. An example will illustrate the point. Given that a certain computer sells for $1,546,100. A company wishes to finance the purchase of this CPU over 84 months and assign a residual value of "0" for our example. ITC is $15,461 and an accelerated depreciation of 0.08 (percent of purchase price) is used. The effect on the monthly cash flow would be as follows.

| Interest | Monthly Cost ($) |
| --- | --- |
| 0 | 14,700 |
| 6 | 18,000 |
| 8 | 19,300 |
| 10 | 20,500 |
| 12 | 21,800 |
| 14 | 23,200 |

The numbers suggest that the cost (and its justification) can vary significantly depending on the carrying costs involved and thus should be given considerable thought during the early stages of defining options.

## Impact of Varying Term on Financial Analysis

Closely related to the changing cost of capital is the period of capitalization. The length of time involved is very sensitive, since the shorter the term of capitalization the higher the cost per month. On the other hand, the longer the term in which financing is done, the lesser the cost per month. Using the previous case with 10% cost of capital the results would be as follows.

| Months | Monthly Cost ($) |
| --- | --- |
| 12 | 108,700 |
| 24 | 57,000 |
| 36 | 40,000 |
| 48 | 31,000 |
| 60 | 26,300 |
| 72 | 23,000 |

Keep in mind, however, that in exchange for longer periods of time, the total cost of capital will rise with the length of time of a loan. With the amounts of money involved in DP hardware decisions, an extended period of payment may drive up the overall costs considerably.

## Impact of Other Variables on Financial Analysis

Other common variables in any computer (or I/O analysis) have varying degrees of impact with the possible exception of ITC. Fluctuating the residual value, for example, will usually be less significant in comparison to the term and interest, although it would still be extremely important in measuring overall cash flow. Once a computer is resold, of course, the company has cash to invest in something else so a certain amount of flexibility is there. Using our case again, for each 10% increase in the residual value, the monthly cash flow drops about $1,100. Depreciation affects only the cash flow and not the total cash outlay for the computer. Thus straight-line would simply spread the depreciation evenly over the period of time while double-declining would bring the bulk of the cost (with its tax implications) into the early years of the analysis.

A variable which is increasingly important in regard to justifying new data processing equipment is the ITC or Investment Tax Credit. This is a tax credit (as opposed to a tax deduction) that is given for the installation of new equipment. It is a credit against federal taxes owed. The ITC is allowable against certain kinds of capital equipment such as computers and peripheral devices. Under the current law, a maximum of 10% of the hardware's price of purchase can be deducted (after tax). Some computer vendors will also pass on to their customers the amount of ITC which is allowable for leased equipment. On purchased hardware the government of the United States will allow the deduction to be 20%

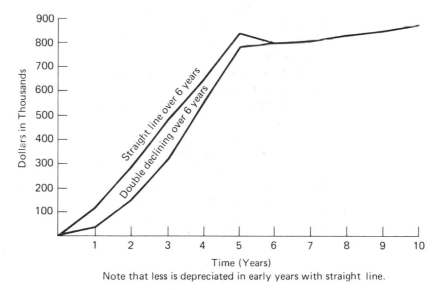

Note that less is depreciated in early years with straight line.

**Figure 4-4**   Example of depreciation impact on cash flow.

137

before tax if the accounting department of a company assumes a 50% tax rate on income. The amount of deduction is determined by the useful life category established by the manufacturer of the hardware in question. Thus as of this writing the ITC amounts are as follows.

|              | Useful Life | ITC (after tax) | ITC (pretax)   |
| ------------ | ----------- | --------------- | -------------- |
| Category 1   | 3–5 years   | 3.3% of cost    | 6.7% of cost   |
| Category 2   | 5–7 years   | 6.7% of cost    | 13.3% of cost  |
| Category 3   | 7+ years    | 10.0% of cost   | 20.0% of cost  |

There are several rules to keep in mind. First, a company must keep the equipment installed for the period of the useful life as determined by the manufacturer. Second, ITC is taken the year the equipment is installed. If the machine is removed prior to the completion of the useful life period then part of the ITC must be "recaptured" or in other words, paid to IRS. The amount due to the government depends on schedules applicable at the time tax must be paid. ITC does not apply to equipment that has been acquired second-hand or, in other words, has been used by someone else first. Since ITC is significant, it becomes an important factor in costing out new equipment. In rough numbers, a CPU purchased for one million dollars would result in an ITC of $100,000 the first year it was installed, bringing its expense down to $900,000 before depreciation or resale (residual) values were even taken into consideration. Thus, for example, the acquisition of a new computer, purchased over time, would in the first year of use probably be less expensive than other computers of comparable power of older vintage.

Other factors are influencing financial decisions in ways which might not be reflected in a formal financial analysis but that may also impact any examination of the variables. For example, the attitude of the U.S. Government toward ITC, tax deductions, and accounting principles affecting the nature of leases are issues of major concern. On the other hand there are questions which are reflected in financial numbers. For instance, since the major manufacturers of computers are introducing new products faster than ever before, many customers are using accelerated depreciation methods more often than in the past. Inflation and business uncertainties also encourage such a tactic. The period of depreciation is rapidly dropping from an average of seven years down to five. Purchase appears more attractive with lower book values than ever, resulting in greater tax deductions.

The evolution of accounting methods in the past few years also is influencing financial analysis. Companies are increasingly capitalizing previous leases under new guidelines. Many are restating older financial reports. If commitments have to be made for more than five years, purchase has to be seen as extremely attractive since the commitment has to appear on the balance sheet or in more detail in other reports. Simultaneously, vendor leases (see Chapter 5 for more details), otherwise known as operating leases, are becoming shorter and more competitive with each other. With purchase becoming more attractive for periods over four years, longer leases no longer seem as advantageous as in the 1960s or early 1970s. Thus a combination of national political concerns, changes in tax and accounting procedures, and the increased speed in the evolution of DP technology with a history of performance and identifiable costs, are all leading companies to consider various options and to place a premium on analyzing the significance of shorter commitments and added flexibility.

Later we shall consider some cases showing how the variables discussed above impact a financial analysis. But there are two other effects on finances that one should be aware of: the influence of cumulative after-tax cash outflows on rent, purchase, and purchase with resale and second, the role of rent and purchase on a company's profits—the bottom line. For our purposes, the impact of each is illustrated in a simple fashion by Figures 4-5 and 4-6. The effect is much the same in most financial analyses. Thus to improve profitability one looks at purchase and if

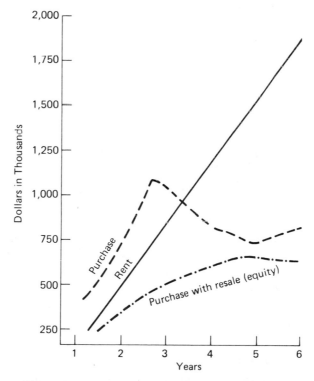

**Figure 4-5**    After-tax cash outflow (cumulative).

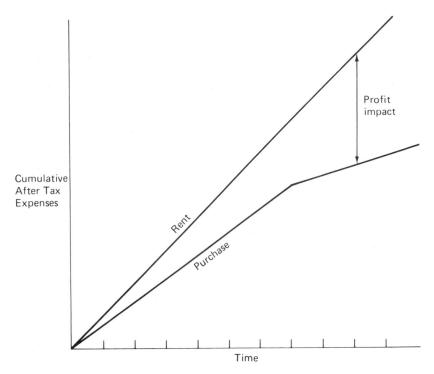

**Figure 4-6**    Effect on profit.

interested in keeping the after-tax cash flow low, the company looks at purchase with resale. One small warning: The resale quoted in financial calculations should be a reliable residual value and not just a safety margin caused by simply using a low salvage value.

## Factors Influencing Accounting Books

Before getting to a set of cases to illustrate purchasing and leasing relationships, and the financial implications involved, it is important to understand the effects any analysis might have on budgets, income statement expenses, cash flow, balance sheet, and on cumulative discounted cash flow. Since any computer acquisition (and often for peripheral equipment too) is usually subjected to such measurements, it is relevant to appreciate them. A sample case will illustrate the relationships involved.

**Price**

Purchase price is $773,500; rental is $23,998; and lease is $21,865.

**Maintenance**

$1285 per month if CPU is purchased, otherwise there is no separate charge for maintenance.

**Taxes**

Federal is 48%, state 10%, sales 8%, personal property 3%. Tax life is 7 years, final book value (resale value) is 0% (to simplify the analysis).

**Depreciation**

For tax books double-declining balance to straight-line is used (1.5 to DB to SL calculation). For public books straight-line is used again, a useful life of 7 years applied, and a residual value of 0%.

**Discount**

The discount factor used is 9% after tax.

Figures 4–7, 4–8, and 4–9 illustrate what the financial and dollar numbers would look like for a cash purchase, a financed purchase, and a computer lease. In each instance the numbers presented are in budget, income statement, profit and loss, cash flow after tax, and in balance sheet forms. To illustrate graphically how each of these forms of financial measurements looks, Figures 4–10, 4–11, 4–12, and 4–13 chart each major pattern.

| | Cash Purchase ($ in Thousands) | | | | | | | |
|---|---|---|---|---|---|---|---|---|
| | '79 | '80 | '81 | '82 | '83 | '84 | '85 | '86 |
| Budget Expense | | | | | | | | |
| Depreciation | 0 | 119.3 | 119.3 | 119.3 | 119.3 | 119.3 | 119.3 | 119.3 |
| Maintenance | 0 | | 16.6 | 16.6 | 16.6 | 16.6 | 16.6 | 16.6 |
| Insurance | 0 | 3.8 | 3.8 | 3.8 | 3.8 | 3.8 | 3.8 | 3.8 |
| Total | 0 | 123.1 | 139.7 | 139.7 | 139.7 | 139.7 | 139.7 | 139.7 |
| Income Statement Impact | | | | | | | | |
| Budget Expense | 0 | 123.1 | 139.7 | 139.7 | 139.7 | 139.7 | 139.7 | 139.7 |
| Pers. Prop. Tax | 0 | 19.6 | 14.0 | 10.0 | 7.1 | 4.9 | 2.9 | .8 |
| P & L Expense | 0 | 142.7 | 153.7 | 149.7 | 146.8 | 144.6 | 142.6 | 140.6 |
| Less: | | | | | | | | |
| Tax Deduction | 0 | 75.9 | 86.8 | 79.6 | 78.1 | 76.9 | 75.9 | 74.8 |
| ITC | 72.3 | 0 | 0 | 0 | 0 | 0 | 0 | 0 |
| P & L Impact (after tax) | −72.3 | 66.8 | 76.8 | 70.1 | 78.7 | 67.7 | 66.7 | 65.7 |
| Balance Sheet Impact | | | | | | | | |
| Assets | 834.8 | 596.3 | 425.9 | 304.2 | 212.3 | 144.8 | 71.4 | 0 |
| Cash Flow (after tax) | −77.3 | 685.5 | −62.2 | −38.6 | −23.4 | −17.1 | −16.3 | −15.4 |
| Cumulative Discounted Cash Flow (after tax) | −77.3 | 609.0 | 547.0 | 508.3 | 484.9 | 467.7 | 451.4 | 435.9 |

Figure 4–7

| | Financed Purchase ($ in Thousands) | | | | | | | |
|---|---|---|---|---|---|---|---|---|
| | '79 | '80 | '81 | '82 | '83 | '84 | '85 | '86 |
| **Budget Expense** | | | | | | | | |
| Depreciation | 0 | 119.3 | 119.3 | 119.3 | 119.3 | 119.3 | 119.3 | 119.3 |
| Maintenance | 0 | 0 | 16.6 | 16.6 | 16.6 | 16.6 | 16.6 | 16.6 |
| Insurance | 0 | 3.8 | 3.8 | 3.8 | 3.8 | 3.8 | 3.8 | 3.8 |
| Total | 0 | 123.1 | 139.7 | 139.7 | 139.7 | 139.7 | 139.7 | 139.7 |
| **Income Statement Impact** | | | | | | | | |
| Budget Expense | 0 | 123.1 | 139.7 | 139.7 | 139.7 | 139.7 | 139.7 | 139.7 |
| Pers. Prop. Tax | 0 | 19.6 | 14.0 | 10.0 | 7.1 | 4.9 | 2.9 | .9 |
| Interest | 0 | 71.5 | 63.0 | 53.8 | 43.8 | 32.8 | 20.7 | 7.5 |
| P & L Expenses | 0 | 214.2 | 216.7 | 203.6 | 190.6 | 177.4 | 163.3 | 148.1 |
| Less: | | | | | | | | |
| Tax Deduction | 0 | 113.9 | 115.3 | 108.3 | 101.4 | 94.4 | 86.9 | 78.8 |
| ITC | −72.3 | 0 | 0 | 0 | 0 | 0 | 0 | 0 |
| P & L Impact | | | | | | | | |
| (after tax) | −72.3 | 100.2 | 101.4 | 95.2 | 89.2 | 83.0 | 76.4 | 69.3 |
| **Balance Sheet Impact** | | | | | | | | |
| Assets | 834.8 | 596.3 | 425.9 | 304.2 | 217.3 | 144.8 | 71.4 | 0 |
| Liabilities | 834.8 | 745.2 | 647.0 | 539.7 | 422.4 | 294.0 | 153.6 | 0 |
| Cash Flow (after tax) | −72.3 | 7.2 | 53.1 | 82.0 | 104.5 | 117.1 | 122.5 | 128.6 |
| Cumulative Discounted | | | | | | | | |
| Cash Flow (after tax) | −72.3 | −69.6 | −25.2 | 37.7 | 111.2 | 186.8 | 259.4 | 329.2 |

**Figure 4-8**

| | Lease ($ in Thousands) | | | | | | | |
|---|---|---|---|---|---|---|---|---|
| | '79 | '80 | '81 | '82 | '83 | '84 | '85 | '86 |
| **Budget Expense** | | | | | | | | |
| Lease + Tax | 0 | 145.6 | 145.6 | 145.6 | 145.6 | 145.6 | 145.6 | 145.6 |
| Maintenance | 0 | 0 | 0 | 0 | 0 | 0 | 0 | 0 |
| Insurance | 0 | 3.8 | 3.8 | 3.8 | 3.8 | 3.8 | 3.8 | 3.8 |
| Total | 0 | 149.4 | 149.4 | 149.4 | 149.4 | 149.4 | 149.4 | 149.4 |
| **Income Statement Impact** | | | | | | | | |
| Budget Expense | 0 | 149.4 | 149.4 | 149.4 | 149.4 | 149.4 | 149.4 | 149.4 |
| Pers. Prop. Tax | 0 | 19.6 | 14.0 | 10.0 | 7.1 | 4.9 | 2.9 | .9 |
| P & L Expense | 0 | 169.0 | 163.4 | 159.4 | 156.5 | 154.3 | 152.3 | 150.3 |
| Less: | | | | | | | | |
| Tax Deduction | 0 | 77.4 | 77.4 | 77.4 | 77.4 | 77.4 | 77.4 | 77.4 |
| ITC | 0 | 0 | 0 | 0 | 0 | 0 | 0 | 0 |
| P & L Impact | | | | | | | | |
| (after tax) | 0 | 91.6 | 86.0 | 82.0 | 79.1 | 76.9 | 74.9 | 72.9 |
| Balance Sheet Impact | 1019.2 | 873.6 | 728.0 | 582.4 | 436.8 | 291.2 | 14.6 | 0 |
| Cash Flow (after tax) | 0 | 80.1 | 77.1 | 75.1 | 73.6 | 72.0 | 70.0 | 68.5 |
| Cumulative Discounted | | | | | | | | |
| Cash Flow (after tax) | 0 | 80.1 | 123.6 | 175.0 | 222.0 | 266.2 | 305.5 | 342.1 |

**Figure 4-9**

142

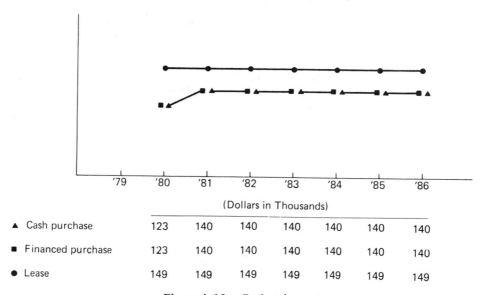

| (Dollars in Thousands) | | | | | | |
|---|---|---|---|---|---|---|
| ▲ Cash purchase | 123 | 140 | 140 | 140 | 140 | 140 | 140 |
| ■ Financed purchase | 123 | 140 | 140 | 140 | 140 | 140 | 140 |
| ● Lease | 149 | 149 | 149 | 149 | 149 | 149 | 149 |

**Figure 4-10**    Budget impact.

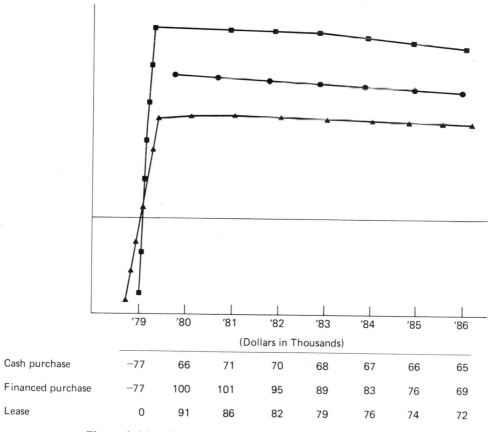

| (Dollars in Thousands) | | | | | | |
|---|---|---|---|---|---|---|
| ▲ Cash purchase | −77 | 66 | 71 | 70 | 68 | 67 | 66 | 65 |
| ■ Financed purchase | −77 | 100 | 101 | 95 | 89 | 83 | 76 | 69 |
| ● Lease | 0 | 91 | 86 | 82 | 79 | 76 | 74 | 72 |

**Figure 4-11**    Income statement impact (after tax P+L).

143

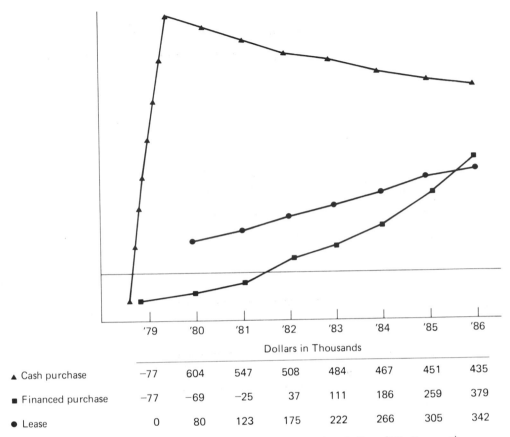

Dollars in Thousands

| | '79 | '80 | '81 | '82 | '83 | '84 | '85 | '86 |
|---|---|---|---|---|---|---|---|---|
| ▲ Cash purchase | −77 | 604 | 547 | 508 | 484 | 467 | 451 | 435 |
| ■ Financed purchase | −77 | −69 | −25 | 37 | 111 | 186 | 259 | 379 |
| ● Lease | 0 | 80 | 123 | 175 | 222 | 266 | 305 | 342 |

**Figure 4-12**    Cumulative discounted cash flow (9% discount).

Depending on which measurement is assigned the greatest weight, the financial analysis can lead to different conclusions. To the executive concerned about cash outlay, leasing is most tempting. Yet from an income statement point of view, a cash purchase is even more appealing. But to the company with little debt and perhaps cash flow needs for other projects right now, a financed purchase might seem the only way to go.

The key point to remember is that in any analysis, the same numbers provide a variety of interpretations. Thus for a particular company, key sets of figures should be calculated and balanced against each other on the one hand, and measured against your management's current financial environment on the other. In short, the exercise is no different than for any other piece of equipment and once again management is given the capability of measuring a DP proposal against other nondata processing

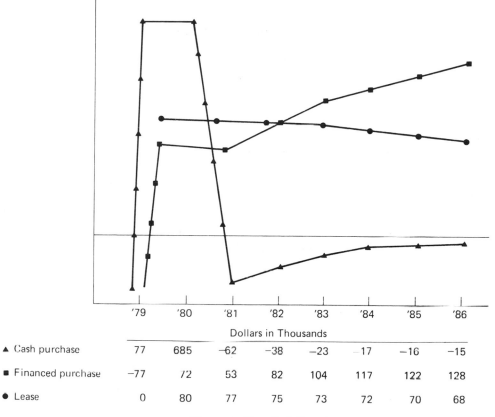

| Dollars in Thousands | '79 | '80 | '81 | '82 | '83 | '84 | '85 | '86 |
|---|---|---|---|---|---|---|---|---|
| ▲ Cash purchase | 77 | 685 | −62 | −38 | −23 | −17 | −16 | −15 |
| ■ Financed purchase | −77 | 72 | 53 | 82 | 104 | 117 | 122 | 128 |
| ● Lease | 0 | 80 | 77 | 75 | 73 | 72 | 70 | 68 |

**Figure 4-13**    Cash flow impact.

options using the same terms and methods of measurements throughout the company.

## SAMPLES OF COMPUTER FINANCIAL ANALYSIS

Hardly any major computer decision is made today without a formal analysis of options and costs in some detail. No two companies are alike in the way this analysis is done or in the options selected. However, they all have in common the kinds of elements discussed previously. There is no better way to illustrate the process than to actually go through some case studies. Typically the financial analysis will either be performed using a computerized financial analysis package already available within the company, or a time-sharing connection to a service bureau's program, or with the aid of a computer vendor who usually has a com-

FINANCIAL ANALYSIS WORK SHEET

Department _____  Date _____

Case Title _____

I. Work Load Forecast

Time Periods

Growth (%) _____

II. Configurations

| Device | Vendor | From | To | Comments | Rel/Per |
|--------|--------|------|-----|----------|---------|
| | | | | | |
| | | | | | |
| | | | | | |
| | | | | | |
| | | | | | |
| | | | | | |
| | | | | | |
| | | | | | |
| | | | | | |

**Figure 4-14**   Sample form.

WORKSHEET

Vendor _____

| Device | Item | Amount | % | From | To | 1 | 2 | 3 | 4 | 5 | 6 | 7 | 8 | 9 |
|--------|------|--------|---|------|----|---|---|---|---|---|---|---|---|---|
| | Cost | | | | | | | | | | | | | |
| | Maint. | | | | | | | | | | | | | |
| | ITC | | | | | | | | | | | | | |
| | Resl | | | | | | | | | | | | | |
| Total | | | | | | | | | | | | | | |
| | Cost | | | | | | | | | | | | | |
| | Maint. | | | | | | | | | | | | | |
| | ITC | | | | | | | | | | | | | |
| | Resl | | | | | | | | | | | | | |
| Total | | | | | | | | | | | | | | |
| | Cost | | | | | | | | | | | | | |
| | Maint. | | | | | | | | | | | | | |
| | ITC | | | | | | | | | | | | | |
| | Resl | | | | | | | | | | | | | |
| Total | | | | | | | | | | | | | | |
| | Cost | | | | | | | | | | | | | |
| | Maint. | | | | | | | | | | | | | |
| | ITC | | | | | | | | | | | | | |
| | Resl | | | | | | | | | | | | | |
| Total | | | | | | | | | | | | | | |
| | Cost | | | | | | | | | | | | | |
| | Maint. | | | | | | | | | | | | | |
| | ITC | | | | | | | | | | | | | |
| | Resl | | | | | | | | | | | | | |
| Total | | | | | | | | | | | | | | |
| Grand Total | | | | | | | | | | | | | | |

**Figure 4-15**

puterized financial application available to him for marketing purposes. Thus most of the mathematics is taken care of through automation. The definition of the cases and their inputs clearly remain very much a judgmental matter for managers assessing DP products, internal business needs, and the corporate political environment. However, in the pages to come, various situations will be shown, including the use of simple input forms for defining options and the variables. There is nothing sacred about any of these models. In fact, a DP department should either use an existing company-wide form for inputs or work with the financial group to tailor one to the company's needs.

| | | Comparison | |
|---|---|---|---|
| Time Period | Vendor | Vendor | Delta |
| ———— | ———— | ———— | ———— |
| ———— | ———— | ———— | ———— |
| ———— | ———— | ———— | ———— |
| ———— | ———— | ———— | ———— |
| ———— | ———— | ———— | ———— |
| ———— | ———— | ———— | ———— |
| ———— | ———— | ———— | ———— |
| ———— | ———— | ———— | ———— |
| ———— | ———— | ———— | ———— |
| ———— | ———— | ———— | ———— |
| Total | ———— | ———— | ———— |
| Comments | | | |

**Figure 4-16**

## Purchase versus Lease

Figures 4-18, 4-19, and 4-20 show a comparative analysis between purchasing and leasing a computer from the first day of installation. In this particular case, it is clearly evident that purchase is less costly. But, as the numbers suggest, the machine should be kept for a longer period of time than if leased. With such an analysis, it is easier for management to assess various options quickly and to appreciate the possible cash-flow and financial impacts.

## Analysis by Relative Performance

Another popular way to measure options, particularly complex scenarios, is by the value and financial impact of various amounts of horse power. Take the situation involving four options defined by DP management:

**Case A**

> Purchase a computer red now and purchase computer green later
> or rent computer red until delivery can be made of computer blue.

# Breakeven Point Analysis

Interim Capacity_____ ARIP*          Eventual Capacity_____ Case No.: _____

| | On Order or to Order | |
| Installed | Current Product | Announced |
|---|---|---|
xxx

xxx

Resale Assumptions

($ in Thousands)

in months

| | Buy/ | | | | Rent(lease)/Buy | | | | |
| | 1–12 | Per Month | 13–24 | Per Month | 1–3 | Per Month | 4–12 | Per Month | 13–24 | Per Month |
|---|---|---|---|---|---|---|---|---|---|---|
| Purchase Price | ____ | ____ | | | ____ | ____ | | | ____ | |
| Insurance | ____ | ____ | ____ | ____ | ____ | ____ | ____ | ____ | ____ | ____ |
| Maintenance | ____ | ____ | ____ | ____ | ____ | ____ | ____ | ____ | ____ | ____ |
| Per. Prop. Tax | ____ | ____ | ____ | ____ | ____ | ____ | ____ | ____ | ____ | ____ |
| Rent | ____ | ____ | ____ | ____ | ____ | ____ | ____ | ____ | ____ | ____ |
| ITC | ____ | ____ | | | ____ | | ____ | | | |
| ITC Recapture | ____ | ____ | | | ____ | | ____ | | ____ | |
| Sub Total | $____ | | $____ | | $____ | | $____ | | $____ | |
| 24 Month Total | | | $____ | | | | | | $____ | |
| Per Month | | $____ | | $____ | | $____ | | $____ | | $____ |

Per Month Delta ($\Delta$)                    $____          $____        $____

24 Month Total Delta ($\Delta$)      $____

24 Month $\Delta \div$ Per Month      $____  $\Delta$ Months

Breakeven = 24 Mo. + $\Delta$ Mo.      ____  Months

Termination Charges      ____  Months

Breakeven with Termination Charge      ____  Months

*ARIP (Approximate relative internal performance of computers compared to various other models).

**Figure 4–17**

149

COMPUTER PURCHASE VS. LEASE ANALYSIS
1980 THROUGH 1986

| Income Tax | | Insurance | | Sales Tax Capitalized | | | Personal Property Tax | | | |
| Fed | State | (pct/yr) | | Purch | Lease | Maint | Rate: | Life: | Final Book Value: 46.00 | Method: Straight-line |
|---|---|---|---|---|---|---|---|---|---|---|
| 48.00 | 7.00 | .05 | | 5.00 | 5.00 | 5.00 | .00 | 6 yrs | | |

| Ident | Shipd mo/yr | L=Lease R=Rent | Rent | Purchase Cost | Total Amnt Installed | Maint | Wrnty Mos | Pct Down | Intrst Rate | Term Mos | Tax Life | Deprec Method | Final Tx NBV | Depr Adj |
|---|---|---|---|---|---|---|---|---|---|---|---|---|---|---|
| Computer | 1 80 | L | 10000 | 500000 | 500000 | 1000 | 12 | .00 | 9.00 | 60 | 6 | Straight-line | 46.00 | 0 |

| Purchase | Other Charges | 80 | 81 | 82 | 83 | 84 | 85 | Term Mos |
|---|---|---|---|---|---|---|---|---|
| ITC | TC | -50000 | 0 | 0 | 0 | 0 | 0 | 0 |
| Resale | TX | 0 | 0 | 0 | 0 | 0 | 0 | -230000 |

| System | Sales Tax | Down Payment | Due Mo/Yr | Amount Financed | Due Mo/Yr | Monthly Payment | Due Mo/Yr |
|---|---|---|---|---|---|---|---|
| 1 | 25000 | 0 | 2 80 | 525000 | 2 80 | 10898 | 2 80 |

**Figure 4-18**  Input data for estimated cash flow and expense analysis.

# COMPUTER PURCHASE VS. LEASE ANALYSIS
## 1980 THROUGH 1986

### Estimated Cash Flow if Purchased

| | | 80 | 81 | 82 | 83 | 84 | 85 | 86 |
|---|---|---|---|---|---|---|---|---|
| Cash Outflow Before Tax: | | | | | | | | |
| Principal | | 79504 | 94519 | 103305 | 113004 | 123692 | 10817 | 0 |
| Interest | TX | 40376 | 36259 | 27392 | 17694 | 7086 | 81 | 0 |
| Total Installment | | 119880 | 130778 | 130778 | 130778 | 130778 | 10898 | 0 |
| Maintenance | TX | 0 | 11550 | 12600 | 12600 | 12600 | 12600 | 12600 |
| Insurance | TX | 229 | 250 | 250 | 250 | 250 | 250 | 250 |
| Resale | TX | 0 | 0 | 0 | 0 | 0 | 0 | −230000 |
| Total Cash Outflow | | 120109 | 142578 | 143628 | 143628 | 143628 | 23748 | −217150 |
| (Cumulative) | | | 262686 | 406314 | 549942 | 693569 | 717317 | 500167 |
| Tax Calculation: | | | | | | | | |
| Deductible Expenses | | | | | | | | |
| Tax Depreciation | | 43312 | 47250 | 47250 | 47250 | 47250 | 47250 | 3937 |
| Ded Exp (Sum TX) | | 40605 | 48059 | 40242 | 30544 | 19936 | 12931 | −217150 |
| Total Expenses | | 83917 | 95309 | 87492 | 77794 | 67186 | 60181 | −213213 |
| X .5164 Tax Rate | | | | | | | | |
| Tax Deduction | | 43335 | 49217 | 45181 | 40173 | 34695 | 31078 | −110103 |
| ITC | TC | 50000 | 0 | 0 | 0 | 0 | 0 | 0 |
| Tax Effect | | 93335 | 49217 | 45181 | 40173 | 34695 | 31078 | −110103 |
| Cash Outflow After Tax: | | | | | | | | |
| Total Cash Outflow | | 120109 | 142578 | 143628 | 143628 | 143628 | 23748 | −217150 |
| Less Tax Effect | | 93335 | 49217 | 45181 | 40173 | 34695 | 31078 | −110103 |
| Cash Flo Aft Tax | | 26774 | 93361 | 98447 | 103455 | 108933 | −7330 | −107047 |
| (Cumulative) | | | 120134 | 218581 | 322036 | 430968 | 423638 | 316591 |
| Present Value at 9.00 Pct (1/1/80) | | | | | | | | |
| Cash Flo Aft Tax | | 25364 | 82019 | 79363 | 76513 | 73911 | −4294 | −61202 |
| (Cumulative) | | | 107383 | 186746 | 263259 | 337170 | 332876 | 271674 |

### Estimated Cash Flow if Rented

| | | 80 | 81 | 82 | 83 | 84 | 85 | 86 |
|---|---|---|---|---|---|---|---|---|
| Cash Outflow Before Tax: | | | | | | | | |
| Rent + S.TX | TX | 115500 | 126000 | 126000 | 126000 | 126000 | 126000 | 126000 |
| Total Cash Outflow | | 115500 | 126000 | 126000 | 126000 | 126000 | 126000 | 126000 |
| (Cumulative) | | | 241500 | 367500 | 493500 | 619500 | 745500 | 871500 |
| Tax Calculation: | | | | | | | | |
| Deductible Expenses | | | | | | | | |
| Ded Exp (Sum TX) | | 115500 | 126000 | 126000 | 126000 | 126000 | 126000 | 126000 |
| Total Expenses | | 115500 | 126000 | 126000 | 126000 | 126000 | 126000 | 126000 |
| X .5164 Tax Rate | | | | | | | | |

**Figure 4-19** Estimated annual cash flow and expense summary.

151

| Tax Deduction | 59644 | 65066 | 65066 | 65066 | 65066 | 65066 | 65066 |
|---|---|---|---|---|---|---|---|
| Tax Effect | 59644 | 65066 | 65066 | 65066 | 65066 | 65066 | 65066 |
| Cash Outflow After Tax: | | | | | | | |
| Tot Cash Outflow | 115500 | 126000 | 126000 | 126000 | 126000 | 126000 | 126000 |
| Less Tax Effect | 59644 | 65066 | 65066 | 65066 | 65066 | 65066 | 65066 |
| Cash Flo Aft Tax | 50856 | 60934 | 60934 | 60934 | 60934 | 60934 | 60934 |
| (Cumulative) | | 116790 | 177724 | 238658 | 299592 | 360526 | 421460 |

Estimated Cash Flow, Purchase Less Rent

| | 80 | 81 | 82 | 83 | 84 | 85 | 86 |
|---|---|---|---|---|---|---|---|
| Before Taxes: | | | | | | | |
| If Purchased | 120109 | 142578 | 143628 | 143628 | 143628 | 23748 | −217150 |
| If Leased | 115500 | 126000 | 126000 | 126000 | 126000 | 126000 | 126000 |
| Difference | 4609 | 16578 | 17628 | 17628 | 17628 | −102252 | −343150 |
| (Cumulative) | | 21186 | 38814 | 56442 | 74069 | −28183 | −371333 |
| After Taxes: | | | | | | | |
| If Purchased | 26774 | 93361 | 98447 | 103455 | 108933 | −7330 | −107047 |
| If Leased | 55856 | 60934 | 60934 | 60934 | 60934 | 60934 | 60934 |
| Difference | −29082 | 32427 | 37513 | 42521 | 47999 | −68264 | −167981 |
| (Cumulative) | | 3344 | 40857 | 83378 | 131376 | 63112 | −104869 |
| Present Value at 9.00 Pct (1/1/80) | | | | | | | |
| Cash Flo Aft Tax | −27958 | 28458 | 30224 | 31432 | 32552 | −42238 | −96013 |
| (Cumulative) | | 500 | 30724 | 62156 | 94708 | 52470 | −43543 |

**Figure 4–20**

### Case B

Purchase the installed computer red with its accruals now and later computer green or continue renting computer red until computer blue can be delivered.

### Case C

Purchase computer red now or rent it until computer blue is delivered.

### Case D

Purchase the installed computer red with its accruals or lease it until computer blue is delivered.

Additional usage was calculated at about 20% for rented machines while insurance was set at 0.5% of the purchase price. Personal property tax in the particular state where the computers would be used was 2.75% of their purchase price and declined annually at 14%. The ITC was valued at 10% of the purchase price.

In the particular situation described above, the management went through an exercise to determine a reasonable resale value for purposes of their calculations. They assumed that if a computer provided a two-for-one price performance increase then any resale value of the older equipment must decline by 50%. Taking into account the 10% ITC available on newer products, this same logic would suggest that the older computer would decline in value by an additional 10% to 40% of the purchase price. Computer blue was new. Management said that the cost per approximate relative internal performance (ARIP) was valued at the purchase price of the product ($1.7 million), divided by 4.40 ARIP (to compare against installed power), equaled $385,000 per ARIP. The resale value of $385,000/ARIP or 57% of the purchase of a computer red was thus easily determined.

Next taking the ITC impact, in a 50% tax bracket, the 10% ITC offers a 20% discount after taxes on new computers. Thus the cost per ARIP for a computer blue would in reality be 80% X 385,000 or $308,000. Economic substitution suggests that $308,000 was the resale value per ARIP for computer red. Put another way, the resale value of computer red equals 46% of the purchase price new. Going through this exercise yielded the following data for the purchase cost for relative performance by taking the purchase price divided by ARIPs.

| | |
|---|---|
| Computer brown | $0.85/1.00 – $0.85 |
| Computer red | $1.85/2.75 = $0.67 |
| Computer green | $0.90/1.87 = $0.48 |
| Computer blue | $1.70/4.40 = $0.38 |

The ARIPS were drawn from the vendors of the various computers and from data processing literature. With that information an estimated resale value percent could be calculated:

| | Purchase Cost/ARIP | ITC Impact | | | % Purchase Price |
|---|---|---|---|---|---|
| Computer blue<br>————————<br>Computer red | $0.38<br>———<br>$0.67 | X | 0.80 | = | 46% |
| Computer blue<br>————————<br>Computer green | $0.38<br>———<br>$0.48 | X | 0.80 | = | 64% |

Relationships of resale can be graphed for various risk scenarios as, for example, 46% against 64% or 23% against 32%. And although there is never any guarantee that the resale will either match the kind of exercise illustrated above or historical trends, management in this instance felt comfortable with the numbers they generated.

The actual base prices for all the calculations were as follows:

| Computer | Memory Size | ARIP | Lease | Purchase | Maintenance |
|----------|-------------|------|-------|----------|-------------|
| Brown | 3 meg | 1.00 | 26K | 0.85M | 1.4K |
| Red | 4 meg | 2.75 | 58.5K | 1.85M | 4.75K |
| Green | 2 meg | 1.87 | 38.5K | 0.9 M | 3.75K |
| Blue | 4 meg | 4.40 | 38K | 1.7 M | N/A |
| Blue | 6 meg | 4.40 | 42K | 1.8 M | N/A |

Taking all this data, management came up with the following breakeven analysis which then could become the basis for a decision that told how much horsepower could be had for what breakeven point. Figures 4-21, 4-22, 4-23, 4-24, 4-25, 4-26 are the worksheets for each case. The data from each of the worksheets was summarized in the following way:

### Breakeven Analysis

| Case | Eventual Capacity Needed | Installed | On Order Current | On Order Announced | Resale | Breakeven Months |
|------|--------------------------|-----------|---------|-----------|--------|------------------|
| A | 4.40 | | Red/Green (later) | Blue | Hold | 13 |
| B | 4.40 | Red(1) | Green (later) | Blue | Hold | 10 |
| C1 | 2.75 | | Red | Blue | Hold | 2 |
| C2 | 4.40 | | Red | Blue | 46% | 17 |
| D1 | 2.75 | Red(2) | | Blue | Hold | (12) |
| D2 | 4.40 | Red(2) | | Blue | 46% | 5 |

The decision as to which choice to select is still a complex one suggesting that more than numbers and dollars are involved. However, the cases above, as complex as they are, indicate that the options could nevertheless be quantified and measured. Thus in the situation above, if 4.40 times the current power is needed in the shortest period of time for breakeven, option D2 looks quite attractive. On the other hand, if growth to the 4.40 power over time is in line with anticipated growth then either C1 or D1 would be advantageous.

Breakeven Point Analysis

Interim Capacity __2.75__ ARIP*          Eventual Capacity __4.40__          Case No.: __A__

On Order or to Order

|  | Installed | Current Product | Announced |
|---|---|---|---|
| xxx |  —  | RED/GREEN (LATER) | BLUE |
| Resale Assumptions | — | | |

($ in Thousands)

in months

| | Buy/HOLD | | | | Rent(lease)/Buy | | | | | |
|---|---|---|---|---|---|---|---|---|---|---|
| | 1–12 | Per Month | 13–24 | Per Month | 1–3 | Per Month | 4–12 | Per Month | 13–24 | Per Month |
| Purchase Price | 1850 | | 900 | | | | | | 1800 | |
| Insurance | 9.5 | .8 | 9.5 | .8 | | | | | | |
| Maintenance | | | 57 | 4.75 | | | | | | |
| Per. Prop. Tax | 51 | 4.25 | 44 | 3.65 | | | | | | |
| Rent | | | | | 166.5 | 55.5 | 599.5 | 66.6 | 799 | 66.6 |
| ITC | (370) | | (180) | | | | | | (360) | |
| ITC Recapture | — | | — | | | | | | | |
| Sub Total | $1540.5 | | $830.5 | | $166.5 | | $599.5 | | $2239 | |
| 24 Month Total | | | $2371 | | | | | | $3005 | |
| Per Month | | $5.05 | | $9.2 | | $55.5 | | $66.6 | | $66.6 |

| | | | | |
|---|---|---|---|---|
| Per Month Delta (Δ) | | $50.45 | $61.55 | $57.4 |
| 24 Month Total Delta (Δ) | $(634) | | | |
| 24 Month Δ ÷ Per Month | $(5.5) Δ Months | | | |
| Breakeven = 24 Mo. + Δ Mo. | 6.5 Months | | | |

Termination Charges          N/A Months

Breakeven with Termination Charge          _____ Months

*ARIP (Approximate relative internal performance of computers compared to various other models).

Figure 4-21

155

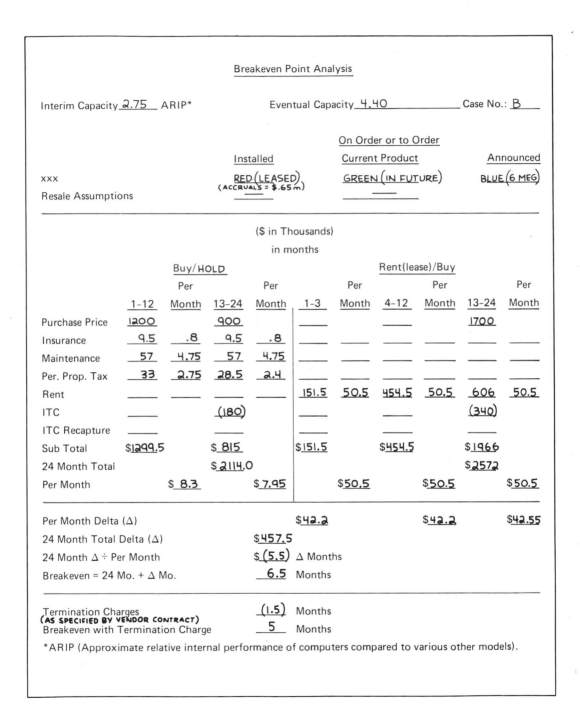

Breakeven Point Analysis

Interim Capacity __2.75__ ARIP*     Eventual Capacity __4.40_____     Case No.: __B__

|  | Installed | On Order or to Order Current Product | Announced |
|---|---|---|---|
| xxx | RED (LEASED) | GREEN (IN FUTURE) | BLUE (6 MEG) |
| Resale Assumptions | (ACCRUALS = $.65m) | ———— | ———— |

($ in Thousands)

in months

|  | Buy/HOLD | | | | Rent(lease)/Buy | | | | | |
|---|---|---|---|---|---|---|---|---|---|---|
|  | 1–12 | Per Month | 13–24 | Per Month | 1–3 | Per Month | 4–12 | Per Month | 13–24 | Per Month |
| Purchase Price | 1200 |  | 900 |  | ——— |  | ——— |  | 1700 |  |
| Insurance | 9.5 | .8 | 9.5 | .8 | ——— | ——— | ——— | ——— | ——— | ——— |
| Maintenance | 57 | 4.75 | 57 | 4.75 | ——— | ——— | ——— | ——— | ——— | ——— |
| Per. Prop. Tax | 33 | 2.75 | 28.5 | 2.4 | ——— | ——— | ——— | ——— | ——— | ——— |
| Rent | ——— | ——— | ——— | ——— | 151.5 | 50.5 | 454.5 | 50.5 | 606 | 50.5 |
| ITC | ——— |  | (180) |  | ——— |  | ——— |  | (340) |  |
| ITC Recapture | ——— |  | ——— |  |  |  |  |  | ——— |  |
| Sub Total | $1299.5 |  | $ 815 |  | $151.5 |  | $454.5 |  | $1966 |  |
| 24 Month Total |  |  | $ 2114.0 |  |  |  |  |  | $2572 |  |
| Per Month |  | $ 8.3 |  | $ 7.95 |  | $50.5 |  | $50.5 |  | $50.5 |

Per Month Delta (Δ)                                $42.2                $42.2                $42.55

24 Month Total Delta (Δ)              $457.5

24 Month Δ ÷ Per Month               $ (5.5) Δ Months

Breakeven = 24 Mo. + Δ Mo.            6.5  Months

Termination Charges                      (1.5) Months
(AS SPECIFIED BY VENDOR CONTRACT)
Breakeven with Termination Charge         5   Months

*ARIP (Approximate relative internal performance of computers compared to various other models).

**Figure 4–22**

156

**Breakeven Point Analysis**

Interim Capacity **2.75** ARIP*　　　　　Eventual Capacity **2.75**　　　　　Case No.: **C1**

|  | Installed | On Order or to Order Current Product | Announced |
|---|---|---|---|
| xxx | — | **RED** | **BLUE (4 MEG)** |
| Resale Assumptions | — | | |

($ in Thousands)

in months

| | Buy/HOLD | | | | Rent(lease)/Buy | | | | | |
|---|---|---|---|---|---|---|---|---|---|---|
| | 1–12 | Per Month | 13–24 | Per Month | 1–3 | Per Month | 4–12 | Per Month | 13–24 | Per Month |
| Purchase Price | 1850 | | 1700 | | | | | | 1700 | |
| Insurance | 9.5 | .8 | 9.5 | .8 | | | | | | |
| Maintenance | | | 57 | 4.75 | | | | | | |
| Per. Prop. Tax | 51 | 4.25 | 44 | 3.65 | | | | | | |
| Rent | | | | | 166.5 | 55.5 | 599.5 | 66.6 | 799 | 66.6 |
| ITC | (370) | | | | (123.5) | | | | (340) | |
| ITC Recapture | | | | | | | | | 123.5 | |
| Sub Total | $1540.5 | | $110.5 | | $43 | | $599.5 | | $2282.5 | |
| 24 Month Total | | | $1651 | | | | | | $2925 | |
| Per Month | | $5.05 | | $9.2 | | $55.5 | | $66.6 | | $66.6 |

| | | | |
|---|---|---|---|
| Per Month Delta (Δ) | $50.45 | $61.55 | $57.4 |
| 24 Month Total Delta (Δ) | $(1274) | | |
| 24 Month Δ ÷ Per Month | $(11) Δ Months | | |
| Breakeven = 24 Mo. + Δ Mo. | 1 Months | | |

Termination Charges　　　　**N/A** Months

Breakeven with Termination Charge　　　—— Months

*ARIP (Approximate relative internal performance of computers compared to various other models).

Figure 4-23

157

Breakeven Point Analysis

Interim Capacity __2.75__ ARIP*          Eventual Capacity __4.40__          Case No.: __C2__

|  | Installed | On Order or to Order Current Product | Announced |
|---|---|---|---|
| xxx | — | RED | BLUE (4 MEG) |
| Resale Assumptions | — | 46% | |

($ in Thousands)
in months

| | Buy/ BUY | | | | Rent(lease)/Buy | | | | | |
|---|---|---|---|---|---|---|---|---|---|---|
| | 1–12 | Per Month | 13–24 | Per Month | 1–3 | Per Month | 4–12 | Per Month | 13–24 | Per Month |
| Purchase Price | 1850 | | 1700 | | | | | | 1700 | |
| Insurance | 9.5 | .8 | 9.5 | .8 | | | | | | |
| Maintenance | | | 57 | 4.75 | | | | | | |
| Per. Prop. Tax | 51 | 4.25 | 44 | 3.65 | | | | | | |
| Rent | | | | | 166.5 | 55.5 | 599.5 | 66.6 | 799 | 66.6 |
| ITC | (370) | | (340) | | (123.5) | | | | (340) | |
| ITC Recapture | | (851) | 370 | | | | | | 123.5 | |
| RESALE Sub Total | $1540.5 | | $989.5 | | $43 | | $599.5 | | $2273 | |
| 24 Month Total | | | $2530 | | | | | | $2925 | |
| Per Month | | $5.05 | | $9.2 | | $55.5 | | $66.6 | | $66.6 |

| | | | |
|---|---|---|---|
| Per Month Delta (Δ) | | $50.45 | $615.5 | $70.4 |
| 24 Month Total Delta (Δ) | $(395) | | | |
| 24 Month Δ ÷ Per Month | $(3.5) Δ Months | | | |
| Breakeven = 24 Mo. + Δ Mo. | 8.5 Months | | | |

Termination Charges          N/A Months

Breakeven with Termination Charge          _____ Months

*ARIP (Approximate relative internal performance of computers compared to various other models).

**Figure 4-24**

Breakeven Point Analysis

Interim Capacity __2.75__ ARIP*          Eventual Capacity __2.75_____          Case No.: __D1__

|  | | On Order or to Order | |
|---|---|---|---|
|  | Installed | Current Product | Announced |
| xxx | RED-LEASED <br> (ACCRUALS = $.65m) | — | BLUE (4 MEG) |
| Resale Assumptions | ___ | — | |

($ in Thousands)

in months

| | Buy/HOLD | | | | Rent(lease)/Buy | | | | | |
|---|---|---|---|---|---|---|---|---|---|---|
| | | Per | | Per | | Per | | Per | | Per |
| | 1-12 | Month | 13-24 | Month | 1-3 | Month | 4-12 | Month | 13-24 | Month |
| Purchase Price | 1200 | ___ | ___ | | ___ | | ___ | | 1700 | |
| Insurance | 9.5 | .8 | 9.5 | .8 | ___ | ___ | ___ | ___ | ___ | ___ |
| Maintenance | 57 | 4.75 | 57 | 4.75 | ___ | ___ | ___ | ___ | ___ | ___ |
| Per. Prop. Tax | 33 | 2.75 | 28.5 | 2.4 | ___ | ___ | ___ | ___ | ___ | ___ |
| Rent | ___ | ___ | ___ | ___ | 151.5 | 50.5 | 454.5 | 50.5 | 606 | 50.5 |
| ITC | ___ | | ___ | | ___ | | ___ | | (340) | |
| ITC Recapture | ___ | | ___ | | | | | | | |
| Sub Total | $1299.5 | | $95 | | $151.5 | | $454.5 | | $(1966) | |
| 24 Month Total | | | $1393.5 | | | | | | $2572 | |
| Per Month | | $8.3 | | $7.95 | | $50.5 | | $50.5 | | $50.5 |

| | | |
|---|---|---|
| Per Month Delta (Δ) | $42.2 | $42.2     $42.55 |
| 24 Month Total Delta (Δ) | $(1178.5) | |
| 24 Month Δ ÷ Per Month | $(14) Δ Months | |
| Breakeven = 24 Mo. + Δ Mo. | (2) Months | |

Termination Charges          (4) Months
BASED ON VENDOR CONTRACT TERMS
Breakeven with Termination Charge          (6) Months

*ARIP (Approximate relative internal performance of computers compared to various other models).

**Figure 4-25**

## Breakeven Point Analysis

Interim Capacity **2.75** ARIP*     Eventual Capacity **4.40**     Case No.: **D2**

|  | Installed | On Order or to Order<br>Current Product | Announced |
|---|---|---|---|
| XXX | RED-LEASED<br>(ACCRUALS = $.65) | ——— | BLUE (4 MEG) |
| Resale Assumptions | 46% | ——— | ——— |

($ in Thousands)

in months

| | Buy/BUY | | | | Rent(lease)/Buy | | | | | |
|---|---|---|---|---|---|---|---|---|---|---|
| | 1-12 | Per Month | 13-24 | Per Month | 1-3 | Per Month | 4-12 | Per Month | 13-24 | Per Month |
| Purchase Price | 1200 | | ——— | | ——— | | ——— | | 1700 | |
| Insurance | 9.5 | .8 | 9.5 | .8 | ——— | ——— | ——— | ——— | ——— | ——— |
| Maintenance | 57 | 4.75 | 57 | 4.75 | ——— | ——— | ——— | ——— | ——— | ——— |
| Per. Prop. Tax | 33 | 2.75 | 28.5 | 2.4 | ——— | ——— | ——— | ——— | ——— | ——— |
| Rent | ——— | ——— | ——— | ——— | 151.5 | 50.5 | 454.5 | 50.5 | 606 | 50.5 |
| ITC | ——— | | (340) | | ——— | | ——— | | (340) | |
| ITC Recapture<br>RESALE | ——— | | (851) | | ——— | | ——— | | ——— | |
| Sub Total | $1299.5 | | $604 | | $151.5 | | $454.5 | | $(1966) | |
| 24 Month Total | | | $1903.5 | | | | | | $2572 | |
| Per Month | | $8.3 | | $7.95 | | $50.5 | | $50.5 | | $50.5 |

| | | |
|---|---|---|
| Per Month Delta (Δ) | $42.2 | $42.2 | $42.55 |
| 24 Month Total Delta (Δ) | $(668.5) | |
| 24 Month Δ ÷ Per Month | $(8) | Δ Months |
| Breakeven = 24 Mo. + Δ Mo. | 4 | Months |

Termination Charges<br>BASED ON VENDOR CONTRACT TERMS     (1.5) Months

Breakeven with Termination Charge     2.5 Months

*ARIP (Approximate relative internal performance of computers compared to various other models).

**Figure 4-26**

## Analysis by Cash Flow

The most common method of analysis is to structure several options listing all the expenses and quantifiable cash benefits (ITC for example). Then one does a cash flow analysis to study the impact of taxes, resale, internal rate of return, and profit vs. loss on each option. Two simple situations illustrate how it is done. Case A assumes a CPU being purchased, leasing the necessary I/O devices, expensing physical site preparation, and selling the computer six years later. Case B considers what might happen if the CPU and I/O were rented or leased. The two cases are then compared. In this situation B was compared against A. Since such a cash flow analysis is almost always done today by means of a computerized financial program, our cases are handled in the same way. Figures 4-27, 4-28, 4-29, 4-30, and 4-31 show the inputs and outputs. Next, simple graphs (Figures 4-32 and 4-33) illustrate the cash flow and profit and loss impact for any formal presentation or documented recommendation. The graphs clearly show that purchase looks favorable. To determine which purchase is best would depend upon the kinds of variables, discussed in this chapter, that influence management at the moment. This exercise is very much like a classic purchase versus lease analysis with the exception that more variables are handled along with an increased number of options.

## I/O ACQUISITION CONSIDERATIONS

Almost everything that has been said about computers in this chapter applies in the same way to peripheral and terminal equipment. There is still the concern for flexibility in acquisition and disposal, in resale prices, ITC, depreciation, cost, P & L impact, and maintenance expense. Although the tendency to treat much of this equipment as expensable items and not as capital acquisitions is still common, when one looks at all the I/O (peripheral) devices in a company as a whole, their value may far exceed that of a large CPU. Thus the need to plan for the acquisition and costing of I/O is just as important as for computers.

## Financial Considerations Checklist

Often the wrong questions are asked prior to making a commitment toward peripherals. Consider the following points in making any decision:

- The number of control units required, channels on the CPU, and how many of each.

XYZ COMPANY
CASE A
1981 THROUGH 1987

| Income Tax | | Insurance | L = Lease | Personal Property Tax | | | |
|---|---|---|---|---|---|---|---|
| Fed | State | (Pct/Yr) | R = Rent | Rate: .00 | Final Book Value: 45.00 | | |
| 48.00 | 7.00 | .02 | | Life: 7 Yrs | Method: Dbl. Dcl. Bal. | | |

| Ident | Shipd Mo/Yr | L=Lease R=Rent | Rent | Purchase Cost | Total Amnt Installed | Maint | Wrnty Mos | Pct Down | Intrst Rate | Term Mos | Tax Life | Deprec Method | Final TX NBV | Depr Adj |
|---|---|---|---|---|---|---|---|---|---|---|---|---|---|---|
| Computer | 6 81 | | 0 | 500000 | 500000 | 1000 | 12 | 25.00 | 9.00 | 72 | 7 | Dbl. Dcl. Bal | 45.00 | 0 |
| I/O | 6 81 | L | 6000 | 0 | 500000 | 0 | 3 | .00 | .00 | 72 | 7 | Dbl. Dcl. Bal | .00 | 0 |

Sales Tax Expensed — Purch 5.00  Lease 5.00  Maint 5.00

Other Charges:

| | | 81 | 82 | 83 | 84 | 85 | 86 | 87 |
|---|---|---|---|---|---|---|---|---|
| ITC | TC | -50000 | | | | | | |
| Sale of CPU | TX | 0 | | | | | -225000 | |
| Site Prep. | EO | 1000 | | | | | | |

| | Due Mo/Yr | Gross Resale | Resale Book Val | Tax Due On Sale | Principal Due | Net Resale | Inflo Mo/Yr |
|---|---|---|---|---|---|---|---|
| ITC | 0 | 0 | 0 | 0 | 0 | 0 | 0 |
| Sale of CPU | 0 | 0 | -225000 | 0 | 0 | 0 | 0 |
| Site Prep. | 0 | 0 | 0 | 0 | 0 | 0 | 0 |

| System | Sales Tax | Down Payment | Due Mo/Yr | Amount Financed | Monthly Payment | Due Mo/Yr | Term Mos |
|---|---|---|---|---|---|---|---|
| 1 | 25000 | 125000 | 7 81 | 400000 | 7210 | 7 81 | 87 |

**Figure 4-27**   Input data for estimated cash flow and expense analysis.

Estimated Cash Flow Analysis

| | | 81 | 82 | 83 | 84 | 85 | 86 |
|---|---|---|---|---|---|---|---|
| Cash Outflow Before Tax: | | | | | | | |
| Purchased Equipment | | | | | | | |
| Principal | | 25740 | 55074 | 60241 | 65892 | 72073 | 78833 |
| Interest | TX | 17522 | 31448 | 26282 | 20631 | 14450 | 7689 |
| Total Installment | | 43261 | 86523 | 86523 | 86523 | 86523 | 86523 |
| Down Payment(s) | | 125000 | 0 | 0 | 0 | 0 | 0 |
| Maintenance | TX | 0 | 6300 | 12600 | 12600 | 12600 | 12600 |
| Insurance | TX | 62 | 125 | 125 | 125 | 125 | 125 |
| Sale of CPU | TX | 0 | 0 | 0 | 0 | 0 | −225000 |
| Rented Equip | TX | 37800 | 75600 | 75600 | 75600 | 75600 | 75600 |
| Total Cash Outflow | | 206124 | 168548 | 174848 | 174848 | 174848 | −50152 |
| (Cumulative) | | | 374671 | 549519 | 724366 | 899214 | 849062 |
| Tax Calculation: | | | | | | | |
| Deductible Expenses | | | | | | | |
| Tax Depreciation | | 71429 | 122449 | 66071 | 15051 | 0 | 0 |
| Ded Exp (Sum TX) | | 55384 | 113473 | 114607 | 108956 | 102775 | −128986 |
| Sales Tax Purch | | 25000 | 0 | 0 | 0 | 0 | 0 |
| Site Prep. | EO | 1000 | 0 | 0 | 0 | 0 | 0 |
| Total Expenses | | 152813 | 235922 | 180678 | 124007 | 102775 | −128986 |
| X .5164 Tax Rate | | | | | | | |
| Tax Deduction | | 78912 | 121830 | 93302 | 64037 | 53073 | −66608 |
| ITC | TC | 50000 | 0 | 0 | 0 | 0 | 0 |
| Tax Effect | | 128912 | 121830 | 93302 | 64037 | 53073 | −66608 |
| Cash Outflow After Tax: | | | | | | | |
| Total Cash Outflow | | 206124 | 168548 | 174848 | 174848 | 174848 | −50152 |
| Less Tax Effect | | 128912 | 121830 | 93302 | 64037 | 53073 | −66608 |
| Cash Flo Aft Tax | | 77212 | 46718 | 81546 | 110811 | 121775 | 16456 |
| (Cumulative) | | | 123929 | 205475 | 316285 | 438060 | 454516 |
| Present Value at 9.00 Pct (6/1/81) | | | | | | | |
| Cash Flo Aft Tax | | 76295 | 42283 | 67814 | 84835 | 85660 | 10605 |
| (Cumulative) | | | 118578 | 186392 | 271227 | 356887 | 367492 |

Estimated Profit-and-Loss-Statement Impact
(Purchase Cost and Sales Tax Depreciated Over 7 Years to 45 Pct Using Dbl. Dcl. Bal Method)

| | | 81 | 82 | 83 | 84 | 85 | 86 |
|---|---|---|---|---|---|---|---|
| P + L Impact Before Tax: | | | | | | | |
| P + L Depreciation | | 75000 | 128571 | 69375 | 15804 | 0 | 0 |
| Ded Exp (Sum TX) | | 55384 | 113473 | 114607 | 108956 | 102775 | −128986 |
| Site Prep. | EO | 1000 | 0 | 0 | 0 | 0 | 0 |
| Tot P + L Expenses | | 131384 | 242045 | 183982 | 124760 | 102775 | −128986 |

**Figure 4-28**  Estimated annual cash flow and expense summary.

163

XYZ COMPANY
CASE B
1981 THROUGH 1987

| Income Tax Fed | State | Insurance (Pct/Yr) |
|---|---|---|
| 48.00 | 7.00 | .02 |

| | | | | | | Sales Tax Expensed | | | Personal Property Tax | | | | |
|---|---|---|---|---|---|---|---|---|---|---|---|---|---|
| | | | | | | Purch | Lease | Maint | Rate: .00 | Final Book Value: 45.00 | | | |
| | | | | | | 5.00 | 5.00 | 5.00 | Life: 7 Yrs | Method: Dbl. Dcl. Bal | | | |

| Ident | Shipd Mo/Yr | L = Lease R = Rent | Rent | Purchase Cost | Total Amnt Installed | Maint | Wrnty Mos | Pct Down | Intrst Rate | Term Mos | Tax Life | Deprec Method | Final TX NBV | Depr Adj |
|---|---|---|---|---|---|---|---|---|---|---|---|---|---|---|
| Computer | 6 81 | L | 10000 | 0 | 0 | 0 | 0 | .00 | .00 | 72 | 7 | Dbl. Dcl. Bal | .00 | 0 |
| I/O | 6 81 | L | 6000 | 0 | 0 | 0 | 0 | .00 | .00 | 72 | 0 | Dbl. Dcl. Bal | .00 | 0 |
| | | *81* | | *82* | *83* | *84* | *85* | | *86* | *87* | | | | |

| Other Charges: | | | | | | | | |
|---|---|---|---|---|---|---|---|---|
| Site Prep. | EO | 1000 | 0 | 0 | 0 | 0 | 0 | 0 |
| ITC | TC | −30000 | 0 | 0 | 0 | 0 | 0 | 0 |

**Figure 4-29**  Input data for estimated cash flow and expense analysis.

Estimated Cash Flow Analysis

| | 81 | 82 | 83 | 84 | 85 | 86 |
|---|---|---|---|---|---|---|
| Cash Outflow Before Tax: | | | | | | |
| No Purchased Equipment | | | | | | |
| Rented Equip.　TX | 100800 | 201600 | 201600 | 201600 | 201600 | 201600 |
| Total Cash Outflow | 100800 | 201600 | 201600 | 201600 | 201600 | 201600 |
| (Cumulative) | | 302400 | 504000 | 705600 | 907200 | 1108800 |
| Tax Calculation: | | | | | | |
| Deductible Expenses | | | | | | |
| Tax Depreciation | 0 | 0 | 0 | 0 | 0 | 0 |
| Ded Exp (Sum TX) | 100800 | 201600 | 201600 | 201600 | 201600 | 201600 |
| Site Prep.　　EO | 1000 | 0 | 0 | 0 | 0 | 0 |
| Total Expenses | 101800 | 201600 | 201600 | 201600 | 201600 | 201600 |
| X .5164 Tax Rate | | | | | | |
| Tax Deduction | 52570 | 104106 | 104106 | 104106 | 104106 | 104106 |
| ITC　　　　TC | 30000 | 0 | 0 | 0 | 0 | 0 |
| Tax Effect | 82570 | 104106 | 104106 | 104106 | 104106 | 104106 |
| Cash Outflow After Tax: | | | | | | |
| Total Cash Outflow | 100800 | 201600 | 201600 | 201600 | 201600 | 201600 |
| Less Tax Effect | 82570 | 104106 | 104106 | 104106 | 104106 | 104106 |
| Cash Flo Aft Tax | 18230 | 97494 | 97494 | 97494 | 97494 | 97494 |
| (Cumulative) | | 115724 | 213218 | 310712 | 408206 | 505700 |
| Present Value at 9.00 Pct (6/1/81) | | | | | | |
| Cash Flo Aft Tax | 17294 | 88831 | 81496 | 74767 | 68594 | 62930 |
| (Cumulative) | | 106125 | 187621 | 262388 | 330982 | 393912 |

Estimated Profit-and-Loss-Statement Impact

(Purchase Cost and Sales Tax Depreciated Over 7 Years to 45 Pct Using Dbl. Dcl. Bal Method)

| | | | | | | |
|---|---|---|---|---|---|---|
| P + L Impact Before Tax: | | | | | | |
| P + L Depreciation | 0 | 0 | 0 | 0 | 0 | 0 |
| Ded Exp (Sum TX) | 100800 | 201600 | 201600 | 201600 | 201600 | 201600 |
| Site Prep.　　EO | 1000 | 0 | 0 | 0 | 0 | 0 |
| Tot P + L Expenses | 101800 | 201600 | 201600 | 201600 | 201600 | 201600 |
| Tax Calculation: | | | | | | |
| Tot P + L Expenses | 101800 | 201600 | 201600 | 201600 | 201600 | 201600 |
| X .5164 Tax Rate | | | | | | |
| Tax Deduction | 52570 | 104106 | 104106 | 104106 | 104106 | 104106 |
| ITC　　　　TC | 30000 | 0 | 0 | 0 | 0 | 0 |
| Tax Effect | 82570 | 104106 | 104106 | 104106 | 104106 | 104106 |
| P + L Impact After Tax: | | | | | | |
| Tot P + L Expenses | 101800 | 201600 | 201600 | 201600 | 201600 | 201600 |
| Less Tax Effect | 82570 | 104106 | 104106 | 104106 | 104106 | 104106 |
| P + L Impact After Tax | 19230 | 97494 | 97494 | 97494 | 97494 | 97494 |
| (Cumulative) | | 116724 | 214218 | 311712 | 409206 | 506700 |

**Figure 4-30**　Estimated annual cash flow and expense summary.

165

XYZ COMPANY
1981 THROUGH 1987

Case A:  CPU Purchased I/O Leased

Case B:  CPU Leased I/O Leased

Present Value of Cumulative Estimated Cash Flows (at 9.0 Pct), as of 6/01/81

| Year-End: | 81 | 82 | 83 | 84 | 85 | 86 |
|---|---|---|---|---|---|---|
| Case | | | | | | |
| A | 76295 | 118578 | 186392 | 271227 | 356887 | 367492 |
| B | 17294 | 106125 | 187621 | 262388 | 330982 | 393912 |
| Difference: | | | | | | |
| A − B | 59001 | 12453 | −1229 | 8839 | 25905 | −26420 |
| Ratio: | | | | | | |
| A % B | 4.41 | 1.12 | .99 | 1.03 | 1.08 | .93 |

Estimated Cumulative Profit and Loss Impact

| Case | | | | | | |
|---|---|---|---|---|---|---|
| A | 13537 | 130590 | 219564 | 279898 | 329600 | 267222 |
| B | 19230 | 116724 | 214218 | 311712 | 409206 | 506700 |
| Difference | | | | | | |
| A − B | −5693 | 13866 | 5346 | −31814 | −79606 | −239478 |
| Ratio: | | | | | | |
| A % B | .70 | 1.12 | 1.02 | .90 | .81 | .53 |

**Figure 4-31**    Comparison of cases.

- Consider total subsystem costs and not just that of individual units.
- With DASD and tape, break down the cost to dollars per byte to arrive at the true expense of all charges for storage. The result is a thorough apples-to-apples comparison of devices.
- How much error information is provided by a control unit? Lack of adequate reporting will make maintenance and recovery of equipment and applications more costly.
- Quantify availability. How often does this particular device go down? What does downtime cost in lost production (for example lost sales due to the order entry system not working)?
- Understand precisely what the termination charges will be should you break the lease. This is a serious problem because peripheral

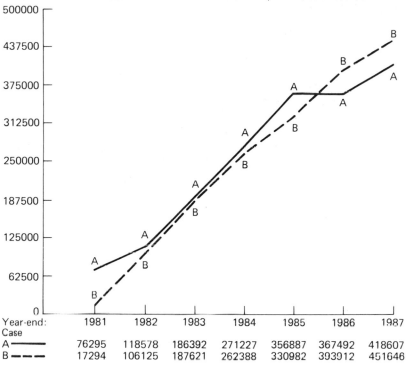

XYZ COMPANY
1981 THROUGH 1987

Case A:
Case B:
Present value of cumulative estimated cash flows (at 9.0 percent) as of 6/01/81:

| Year-end: | 1981 | 1982 | 1983 | 1984 | 1985 | 1986 | 1987 |
|---|---|---|---|---|---|---|---|
| Case | | | | | | | |
| A ——— | 76295 | 118578 | 186392 | 271227 | 356887 | 367492 | 418607 |
| B — — — | 17294 | 106125 | 187621 | 262388 | 330982 | 393912 | 451646 |

**Figure 4-32**   Comparison of cumulative cash flows.

equipment is changed more frequently than CPUs. Often charges are eliminated if you upgrade—but not always.

- Understand what your capacity requirements will be vs. length of contract. Do the same exercise as if it were a CPU.

- Consider making a grid of options over time with probabilities of each option happening to show what the relative costs of flexibility would be. Consider the technique used in Chapter 2 in assessing risk.

- Look at total I/O needs. For example with storage devices, consider total capacity and storage needs over a period of time and then decide how much should be on tape or DASD and when.

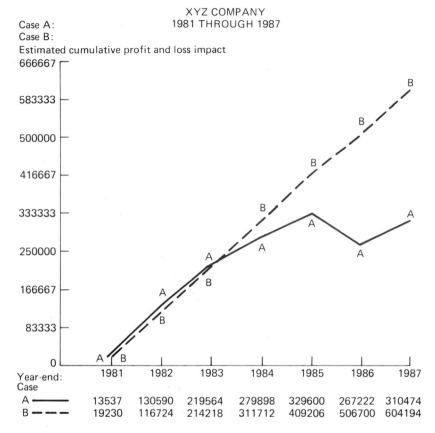

| Year-end: Case | 1981 | 1982 | 1983 | 1984 | 1985 | 1986 | 1987 |
|---|---|---|---|---|---|---|---|
| A ——— | 13537 | 130590 | 219564 | 279898 | 329600 | 267222 | 310474 |
| B – – – | 19230 | 116724 | 214218 | 311712 | 409206 | 506700 | 604194 |

**Figure 4-33**    Comparison of cumulative profit and loss impact.

## Strategic Considerations Checklist

Besides the functional and monetary considerations, there are some simple strategic concerns which must be kept in mind to keep costs under control.

- Look at all pieces of a proposed deal or contract.

     (1)    Availability: maintenance record, service level.

     (2)    Contractual obligations (for example, start dates of trial test periods, whose specifications and ground rules are used, vendor's or yours)?

     (3)    Price vs. cost. Price may simply be a rental fee while cost includes maintenance, depreciation, resale value, etc.

- Vendor support issues.

    (1) What kind of migration assistance will be rendered to move from one type of device to another? Quantify and document this support, otherwise the cost in manpower and lost usage of new devices can be expensive to you.

    (2) Understand your major vendor's storage products strategy so that your plans and supplier's direction will complement each other. That way the possibility of taking advantage of future improvements in cost/performance is there.

    (3) When checking out a vendor's references, do not consult with DP managers; discuss performance with operational managers directly responsible for the maintenance and use of peripherals.

- Remember that the highest price does not mean the highest cost.

    (1) Residual value is key in many lease and purchase contracts. Factors involved include:

        (a) Supply and demand by class of product on the open market (for example, newest technology is always in greatest demand and thus has tightest availability).

        (b) Maintenance costs and availability of warranties.

        (c) Price/performance ratio.

        (d) Technological changes—older equipment drops in price as newer devices are installed.

        (e) Vendor pricing practices: used equipment vs. new equipment prices.

        (f) Does a market exist for specific types of devices? (For

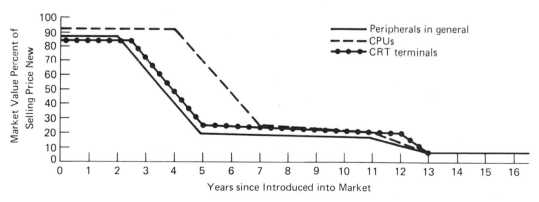

**Figure 4-34**    Used equipment value trends.

example, tape drives from the 1950s are hard to sell today.)

(2)   DASD prices have improved by a factor of six between 1970 and 1977. Thus long-term commitments today may not be wise if you expect further improvements in price/performance. Therefore weigh this possibility in your thinking.

## Case Approach to Analysis of Cost

Throughout this book we have suggested that defining several options and quantifying their costs and benefits lead to the most cost-effective decision. The same kind of analysis one performs on a computer decision should be done with peripherals. Figures 4–35 and 4–36 offer two sample forms that could be used to study rental, lease, and purchase of equipment. Again, remember that these aids are not necessarily the best for all companies, and it would be worthwhile to tailor one for yours. However, note the items listed in each document because they suggest the kind of data that one needs to gather. With such information a financial group can assess costs and investments in terms used to analyze expenditures in other departments.

Another common approach is to take a list of financial formulas provided by the accounting department and have DP management prepare the initial set of justification numbers for presentation to upper management. Figure 4–37 illustrates a twelve-step process for doing a simple financial analysis on hardware. Figure 4–38 reflects what the numbers look like for a number of terminals using the twelve-step procedure. With only slight variations, this offers a common-sense, short-hand approach to doing financial analysis which is already currently used in many companies.

## SOME CONCLUDING ADVICE

Decisions regarding hardware acquisitions are often far easier to make than those regarding software and applications. There are more tangible numbers involved and therefore management is usually quick to do more formal analysis regarding equipment than with any other aspect of data processing. Several points, however, are not always kept in mind when doing such analysis. First, the tendency to understate or underestimate capacity requirements in DP is a common pitfall, yet often management is hesitant to study options that provide adequate capacity. Shortsightedness of this sort can be expensive. One has only to define some cases to understand the risks.

| PURCHASE CHECKLIST | | | |
|---|---|---|---|
| (Annualized $) | Option 1 | Option 2 | Option 3 |
| 1. Purchase Price | ____ | ____ | ____ |
| 2. Purchase Accruals | ____ | ____ | ____ |
| 3. ITC | ____ | ____ | ____ |
| 4. Maintenance | | | |
|    1. Cost | ____ | ____ | ____ |
|    2. Vendor | ____ | ____ | ____ |
| 5. Property Tax | ____ | ____ | ____ |
| 6. Insurance | ____ | ____ | ____ |
| 7. Transportation | ____ | ____ | ____ |
| 8. Installation | ____ | ____ | ____ |
| 9. Power & A/C | ____ | ____ | ____ |
| 10. Cables, Supplies | ____ | ____ | ____ |
| 11. Upgrade Cost | | | |
|    1. For Features | ____ | ____ | ____ |
|    2. For Models | ____ | ____ | ____ |
| 12. Downgrade Cost | | | |
|    1. For Features | ____ | ____ | ____ |
|    2. For Models | ____ | ____ | ____ |
| 13. Termination Cost | ____ | ____ | ____ |
|   (rented features) | | | |
| 14. Software Support/Cost | | | |
|    1. Operating System | ____ | ____ | ____ |
|    2. Applications | ____ | ____ | ____ |
| 15. Systems Engineering | ____ | ____ | ____ |
| 16. Delivery Date | ____ | ____ | ____ |
| 17. Interim Costs | ____ | ____ | ____ |
| 18. Estimated Resale Value | ____ | ____ | ____ |
| 19. Other Expenses | | | |
|    1. | ____ | ____ | ____ |
|    2. | ____ | ____ | ____ |
|    3. | ____ | ____ | ____ |
| 20. Total Period Cost | ____ | ____ | ____ |

**Figure 4-35**

Second, the need for DP management to maintain greater flexibility in regard to peripheral and terminal equipment is more essential than with CPUs. Minis and micros would almost fall into the peripheral category simply because changes in this type of computer technology in cost/ performance are taking place faster now than in any other aspect of data

```
┌────────────────────────────────────────────────────────────────────┐
│                      RENT/LEASE CHECKLIST                            │
│                                                                      │
│   (Annualized $)                    Option     Option     Option     │
│                                       1          2          3        │
│                                                                      │
│    1. Price for Configuration                                        │
│       1. Model                      _____     _____     _____     │
│       2. Control Unit(s)            _____     _____     _____     │
│    2. Minimum/Maximum Lease         _____     _____     _____     │
│    3. Delivery Dates                _____     _____     _____     │
│    4. Interim Costs                 _____     _____     _____     │
│    5. Termination Charges                                            │
│       1. When (by yr)               _____     _____     _____     │
│       2. Costs                      _____     _____     _____     │
│       3. Special Provisions         _____     _____     _____     │
│    6. Upgrade Costs                                                  │
│       1. For Features               _____     _____     _____     │
│       2. For Models                 _____     _____     _____     │
│    7. Downgrade Costs                                                │
│       1. For Features               _____     _____     _____     │
│       2. For Models                 _____     _____     _____     │
│    8. ITC                                                            │
│       1. Amount                     _____     _____     _____     │
│       2. Which year earned          _____     _____     _____     │
│    9. State Property Tax            _____     _____     _____     │
│   10. Maintenance                                                    │
│       1. Your Cost                  _____     _____     _____     │
│       2. Vendor                     _____     _____     _____     │
│   11. Purchase Accruals                                              │
│       1. Term                       _____     _____     _____     │
│       2. Percent                    _____     _____     _____     │
│   12. Transportation Cost           _____     _____     _____     │
│   13. Installation Expense          _____     _____     _____     │
│   14. Power and A/C                 _____     _____     _____     │
│   15. Cables & Supplies             _____     _____     _____     │
│   16. Software Support                                               │
│       1. Operating System           _____     _____     _____     │
│       2. Application                _____     _____     _____     │
│       3. Product                    _____     _____     _____     │
│   17. Other Expenses                _____     _____     _____     │
│   18. Total Period Cost             _____     _____     _____     │
└────────────────────────────────────────────────────────────────────┘
```

**Figure 4-36**

172

## Formulas for Hardware Financial Analysis

1. Cost to lease equipment per year.

2. Depreciation — total cost (11) ÷ estimated life @ 1/2 year first year and full years thereafter.

3. Investment Tax Credit _____ % × Cost (11)

4. Income before taxes (1) − (2) − (3) = (4)

5. Tax @ Statutory Rate (4) × .50 = (5)

6. Net Income (4) − (5) = (6)

7. Add Depreciation (2)

8. Cash in (6) − (7) = (8)

9. Cash out. Cost of Maintenance

10. Cash Flow (8) − (9) = (10)

11. Original Cost of Investment

12. Balance (10) − (11) = (12)

**Figure 4-37**

| Year | 1 | 2 | 3 | 4 |
|---|---|---|---|---|
| Savings | 11,928 | 11,928 | 11,928 | 11,928 |
| Depreciation (4 yr.) | 1,813 | 3,626 | 3,626 | 3,626 |
| Investment Tax Credit | — | — | — | — |
| Income before Taxes | 10,115 | 8,302 | 8,302 | 8,302 |
| Tax @ 50% | 5,057 | 4,151 | 4,151 | 4,151 |
| Net Income | 5,058 | 4,151 | 4,151 | 4,151 |
| Depreciation | 1,813 | 3,626 | 3,626 | 3,626 |
| Cash In | 6,871 | 7,777 | 7,777 | 7,777 |
| Cash Out (maint.) | 1,398 | 1,398 | 1,398 | 1,398 |
| Cash Flow | 5,473 | 6,379 | 6,379 | 6,379 |
| Cost of Investment | 14,506 | — | — | — |
| Balance | (9,033) | 6,379 | 6,379 | 6,379 |

**Figure 4-38**   Case study of CRT financial analysis (see Figure 4-37).

processing hardware. With the introduction of more products using lasers, bubble memory, and higher-density chips, the need for a certain amount of flexibility will continue. Thus non-DP management must realize that data processing will continue to insist on short-term commitments on those pieces of hardware which are subject to the greatest change.

Third, terminals are acquired either by lease or purchase faster than any other element in the hardware inventory. They are everywhere, attached to all manner of minis, micros, main CPU, service bureaus, other intelligent or RJE terminals, to DP within the company and out-side. Vendors talk about annual growth rates in sales of 25% to 75% for the next ten years. DASD and other storage subsystems also repre-sent high activity and increased demand. Closely allied to this pattern is the very rapid rise in the demand for mini- and microcomputers which all experts anticipate will rise dramatically in volume and percentage of DP sales in the immediate future. Turnover of CPUs, however, is less than for any of the above-mentioned units. The devices which turnover the least are card I/O: punches and readers. As the amount of card pro-cessing declines, the demand for such units will continue dropping off sharply.

These trends in hardware acquisition and possession suggest that as a general rule longer-term commitments for CPUs will continue to be an attractive source of options, followed by storage and printing sub-systems. Intelligent and RJE and especially distributed processing devices are probably the least attractive prospects for long-term commitments simply because they are constantly changing—particularly the intelligent terminals where entirely new technologies are evident. On the other hand, CRTs have a greater appeal since new models have not been all that different from older devices. CRT printers have changed a great deal, so they do not lend themselves to long-term commitments, and for the same reason neither do control units for terminals.

## Presenting Options for Decisions

In defining options and costs, presenting the key elements for a decision in clear and sensible terms is absolutely essential. Clarity makes manage-ment acceptance easier and facilitates a proposal's incorporation into an overall master plan for data processing. Using the techniques employed in this book can help. Specifically, one should consider the following:

- Define numerous options in columns and rows for comparison to each other.
- Do risk analysis and lay out the results in box charts.
- Use graphs to lay out what the cash flow for a proposed expendi-

ture would be with time along the horizontal line and item expenses along the vertical line.

- Graph options, trends, costs and other key numeric data.
- State what assumptions were used in developing evaluations and identify them in some order of priority.
- Quantify all the expenses and benefits involved as reasonably as possible.

In short, "sell" the options and recommendations much in the same way that computer vendors try to market their products. Keep the issues as simple and nontechnical as possible and the recommendations precise.

How little do they see what
really is, who frame their hasty
judgment upon that which
seems.

*Southey*

*All the best-laid DP plans and tactics can be ruined if you do not have ways of reflecting them in the contracts you sign. The millions of dollars which are wasted each year in contracts that do little good is so common that it hardly needs repeating. This chapter will explain the types of contracts found in the DP industry, what they are designed to do, and how they affect your company. Next we will show how to negotiate these types of contracts and then how to keep track of them so that these documents serve you and not simply a vendor or broker. Finally, the role of contracts, negotiations, and terms are directly related to financial considerations. The objective is to show you how to make your contracts an extension of your DP strategy with you in control.*

# CHAPTER FIVE

# The DP
# Contract

Because of the large amounts of money involved in data processing, almost all business transactions require the execution of a contract. Typically, one thinks of leases for equipment, purchase of other hardware, rental of software (or its purchase), commitment for some software development, or even a contract for work from a service bureau. There is a large body of literature on the subject of DP contracts, leases, service agreements, and on the art of negotiating them. In this chapter the rudiments of contracts often encountered in the DP world will be briefly reviewed, some factors to consider presented, and a few recommendations made about negotiating them. The emphasis will continue—as in previous chapters—to rest on financial and managerial issues. This chapter is not meant to be a detailed discussion such as one might find in a law book.

The pattern of decisions by management to contract for data processing systems clearly should reflect the DP strategy in place and support it. Otherwise an error can be costly, even running into hundreds of thousands of dollars. The difficulties are great, however, because many sources of pressure come together when a manager is trying to decide what kind of contractual obligation to make. Data processing must foresee its capacity requirements over time, understand the capabilities of a particular machine, know the terms and conditions of existing obligations, and have confidence in current plans. Moreover, the monthly costs must be weighed against the need for some flexibility to change DP environments and to adjust for risks. The DP marketplace is also complex because of changing contract trends and prices of new and used hardware. A third source of uncertainty is the company's financial environment, where concern is expressed about ITC, depreciation, cost of capital, cash flow, income, budget issues, and always the allowable risk of any venture. Thus there are no easy guidelines that are applicable to all companies for every situation. Yet there are some general considerations to keep in mind.

## TYPES OF CONTRACTS

More leasing contracts are signed in DP than any other type. Leases for equipment and services, software and space, long-term and short, from vendors and third parties, and leasing companies and banks. Consequently, when talking about DP contracts, much of the discussion must involve leases. What in fact is a lease? How is it different from a sales contract? The two types of contracts are not always apparent to management not trained in the law. The U.S. Internal Revenue Service considers a contract to be a lease if the following conditions describe the agreement:

- The term is less than thirty years; otherwise it is a form of sale.
- The lessor must make a reasonable profit out of the arrangement (somewhere between 6% and 10% for example).
- There must be a genuine renewal option; that is, a lessee (you) has a real option to obtain another contract offer from a different company to provide an equivalent alternative.
- A repurchase option cannot be part of the contract. If it is then there must be a clause that says a lessee will be treated as an equal to any outside offer that matches his.

If the contract is a *true lease* then the company doing the leasing can depreciate the leased item (inventory). The user of the equipment, for example, paying a monthly lease charge can deduct that cost as an operating expense when calculating federal income taxes. Also remember that the IRS will allow the ITC to pass to either party but the contract has to specify who obtains it. Keep this second rule in mind because in negotiating a lease, you will want to try and have ITC pass through to your company thereby making the expense for equipment less in the first year.

If any of the above four conditions is not met then you have a *conditional sales* contract, sometimes also called a "buy-out lease." Basically this says that at the end of the contract period the leasing company no longer owns the item. In fact, the following conditions usually apply:

- You, as the lessee, own the leased items (hold title) from day one and treat it as your property for accounting purposes.
- You can depreciate the item and take the full ITC.
- The only part of the monthly payments which is tax deductible is the interest portion of your payments much like on a house mortgage.

Another way to look at the two general types of leases is to think of them as either being an *operating lease* or a *capital lease*—two terms most often used by DP vendors, data processing's management, and financial managers. If we look at leases from the point of view of accounting, then operating and capital leases take on new meanings. They no longer are just subject to tax considerations. The ground rules are established in the United States by the Financial Accounting Standards Board (FASB) which dictates how balance sheet, income statement, and P & L accounting shall be handled. In the fall of 1976, the FASB stated that data processing equipment under a capital lease would have to be shown on a balance sheet both as an asset and a debt rather than being hidden in other accounting reports. This is significant, particularly with an expensive computer, since the numbers involved might run well over a million dollars. By showing the amounts on a balance sheet, the debt-to-equity ratio (number of dollars available to pay for every dollar of debt) might be affected and thus could reduce the ability of a company to borrow more money or appear as financially strong as it might otherwise be. If the equipment, for example, is under an operating lease, then the cost is expensed and does not impact the debt-to-equity ratio. Management looking at a major acquisition will keep this factor in mind since their objective is to present the company as being able to meet its debts easily. And that means having a low debt-to-equity ratio.

The FASB recognized two types of leases: capital and operating. FASB said a lease is a capital one if it meets any of the following conditions:

- Transfers title of ownership to the lessee (you) by the end of the contract (such contracts are not cancellable).

- Provides the lessee the option to buy the leased item at a "bargain" (reasonably this might be expected to be 15% or less of the purchase price).

- Has a term equal to or greater than 75% of the economic life of the asset as estimated by the lessor (or manufacturer).

- Requires monthly payments equal to or greater than 90% of the fair market value less ITC kept by the lessor.

In other words, if your company has a capital lease on a computer, for instance, your accountant will treat it as if you had bought it. Consequently, it appears on the balance sheet as an asset (property you own) and as a liability (what is left to be paid on it).

An operating lease is simply a contract which does not meet any of the four conditions listed above. They are usually short-term (for example, two to four years) and thus only cover a small part of the useful economic life of an item. For example, a disk drive which the manufacturer feels will have a useful life for seven years is leased for two, which makes the contract an operating lease. Operating leases do not go on the balance sheet and thus are simply treated as an expense to be paid over the term of the lease. Put another way, the expense of an operating lease is buried among other expenses so that the total amount of expense which appears on a balance sheet is taken in the year in which it was incurred and does not become a debt to be carried forward into other years. Most manufacturers of data processing equipment and a number of software producers offer operating leases although all equipment manufacturers allow their customers to purchase their products.

The effects of both kinds of leases are rather interesting. The more expensive the item the greater the possibility that a capital lease will be used. In fact, by the criteria established by FASB, a large majority of DP hardware commitments will have to be capitalized. This forces management to consider carefully the options of leasing and purchasing. That which cannot appear on a balance sheet (for example in a company saddled with a great deal of debt already) must then be covered by an operating lease. Since operating leases carry with them higher monthly cost than capital leases, the effect on net income should be kept in mind. The temptation to buy outright more than in the past is clearly evident in the marketplace today. This also implies a greater risk since a long-term commitment is usually more necessary with any purchase and comes at a time when technological and price/performance changes are taking place faster than ever before.

## Standard Vendor Leases

The most common form of a lease is a standard "boiler-plate" contract from a vendor for hardware or software. Typically this is a preprinted form with the terms and conditions already included. It will state the length of time the contract will be in force, who maintains the product and services it, how the lease can be renewed, and makes an explicit detailed statement of penalties for early cancellation (or perhaps a less clear description of penalties). All leases will declare the name of the owner and define how much the monthly charges are and under what terms and conditions they may be raised or lowered by the vendor. Many vendors will not negotiate separate contracts although they may have a variety of leasing contracts to offer. All do not want to vary from their standard forms. However, each of these documents should be carefully studied so that all terms and conditions are understood. Remember that there are almost as many different kinds of leases and terms as there are vendors, since each one has some clause which makes that particular agreement different from others. If the boiler-plate document is to be used, then questions and problems can usually be resolved in discussions, but the agreements reached outside of the contract which influenced you to sign the preprinted form should be detailed in writing either as appendixes to the contract or on letterhead stationery. Many computers, most unpurchased hardware, and a large amount of software are usually covered by such printed leases. One should remember also that some vendors carrying printed contracts are willing to negotiate special ones, tailored to a particular deal. This is especially so with third-party leasing companies, banks, small manufacturers, and software service groups.

## Vendor versus Third-Party Leases

This subject represents a jungle of operating and capital leases, multiple parties, banks, complex financial and tax considerations, lengthy and complicated contracts and negotiations at various corporate levels. Simply put, a third-party lease is a contract which states that someone other than the manufacturer of an item will lease it to a user. The lease may be for a short or long period and can be an operating lease or a capital lease. The third party makes his profit by gambling that the useful economic life of the item in question is greater than either the manufacturer or user thinks. There are as many different types of contracts as there are individual needs, situations, and leasing groups. Typically, however, a third party will buy equipment from a manufacturer and then lease it to users at a monthly price lower than the original vendor's and usually for a longer period of time. The other approach is to buy either on-order equipment or that which is already installed and lease it back to the same user, again for a lower monthly rate.

In most of these financial arrangements, several conditions exist. First, sales tax is usually paid by the third party even though the user may buy, for example, installed equipment in his company and then resell it five minutes later to a leasing firm. Property taxes may be absorbed by the original manufacturer, the third-party lessor now holding title, or even by the user. Such a lease-back contract typically states who pays insurance, where the equipment is to be used, and which party absorbs its ultimate removal and marketing costs to the next user. These contracts are invariably iron-clad in that they are next to impossible to break except by outright purchase of the installed equipment at prices negotiated at the time of the actual sale. Some leasing companies, however, will be willing to terminate a contract if you are going to sign another, and—for them—more profitable lease from the same firm at the time the contract is cancelled. In addition, there may be some further liquidation costs involved in the earlier contract much like purchasing of installed in order to end an arrangement. Such purchases in a properly drafted contract represent a percentage of the original purchase price at a particular point in the life of the contract or are simply subject to negotiation later. Thus the terms usually have an element of risk for both parties involved.

Escape clauses can be important. For example, a computer is under contract for five years and the user wants out because he needs a larger one. The leasing company says the user is three years into the contract and the only way it will consider cancelling the agreement is by the user purchasing the machine. The contract might have a schedule saying that for every month into the contract the machine is worth ½% less than the original purchase price. Say that they are in the 36th month on the contract for a computer that originally cost one million dollars. The purchase price is 18% less than one million dollars or 80% of that which equals $800,000 at this point in time in the contract. But let us realistically assume that the particular type of computer in question is currently available from second-hand dealers for 50% of original price or $500,000 or that the manufacturer reduced his purchase price by 30% to $700,000 for a new one. The lease-back contract all of a sudden looks awful since to buy the machine the user would have to pay the difference between the market value and his accrual which in this case would run into hundreds of thousands of dollars. This contract just looks too expensive. Purchase clauses thus require considerable thought and negotiation to make the risk involved acceptable.

At the present time, several trends were observable in third-party leases. First, an increasing number of leasing companies were attempting to pass title of equipment on to users by acting more often than ever as brokers, putting together financial packages for a commission of about 3% to 5%. This was due in large part to their attempt not to be caught holding old inventory made less marketable or profitable by the rapid introduction of new cost-effective products by the major DP manufacturers. Second, contracts where leasing firms kept title were becoming more iron-clad and thus difficult to break. Third, there was more flexibility in length of contract available but a more rapid amortization of original costs was taking place thereby raising the cost of such leases. Thus the old rule continued to apply that the longer the lease the lower the monthly cost that would be charged. Fourth, maintenance costs were still the responsibility of the users. Quite often leasing companies holding title will insist that maintenance be done by the field engineers of the equipment's manufacturer because this makes future leasing or sale to another party easier. Fifth, warranties by manufacturers pass through the contracts to users in all cases.

A sixth trend involves the increased concern over obsolescence and being caught with dead inventory by leasing company executives. To minimize the economic impact of such possibilities, they are leaning more in the direction of writing tighter terms in their contracts which make termination clauses difficult to activate. Thus a large number of such third-party leases will not contain as many flexible clauses as those of manufacturers who would want their customers to move on to whatever new product lines they introduce. To illustrate, consider a contract on a piece of equipment for five years. In year three the user wants to add another feature or move to another piece of equipment. The contract from a third party may not be broken because of terms and conditions that leave the user the only option of acquiring the feature. But typically this feature's entire cost might have to be amortized over the remaining period of the contract, making it extremely expensive. Under a lease from a manufacturer for the same period of time, the addition of a new feature may only increase the rent by the same amount per month as if the feature had been put on in year one. In this second circumstance, the feature's cost be amortized only partially by the user, the rest would be absorbed by whomever leased the equipment after year five. Or the lease might have small enough termination charges where it might be cheaper to pay them and move on to newer technology.

A seventh emerging trend among third-party leases is the package lease which involves not only the original piece of equipment which generated the negotiations but other peripheral items as well. Thus a complex deal might emerge for a computer, peripherals of various types and brands all with the objective of reducing the monthly cash outflow while giving the leasing company more business. In short, third-party contracts are complex financial instruments requiring the careful attention not only of DP management, but of a company's legal and financial staff.

## Software Contracts

Contracts for software involve a number of variations. Some vendors will lease a particular piece of software for a specified period of time after which the user continues to use the product but pays no lease charge. Note however, that the manufacturer of the software does not give up titel to it, otherwise customers could make copies and market the product in competition with the real owner. Another common variation is a rental fee that continues until the product is no longer installed. This contract is open-ended with no specific termination date other than notifying the vendor a certain number of months in advance before removing the product from use. Usually a 30-to-90-day notice of termination must be given just as with rental equipment and typically no termination charges are involved. The last kind of software lease involves outright purchase of a package effective after a predefined test period for acceptance running anywhere from 30 to 180 days. The terms and conditions of each of these arrangements are similar to those for hardware since like equipment, they are products and assets belonging to someone. Software leases are in effect licenses to use another company's copyrighted property subject to the owner's terms and conditions.

Another form of software contract is the arrangement for someone to write programs tailored to your firm. This may involve a contract providing you with programmers and analysts for a period of time to do with as you please. There is the fixed price contract that says a particular job will be done for a specified amount of money by a certain date. A third variety involves preparing system designs and code at a cost plus a margin of profit and is open-ended until either the job is done or one party terminates the contract. Each of these three contracts obviously requires careful consideration. All relevant issues should be defined and put in writing. Many of the DP lawsuits today involve software contract services. Invariably what happens is that a poorly prepared set of criteria will become the basis of an ill-defined contract that does not spell out in explicit terms the costs, manpower required, and level of quality of the software to be produced.

The "warm body" type of contract is usually least expensive but requires supervision and project leadership on your part. If the quality of personnel and the leadership is poor the cost can be quite high since the project may take longer and may never be completed. The fixed price contract is beneficial in that you know exactly what it will cost to get a certain job or project done. However, you must define the work expected in great detail and remember that changes along the way may require additional cost or even renegotiation of the contract. Since the risk of not completing a job on time is greatest for the supplier of such services, his charges will be greater than in a "warm body" contract. The third version—cost plus profit as you go along—offers a degree of uncertainty since you the customer do not know exactly what the job will cost, but it does provide flexibility because you can change things along the way or even stop the additional manpower service. The supplier of this extra help carries little risk as long as the quality of his work is acceptable, and typically these arrangements have easy escape clauses for both parties.

The three types of contracts briefly described suggest that the kinds of controls outlined in Chapter 2 for project management are essential in this area as well. Written detailed specifications, target dates, progress reports, checkpoint meetings, etc., all must be part of the written arrangement along with a definition of what will be considered acceptable work. Issues to be discussed include data and coding security, copyright, and availability of software to other users. Any of these contracts can be a useful and cost-effective alternative to going out and hiring more technical personnel but the risks involved must be understood and contained as much as possible. Only then does a software writing contract become a cost-effective tool useful in your environment.

## FACTORS TO CONSIDER IN CONTRACT NEGOTIATIONS

There are obviously a large number of issues to weigh in negotiating contracts. They involve asking questions about how consistent are contract offerings with a company's policies and DP plans. There are factors regarding costs, termination charges, purchase, maintenance, insurance, and resale values to consider.

### Drafting a Contract

Vendors of data processing equipment and services negotiate contracts all the time and therefore are usually better negotiators than data processing management. So the first rule is, involve a company lawyer and a financial specialist in drafting a contract. DP management typically is inept in such negotiations. By involving a lawyer at least, DP management will be forced to specify in detail what they want as terms and conditions. The lawyer will help insure that the language is clear and understandable to all while the financial specialist will consider the economic consequences of various options. Perhaps technical specifications should be part of a contract as an exhibit or as letters of understanding between the two parties but get the terms and conditions in writing before an agreement is signed.

## Termination

Contracts are often terminated because of new conditions in a user's data processing environment. There is nothing wrong with this possibility nor with the termination charges that might result—this is simply an expense of doing business. However, both parties should define in writing what they will be and under what circumstances they will be paid, so that each side understands the risks involved. Always try to have the termination charges specified in amounts (dollars, percentages) and by dates (one year into the contract, two years, etc.). If this is not done, then the possible termination charges remain too risky, perhaps forcing a financial specialist to recommend that a month-to-month rental charge is more attractive or that other alternatives must be developed.

For the sake of argument, let us assume that a particular piece of equipment is to be leased for seven years and that the contract says that the longer the hardware is installed the lower the termination charge would be during the life of the contract. Let us also assume that DP management does not know if the equipment can be kept for seven years, perhaps only four, five, or six. An individual should be able to plot out the costs for each of those years, and then must determine what is the risk of having to terminate in any of those years. On that basis, a decision can be made. Figure 5–1 illustrates such a graph. In our case, termination charges are quite high for the first four years and thus management needs to be quite sure that it will keep the equipment for at least that amount of time. Otherwise, a shorter lease is more appropriate where the termination charges are proportionally less even though the monthly cost is greater.

Pay particular attention to residual value clauses in third-party leases. This is a unique feature of most financial contracts and says that you will pay the leasing company a certain percentage of the original purchase price at a certain time should you terminate the contract. Or, at the time the contract comes to an end, if the value of the machine on the open market is below a certain amount (usually expressed as a percent of original cost) then you pay the difference. Obviously, there is a risk and a lot of gambling going on, particularly if the contract is a long one. Such clauses must be carefully negotiated and understood. As a user you want as low a percentage residual value as possible. The other party wants it as high as he can talk you into. Typically the result of your negotiations will appear in the form of a table. A sample might look like this:

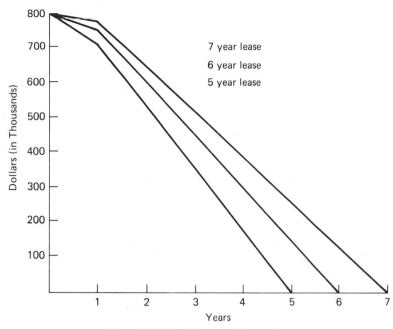

Note: This chart illustrates 3 leases from same
vendor, 3rd party. Could be done for multiple
vendors

**Figure 5-1**    Sample termination charges analysis.

| | |
|---|---|
| Month 22 | 75% |
| Month 23 | 74.5% |
| Month 24 | 74% |
| Month 25 | 73.5% |

The table would go on for as many months as the contract is in force.
Such tables are a result of historical data on resale values, what a leasing
party believes will be the future value of his property at certain given
points in time, and are an outgrowth of negotiations. Having such tables
quantifies in detail the possible cost to you should your anticipated length
of usage vary from original plans. The tables may involve a considerable
cost to you should you terminate at any point, particularly with large
CPUs which originally cost millions of dollars. If at all possible, avoid high
residual percentages, fight hard to keep them down even if it means higher
monthly charges or doing business with someone else. Remember that
right now the cost of computing is dropping very quickly, making the
possibility of high resale values unrealisitc when compared to what took
place in the 1960s and during the first half of the 1970s. Again it becomes
a question of what price for flexibility? Such residual values, it might be

noted, do not exist in software contracts although sometimes termination charges as a flat fee may.

## Disclaimers

Invariably the vendor, third party, bank or broker, will want to insert a clause into the contract disclaiming any liability for the functioning of the equipment or software beyond a certain point, and limiting liability in general or restricting it to a certain amount. Usually few parties have any problems with this clause since such language involves eliminating liability for incorrect use of the item in question or liability for warranties that are already granted by the manufacturer and which are not subject to negotiation anyway since they are already there. Closely related to such clauses might be protection of the confidentiality of software beyond the contract period for an additional time either for competitive reasons or to conform with copyright laws. The only two times the question of disclaimers must become the subject of consideration is when you are contracting for someone to write software or in using the services of a service bureau. More will be said about contracts in the next chapter on the service bureau. However, it only makes sense to realize that some contractual understanding about the quality and nature of the services to be rendered should be placed in writing and a statement as to what services will be paid for should the service bureau fail to deliver on its commitments.

## Insurance

Who will insure the items in question, you or the vendor? This is an important issue. Typically, the owner insures. Thus if you lease, insurance is carried by the vendor. But make sure you have provided the necessary fire prevention facilities, air conditioning and humidity, and physical housing; otherwise any damage to someone else's equipment becomes your expensive liability. And if you buy, the cost of insurance is always yours. Negligence is again yours. Other types of exposure exist as well in a leased environment. For example, if you have a leased computer and one of your operators gets mad and destroys the CPU console with a tape housing, the manufacturer (owner) of the computer will hold your company responsible. Automobiles cost less. Much of this kind of exposure is already controlled by state and local statutes and common civil law experience, but the issue is one that nonetheless must be resolved. When you consider that insurance can amount to ½% to 1% of the purchase price of a product, the sum can be considerable—enough so that it becomes part of any thorough financial analysis.

Remember that manufacturers will usually insure only for those things which happen as a direct result of their malfunctioning products.

For instance, if a computer card valued at $2000 burns out because the CPU's power unit went crazy, the vendor would probably replace it. However, if an electrical power surge in your building burned out the card, your contract might call for you to absorb the $2000 expense.

## Maintenance

Who will pay for maintenance, how much coverage is involved, and what will it cost? These three questions are never asked often enough. Invariably, a DP manager will receive a monthly lease charge quote only to find out later that it did not include maintenance costs which might be as high as an additional 15% over rent or lease. Thus the total monthly expense must include whatever maintenance fees there are so that alternative proposals can be fairly weighed. An illustration shows how it is done.

### Case A

A manufacturer of disk drives proposes a specific product under lease for two years at $1000/month which includes maintenance for parts and labor 24 hours a day.

### Case B

A third-party leasing company proposes the same equipment for $600/month for four years. Maintenance would be provided by the manufacturer at $100/month for similar coverage as in Case A for a total monthly cash outflow of $700 for Case B.

From the point of view of the budget, Case B looks terrific and is accurately portrayed since maintenance costs are included in the $700, all other factors being equal. But it does require a four year commitment. With maintenance being a labor-intensive activity, our DP manager in this instance can assume that his $100-a-month charge will annually rise at about the same level as inflation. Using an inflation rate of 7% per year, by the third year (if he still has the same equipment) his total monthly cost under Case B is $722 a month and still rising. Moreover, in Case A the lease price may have dropped (as is becoming more common today) to reflect new cost/performance ratios. New products and purchase accruals (probable in Case A) might suggest that Case A will become cheaper in year three. Thus along with other factors, maintenance should be explored in some detail. Taken as part of a total picture, it will play a role in the final decision.

## Purchase Options

Most leases will have a purchase option clause. Typically, if from a manufacturer, accruals are earned as a percent of monthly lease payments which can be applied up to a certain amount toward the purchase of a particular piece of equipment. Third-party leases can also have such clauses. They may be expressed either as a percent of the original price at a given point, or of a price which is to be negotiated at the time purchase is considered. The latter type of clause should be avoided if at all possible since it is unclear and even worse, uncertain enough for planning. The more common is the accrual clause from a manufacturer. Take our case of a $1000/month disk drive which brand new sells for $30,000. The manufacturer's contract states that half of the monthly lease charge ($500) will go toward purchase, up to 50% of the purchase price or in our case, $15,000. Dividing $500 into $15,000 (maximum allowable accrual amount) we find that in 30 months the drive will be fully accrued. If purchased at that point for $15,000 and kept for two more years and then sold for 30% (hypothetical market value for our case) of original purchase price the cash flow would look like this:

| | | | |
|---|---|---|---|
| Year 1: | $1,000 × 12 months | = | $12,000 |
| Year 2: | $1,000 × 12 months | = | 12,000 |
| Year 3: | $1,000 × 6 months | = | 6,000 |
| | Purchase amount | = | 15,000 |
| | Maintenance | | |
| | ($122 × 6 months) | = | 732 |
| | *Total Year 3* | = | *21,732* |
| Year 4: | Maintenance | = | 130 |
| **Grand Total Cost 4 Years** | | = | **45,862** |
| Year 5: | In January sold (30% | | |
| | of $30,000) | = | −9,000 |
| **Total Final Cost 4 Years** | | | **= $36,862** |

The total cost of the lease for two years then ownership for two years was $36,862 as opposed to leasing for four years from the manufacturer at $48,000. The accruals thus played a significant role in our case in providing genuine savings on the one hand and flexibility (to buy or not) on the other.

## Terms

Closely tied to the overall question of flexibility and the impact on cash flow analyses is the term of a contract. Leases for peripheral and terminal equipment usually run anywhere from one to four years, computers four to ten years, software from 30 days to open-ended until the customer terminates the use of the product. The longer the term the smaller the monthly charge. Therefore one has to consider the cost and advantages of various length contracts. If you feel that a newer, less expensive technology will be available in two years, then a four-year lease at less cost than currently paid might not be wise, unless the anticipated monthly charge for the forthcoming technology is not believed to be as great as the savings from a longer lease on currently available products. You should ask the vendor if, when his company announces lease price reductions during the life of your contract, will your company then pay the lower charge? The same must be asked about purchase prices and the effects they might have on accruals.

## Costs of Contract

The one question that always seems to be asked is how much will the equipment in question cost per month? What is the lease price? What is not often asked, however, is when the monthly lease must be paid, if there are late payment charges, when purchase of installed hardware becomes effective (not usually when a contract is signed or a check put into the mail but when payment is received by the vendor). Again there is the conflict between price and cost. Price is what the vendor quotes to you out of his sales manual or price sheet. Cost is the expense to you after tax, depreciation, resale, maintenance, etc., and price. Keep in mind that some lease prices do not include maintenance charges or local sales taxes in the dollars quoted to you.

## Transportation and Setup Charges

Some contracts call for the vendor to absorb the cost of transporting to a customer a product and the expense of making it operational. Others more often pass the transportation cost on to their customers. Setup costs are more commonly absorbed by the manufacturer, except for physical site preparation involving such things as building a computer room or adding more electricity. The amount of money that can be consumed in transportation and set up can run into thousands of dollars easily and thus such issues should be addressed in writing in your contracts.

Another consideration involves the movement of installed equipment. Usually the expense involved is not covered under a maintenance contract or a lease agreement and thus must be absorbed by the customer. If that is the case and you plan to rearrange a computer room, for example, or move equipment from one location to another, obtain in writing a price for the moving and setting up of the hardware. Usually an exchange of letters will suffice without the need for a contract.

## Features, Cables, and Testing

What happens if you want to add or delete a feature, upgrade a model or downgrade? Does the contract allow you to do these things and at what cost? Have them specified in writing. Thus your contract should say, for example, that feature deletions will not result in termination charges unless removed within "x" period of time of the end of the contract. Or, feature upgrades will be allowed and the additional lease charge shall be added onto current billing. Does such a change extend upward the life of the contract? This is an extremely important question. Adding a small feature, for instance, onto a computer costing tens of thousands of dollars a month which causes the entire contract to be extended out is not common today but the problem still exists. It is more typical when there is a *model* upgrade.

A number of smaller questions are closely related. Do cables come with the equipment or must you provide them? The cables, particularly for complex peripherals attached to a CPU (disk and tape drives, control units, and power), cost thousands of dollars. Therefore ask for some statement in writing. A good contract will usually specify that cables will be part of the vendor's responsibility.

Test allowances also cause confusion, expense, and irritation if not handled properly. A good contract will usually specify how much test time a customer will have before lease charges apply. This is particularly the case with software. What is not always clear is when the test allowance begins. Does it start when the product is installed by the vendor at your location? Or does it begin when you say it is in productive use? Some vendors take the position that test periods begin a certain number of days after leaving their production plant. The point to remember is that the differences between when you say a test allowance is in effect and when a vendor says it is may vary by several months. That can mean a great deal of rental money in dispute. Another potential bone of contention regards where the testing allowance is applicable. Some vendors will say you can pretest a product at their data processing site and not at yours. Also, if you do not use all of your test allowance (time) will the vendor give you a credit toward future rent? Answering these questions well in advance can reduce your financial exposure while eliminating possible disagreements with a supplier of DP products.

## Overtime Charges

Another source of hidden questions involves overtime costs. Some leases will provide that equipment can be used for a certain number of hours per month at a flat rate. Usage beyond that point will cost more on a surcharge basis and thus generate a larger, usually fluctuating, invoice amount each month. You should examine the machine usuage clause very carefully since overtime charges can easily exceed a flat monthly rate. Heavy overtime usage can even double a normal monthly rental charge. If you rent a machine as opposed to leasing it, you may find that overtime charges can be reduced by going to a lease contract, particularly if the lease contract has a flat charge regardless of how many hours you run.

Some companies are beginning to charge for the number of transactions used with their software products, almost like metering usage. If this is the case, then examine carefully what your monthly billing exposure could be and be prepared to pay it. Ideally, you will want either to buy the software or lease it at a flat rate per month since that way one can use it as much as possible without affecting the cash flow. Some software vendors will offer either plan. In this case, one elects a fixed price if utilization is expected to be high and accepts an overtime charge rate if usage is anticipated to be less than the minimum amount allowed for a fixed price.

## Viability of Your Vendor

Nothing can cause more trouble, worry, and work for your company lawyers than a contract with a defunct company. The problem is not with the IBMs, CDCs, or Honeywells as a rule but with small companies that perhaps sell one or a few products, hardware or software, or who specialize in some product line which might be outmoded by some new technology. In the past, a division of a major corporation not ordinarily specializing in data processing products could pose a similar problem. After small vendors, the irritations are with consortiums of individuals providing the financing for lease-back arrangements who may overextend themselves financially.

These problems will raise a great number of questions about product support, viability, and residual value of their products, and ability to honor contracts. Therefore, to avoid a lot of headaches, try to determine with some reasonable assurance that you are not going to sign a contract with a company, leasing firm, manufacturer, etc., who may go out of business or into receivership before the end of the life of the contract or product. If that should happen, maintenance service would stop, support for software also disappears until some other arrangements are made (usually unsatisfactory ones), and the hardware you own drops in value right through the floor. Third-party contracts are acquired by other organizations that might have policies different from those you are accustomed to as well. Also, in checking out whether you think the company will be around a few years, find out who holds title to leased products. In some cases the firm you lease from is not the owner; its creditors hold the title to do what is necessary should your leasing firm fail to meet its financial obligations to the bank, for example. Moreover, even if the company you lease from is in good condition, it may have the legal right to sell your lease to someone else. Make sure your company lawyer has checked this point out carefully while your financial department examines the business health of the company in question. Obviously you want a statement in the contract about what happens to the title and who holds it.

## Second-Party Support

With the amount of second-hand computer equipment available in the marketplace increasing over the years, several additional questions come up which must be answered during contractual negotiations. There are, for example, manufacturers of data processing equipment who will support and maintain hardware belonging to the first user of that product. But, such vendors may not support the equipment when it finally falls into the hands of a second owner who did not acquire it originally from the manufacturer. This is not a common problem but it exists, as of this writing, primarily with OEM memory sold by the first user to a second. The reason that the problem is not a major one is that most vendors recognize that the attractiveness of their product would decline if they did not support it. The concern remains, however, and thus is worth investigating before making any decisions.

A widespread and more serious problem is the extent and cost of supporting old software, particularly earlier releases of currently available packages. Old operating systems which have not been supported by a manufacturer (who may also be out of business) for computers that are ten years old or more is a clear case in point. In addition, existing support from software houses may not be as good as the manufacturer's, since new fixes may be slow in coming, and the monthly cost in maintenance may be higher than for newer releases. And in the case of certain products, no support from the manufacturer for old releases is any longer available. Finding support for such software in the marketplace may be difficult. The kinds of software that fall into this category are old teleprocessing monitors, the first data base packages, dated access methods, operating systems released over ten years ago, nonvirtual SCPs, and products of companies no longer marketing data processing goods and services. The latter is a serious problem because companies selling software come and go much in the same manner as hand-held calculator manufacturers did in the mid-1970s. Should support disappear and a company be faced with a conversion to a more widely used product, the expense might be greater than the risky item is worth. Therefore, keep in mind who you sign a contract with and be confident the other party will be around to support the product you installed.

# MANAGING DP CONTRACTS

Because the costs of a poorly negotiated contract can be high in dollars—not to mention the expense of system conversion, as well as disruption of DP plans and company policies—some general comments must be made about contract negotiations and key points restated. The first thing to do is to have the company lawyer review all contracts as a minimum step and at best, to have him involved in the negotiations. Second, a formal procedure for evaluating the costs of a particular option must be documented, involving financial specialists if necessary, and the options laid out on paper for management much in the same fashion as illustrated in the previous two chapters. If a DP steering committee exists, then the options should go to it for review and a final determination, along with a statement by the company lawyer defining the value of each option and contract. A lawyer's thoughts and involvement are simply essential.

Even in the case of standard preprinted contracts which data processing already understands and is constantly signing for various items, the procedure of involving a lawyer is still a sound one. Moreover, the number of individuals who can sign such a contract should be restricted to those who understand fully the DP department's policies and plans and of the company in general. Typically this might involve authorizing only a member of a DP steering committee to sign or a high-level DP manager, his boss, and perhaps an operations manager. Contracts submitted to remote data processing locations should always be reviewed by central site data processing management to insure that commonality of commitments exists and that no contract conflicts with preestablished policies and guidelines.

Typically in any company—big or small—DP contracts are scattered about in various departments and are the responsibility of numerous individuals. This is a poor situation that can only lead to multiple contracts being signed for the same equipment, to multiple licenses for software where one license could serve several sites, and to contracts becoming outdated because renewals were not signed on time. The cost can be prohibitively high. Thus an easy step toward controlling contracts is to have them all resident in one location. A lawyer's office or a DP manager's will do but the point is to have them in one place. Second, make one individual responsible for keeping track of what contracts have been signed, continue in force, are coming up for renewal, and are terminated.

To simplify the process of keeping track of what contracts exist, a control log might be appropriate and one should be designed for your particular company. It must be reviewed periodically by DP management and a company lawyer. This should take place at least once a quarter and more frequently if in fact the number of contracts is large. This will result in several benefits to the company:

- Gives times to renegotiate contracts perhaps on more favorable terms without the press of time to worry about.
- Avoids contracts becoming outdated and rental prices automatically taking over from the usual lower leasing prices.
- Prevents leases from being automatically renewed without the foreknowledge of DP management which may have wanted to follow a different path.
- Allows management to assess plans carefully and insure that future contractual obligations support them.

One possible format for such a log is illustrated by Figure 5-2. Note that the format is not as important as the various pieces of information it includes. The key facts are there and can be explored in more detail by studying the contracts themselves.

## FINANCIAL BUYING

Controlling the costs of data processing and translating options and expenses into terms which are uniform throughout the company involves buying and using services and products in an organized and rational fashion. It also involves defining options clearly and in financial terms whether it be for preprinted forms or a computer. To reiterate some of the points made throughout this chapter we list the following areas of concern when negotiating options, financial deals, and contracts. Relate each to the company's data processing and business environment.

*Checklist of Contractual Issues*

(1) Payment timing and level
(2) Term or length of contract
(3) Interest rates
(4) Termination provisions
(5) Flexibility issues
(6) Maintenance coverage (who and how much: parts and labor?)
(7) Taxes and insurance (who pays? how much?)
(8) Sales and lease provisions
(9) Residual values quantified, documented, guaranteed
(10) Purchase options defined
(11) Is the company going to be around as long as this contract? Is it financially sound? Can it honor its commitment to me?

| Contract Number | Vendor | Termina- tion Date | Automatic Renewal Yes | No | Monthly Cost | Device | Service | Mainte- nance | Reviewed | Comments |
|---|---|---|---|---|---|---|---|---|---|---|
| 23 | XYZ | 10-30-81 | X | | 1,000 | Disk | | | 8/81 | Fully accrued purchase? |
| 24 | XYZ | 11-15-81 | X | | 800 | Disk | | X | 8/81 | Tie to No. 23 by 12-15-81 |
| 20 | OEM | 9-30-82 | | X | 8,000 | Memor. | | X | | CPU #197568 |
| 21 | PC Co. | 6-20-81 | | X | 25K | CPU | | | | CPU #197568, Memory date 82 |
| 9 | Code Inc. | Open | | | 500 | TP SCP | X | | | Review 4th Qtr, 1980 |

**Figure 5-2**   Sample DP contract log.

199

(12)    Transportation charges (who pays? how much?)

(13)    Feature/model upgrades, downgrades (cost?)

(14)    Test time (how much? any rebates?)

(15)    Cables

(16)    Lease extensions (lower rates? current rates?)

(17)    Cost of overtime

(18)    Software support (how much and what kind?)

(19)    Have I discussed financial and accounting implications with the finance department? Are their recommendations and guidelines being considered? How?

(20)    How does this contract support my DP department's goals?

(21)    Does this contract support the company's objectives for the period during which the document will be in force?

(22)    Are there any problems associated with a multivendor environment? Is it worth the trouble/benefit?

(23)    Warranties (extent and length of time in effect)

## Special Financial Considerations

One begins by accepting nothing as fact until checked out. What one vendor says about the numbers presented by another must be verified. Recommended resale values and cost of capital should also be validated independently to assure the accuracy of financial analysis. Consider the impct of the following listed items on any proposal, particularly a complex one involving various groups and/or multiple factors:

(1)    Impact on accounting and tax books

(2)    Method of depreciation used

(3)    Capitalization (percentage, sales tax, other costs)

(4)    Eligibility for ITC

(5)    Impact on cash flow, budget, profit and loss

(6)    Formal analysis of before-and after-tax cash flow

(7)    Return and payback factors:

- ROI
- NPV
- IRR
- Budget
- Other hurdle measurements

(8)  Method of acquisition: purchase, lease, rental

(9)  Interest and term for financing

(10)  Conversion cost: expensed? How much?

(11)  Installation expense: how much and when?

(12)  Resale value (market) for purchased hardware now and for next several years

Each of these factors will help you shop wisely by making your personnel take into account various alternative technical solutions, using benchmarks, establishing useful lives for various products, resale values, real capacity requirements, and availability needs. The issues involved are numerous and often time-consuming not to say complex. Perhaps all of these issues are only worth examining in detail for major decisions and a lesser number for lower-priced evaluations. But these are variables to consider, paraemeters for a decision. It is with such questions being asked that the numbers presented by multiple vendors and interest groups within a company can be properly evaluated. Thus it becomes possible to deal with the all-important yet difficult question of how to preserve the greatest amount of flexibility at the lowest possible cost in a new environment? Politics, immediate needs, the responsibility of getting daily work done, and a vendor's product line provide only limited answers.

**Know well the condition of your flocks, and give attention to your herds.**

*Proverbs 27:23*

*Without a doubt, as you read this introduction there is some department in your company that is using the services of a service bureau. More likely as well, few if any personnel in your organization know how much money is being spent on this service or whether it is cost-effective. This chapter explains what a service bureau is, its costs, benefits to you, and the risks involved. How to select a service bureau is defined next. Closely related to the question of outside help in DP is that of the facilities management firm. This option is defined and you are shown how to determine if it is a good choice for your company. Finally the alternative of buying time and services from another data processing department is discussed with the benefits and costs to you and a discussion of how to go about it. In short, this chapter will make it possible for management to analyze the question, "Should all our DP work be done by us?"*

# CHAPTER SIX

# Service Bureaus
# and Facilities Management

Probably every company with sales of over one hundred thousand dollars annually uses a service bureau in one way or another. Larger companies use them even more so, frequently dealing with multiple service bureaus providing data processing support for various specialized administrative activities. In the U.S. economy alone, millions of dollars are spent each year on service bureaus and facilities management companies. And undoubtedly, your organization uses such services. Yet, service bureaus are not well understood, particularly since they tend to have a low profile within a company's organization and their expense is listed under a variety of headings in everyone's budget.

Briefly defined, a service bureau is a company that provides data

205

processing for other companies. This can take various forms from preparing simple payroll checks to offering access to large computers through
terminals located in your company for multiple applications. Facilities management companies are organizations that will run your data
processing department with their personnel on a contract basis. Again,
as with service bureaus, there is an infinite variety of arrangements,
costs, and applications involved. Both groups provide either partial or
total alternatives to doing all data processing within your company.

## WHAT A SERVICE BUREAU DOES

Once a company first determines that it needs data processing services,
typically in accounting, a choice arises: to do it inhouse or to go to a
service bureau. A very small company with no data processing staff or
computers might well want to avoid the expense of creating a DP department and will simply go to a service bureau to process payroll, accounts
payable, accounts receivable, general ledger, and financial reports. Data
for these applications might be keyed onto cards or through a terminal
either at the service bureau or within the company itself. As the organization grows in size, it becomes more practical and less expensive to do your
own accounting applications inhouse with a DP staff and computer.
Then only specialized applications which are done occasionally or that
require large amounts of computer time and power are done at a service
bureau. And as the volume of transactions increases then the option of
bringing this work inhouse becomes more attractive.

With the cost of computing declining, more and more companies are
doing their own data processing inhouse so it is more typical to think
of the work that service bureaus do as that which cannot be done normally with existing internal facilities. Some examples will illustrate the
point. A data processing department may provide all the accounting
applications that a company wants. Yet engineering may have a need for
running some large simulation package once a month that requires the
availability of a computer twice the size of the one in the company.
The engineers might lease a terminal linked to a service bureau and rent
time and the necessary software to run the application. Another common
example can usually be found in the finance department where a need
usually exists to run a financial analysis package occasionally to evaluate
capital acquisitions, model next year's budget, or support other financial
decisions. Again the concern is for a great deal of machine power with
expensive or sophisticated software on occasion. A third illustration
might be the requirement to keypunch thousands of computer cards after
a physical inventory has been taken so that the computerized inventory
file can be brought up to date. Rather than hire extra keypunch operators

and lease keypunch machines, the work would in this case be better farmed out to a service bureau.

There are a number of situations where a service bureau becomes an attractive option to a company instead of using an inhouse DP department.

### Checklist of Reasons for Using a Service Bureau

(1) A need exists to have a large piece of work done quickly which does not justify hiring additional staff and leasing or buying more equipment (for example, to put the results of an annual physical inventory count into machine-readable form).

(2) An application requires large amounts of computer power but is only run occasionally (for example, doing a financial analysis of the budget once a month for about one hour).

(3) An application has to be run only occasionally, but would cost a fortune to design and write in house, when a service bureau could lease a similar code as needed (for example, modeling packages for engineering).

(4) There is no need to use a special application or data available only through a service bureau (for example, a company lawyer wanting to use a computerized data base library of legal cases).

(5) A company that wants an application right now which it cannot wait months or years to develop internally might go to a service bureau which has it or a similar one already (for example, a complex purchasing system needed for a manufacturing plant experiencing dramatic jumps in product demand).

(6) In some cases management feels that the technical expertise of the inhouse DP staff is inadequate for providing certain services or would cost too much to develop when such knowledge can be obtained from a service bureau (for example, a highly specialized interactive scientific package to study weather patterns for aerodynamical engineers).

Thus a number of situations will make the option of a service bureau worth exploring. The variety of services is extensive as well. They fall into several categories. First, service bureaus provide a large number of standard accounting services. Typically the bureau will maintain the programs, modify their applications to reflect changes in local and federal tax laws, and store data. Second, they offer a variety of modeling and simulation packages and services for engineering, mathematics, and finance. Such services are broadening out to include the establishment of data banks on stocks, law cases, current events, scientific and medical data, and economics. These become very attractive because in effect the cost of developing and maintaining such applications is shared by a number of companies.

The ways these applications are used also vary widely. One can take data in English or in machine-readable form down to a service bureau for processing. Such data can be transmitted via terminals from your company. Access to computer power can be by appointment much like you would run a batch job inhouse or simply in real-time by dialing a telephone or signing onto a terminal. Typically the service bureau will establish conventions and procedures for using their services. These rules include the format data that must be submitted to them, times when services will be provided, and formats in which reports can appear. Service bureaus will have established policies regarding who owns the data and the programs you use and will specify their availability.

## COSTS, BENEFITS, AND RISKS OF SERVICE BUREAUS

### Costs

Service bureaus establish pricing policies which measure the amount of computer time you use, the application involved, and the number of reports generated. The cost of supplies consumed is factored into the charges submitted to you as well. Some will also charge for labor, and for terminals which are used in your buildings. Formulas are always used to measure the volume of transactions coming from your company into the system and monthly billing for those services is then generated.

Typically two types of billing arrangements will be negotiated. First, there may be a flat rate for providing a specific service. For example, a service bureau might agree to charge one price for the use (or nonuse) of its accounts receivable application no matter how much it is used. Such an arrangement will specify for how long a contract would be in effect. If you think that there may be heavy usage of an application, try and negotiate a flat monthly fee so that you can control your cash flow and avoid surprises. In the second billing arrangement a service bureau may charge a certain fee by the hour for an application and a specified amount per page for a particular report generated or a fee for every check written (in payroll for instance). If you think utilization will be low, negotiate a contract that says you pay only for what you use.

Charges for specific items vary considerably. Some service bureaus charge you for the paper and forms you need while others want you to bring in your own. Terminals may be provided by the service bureau which then charges you for these or the responsibility for having such a device may be yours. The same may apply to telephone lines and modem costs. Try to negotiate an arrangement whereby you are responsible for renting terminals and modems; you could save a lot of money that way (see Chapter 4 for details). Some service bureaus will charge you for delivering and mailing data and reports while others factor that cost into the applications you use. Contracts can be open-ended with no time limits while others are more restrictive. Typically those with time limits will have specific charges spelled out and that is a feature you want to have so as to control costs. Open-ended contracts with no time limits simply will state how much advance warning you will be given before price increases take effect.

Everything with a service bureau depends on the application involved, the amount of its use, and how it is to be utilized. Therefore, when negotiating with service bureaus remember that various arrangements can be negotiated to your mutual advantage.

## Benefits

Typical benefits one can expect from using a service bureau include the following:

- Cost avoidance by not absorbing the entire expense of developing an application that is insufficiently used to justify inhouse development. This usually applies to small companies that cannot afford to buy a large package or write its own.

- The responsibility for maintaining a system and its applications code is put directly on the shoulders of the service bureau, thus reducing your overhead. For you that means some applications would be less expensive if obtained through a service bureau.

- Closely related, a service bureau will have expensive technical staffs knowledgeable in complex systems and software that you cannot afford to have on your payroll.

- Management of applications is left in the hands of managers who have considerable knowledge of data processing and probably in the application area of interest to you. Therefore, you are taking advantage of experience.

## Risks

A number of risks which are serious at times exist when using service bureaus.

- You are dependent on another company for data processing services. What is the impact to you if they should go out of business? What happens if the costs rise to levels which you consider unreasonable?

- You lose a certain amount of control over the application. It would be rare indeed to find a service bureau that had an application that was designed to be exactly right for your company. So there are some little and large compromises that you will have to make.

- You lose a certain amount of control over when you can execute your applications. Batch jobs may be run at night only, which might delay turn-around time. Weigh the issue of timeliness carefully—it is important.

- Data security becomes a serious problem. What guarantees do you have that a competitor to your company will not have access to data vital to the welfare of your organization?

- With integrated data base environments becoming more common today, having information resident outside of your company makes it difficult if not impossible to integrate all files. Thus you lose some of the advantages of data base files by increasing the possibility of data redundancy, data in different formats than what you have or need, and multiplying the cost of storage devices, tapes and disks.

- You run the very common risk of using a service bureau's service long after you no longer can cost-justify it. What if you have a large DP staff and lots of computer now? It probably would be less expensive to bring the work being done outside back into your system. Your risk lies in the fact that many companies do not systematically review their outside service work regularly to determine whether the work should come inhouse. Thus little pockets of expensive work that should be performed internally continue costing money. It is just that some people find it easier not to make changes, and that can cost a great deal.

## Cost Justification and Control Factors

An application must first be justified in the manner described in Chapter 3. Assuming an application to be justified for data processing, then the cost of doing the work within the company or at a service bureau can be weighed. Typically the infrequently used application is one you might send to a service bureau, particularly if it is a complex and unusual one that gobbles up people and machine resources. However, remember that, as the use of a service increases, the justification for bringing it back inhouse does too and therefore has to be studied. Moreover, the original set of charges by a service bureau will go up over time, raising the question: Has the cost risen enough to cancel the justification for that service? Again the related question is, "Should I do the application inhouse?"

It becomes important to understand what the cost of an application is to a company when done inhouse or externally so that periodically these services can be reexamined. Usually this is not done. Once a service begins it continues for years until the costs have become outrageously high, often because of the increased use of an application over what was originally intended. Further, many data processing services are being used by a company without the knowledge of the DP department. Cost justification thus should be an ongoing activity which takes into account all DP services within and outside of your company as a whole.

And remember that costs from a service bureau invoice do not represent all your expenses. Other factors to weigh besides the actual charges by a service bureau include such expenses as the cost of transmitting data and getting it back, the cost of preprinted forms (can you do it cheaper?), and the cost of availability of data on a timely basis. Would speeding up transactions from a service bureau batch environment to an online inhouse system save money, increase sales, or reduce data errors? Be sure to put a value on these points. In other words, remember as with anything in business, account for all the costs and not just what appears on an invoice or neatly on some line item in a department's budget.

Justification at the beginning is also very much an exercise in common sense. For example, take the case of payroll checks. Some companies will run a payroll application internally and generate all the appropriate reports but may have a service bureau actually print the checks so that no one within the DP department will know how much any individual executive was being paid, or for that matter, anyone else. Suppose that producing checks in this manner cost $2.00 each at the service bureau whereas the cost of doing it inhouse is $2.10 each. One thousand checks are run every week and the cost of check forms is higher for you than for a service bureau, which can order various check forms in greater volumes and thus enjoy quantity discounts. Time passes and inflation forces the service bureau to raise the cost per check to you from $2.00 to $2.50 and the number of checks run grows meantime from 1000 per week to 2000. Now the costs have gone up substantially. Would it cost you less to have check forms printed since they are needed in higher volumes for which a printer might offer a quantity discount? Part of the 50¢ increase in checks might be attributable to inefficient management of human resources at the service bureau, which your data processing shop might be able to beat (possibly with slave wages too!). Or perhaps you have a faster printer on your computer so that now you can print the checks on a timely basis convenient to you and not to a service bureau's schedule.

The example is a simple one but it suggests a line of action. As data processing departments within companies become larger and better staffed and equipped, the trend toward bringing back inhouse the work being done in a service bureau is increasing. Besides having data processing staffs, another reason for this trend is that many companies are consolidating all their service bureau work internally—with very substantial savings. The pattern is very common. Over the years various departments within a company will have farmed out work to service bureaus either because the DP department could not provide them or they were not cost-justifiable internally. A smart data processing executive eventually hits on the idea of surveying exactly who is using what service bureaus, how often, and for how much throughout the company. Shocked at the usually large sums of money being spent he examines the work load and what it would cost to bring some or all of this processing inhouse. Invariably, in companies over $100 million in sales the benefits of such an exercise are significant. Usually the optimal solution would be to provide time-sharing facilities internally on single or multiple computers using a common set of simulation and system software, thus driving down the cost per transaction. Vendors trying to sell additional computer power will often go after service bureau work within a company, knowing perfectly well that their customers could easily and quickly justify doing some of this work themselves and thus would likely buy more computing power.

Thus a major step in controlling the rise in cost of service bureau work is to recognize that there are pockets of services being offered all over your company. Define what they are and ask the following questions of them:

*Checklist on Service Bureau Work*

(1)   What applications are being used with a service bureau?

(2)   How often are these applications run?

(3)   How much data is required to execute them?

(4)   What computer languages are used?

(5)   Are they done in batch or real-time execution?

(6)   What does it cost per transaction?

(7)   Are there any minimum monthly charges whether the application is used or not? If so are there months in which the fee is paid but the application not used or hardly used?

(8)   Could the application code be bought and run more cheaply on our own computer?

(9)   Can the availability of an application on our own computers be improved over the availability a user is getting from a service bureau?

(10)  Are there any security exposures to the company in having data resident elsewhere?

(11)   Should we be using a different service bureau for the same work?

Engineering provides a simple example of the exercise. Industrial engineers in one department might be using Fortran to do their mathematics in developing bills for material. In another department engineers might also be using Fortran and GPSS (a widely used general-purpose modeling package) to design a new product. The development engineers in yet another department might be using GPSS and Fortran to test products for quality control. It would not be unreasonable to assume that each of these three groups was using separate service bureaus with charges being leveled against three budgets in differing amounts. The data processing director might have Fortran already in his DP shop for his programmers and this manager may have a partition in the computer set aside for interactive modeling and testing. A consolidation of the three engineering activities into this already existing partition, which is not being fully utilized but is being paid for anyway, might result in substantial savings to the company in monthly fees to service bureaus. The acquisition of GPSS might also be justified and paid for within a reasonable period of time. Thus the only expense that remains from before might be for terminals and even here the DP director might save money since one or more of the service bureaus could possibly have added a surcharge for placing a terminal in one of your engineering departments in the first place. And now the cost of that software and terminals might be capitalized rather than expensed for tax purposes.

The net result of consolidation would be to force down the cost of data processing in general throughout the company while increasing management's control over such processing. In our simple example, availability of programming and test time for the engineers probably would have increased since there no longer would be any concern on their part about keeping computation down to a minimum in order to keep service bureau bills low.

If there are hundreds of users of time-sharing facilities from service bureaus in your company, then going after consolidation within your data centers can generate real savings. There are several good reasons for this. First, there is a cost associated with each transaction that the service bureau experiences, for example, in leasing or buying computers from manufacturers of such equipment. The service bureau then adds its profit on top of this. If you have enough users you can go to the same computer vendor and buy or lease the same machine and eliminate the service bureau's profit, thus forcing down the cost per transaction. Second, the same reasoning applies for software and personnel expenses. Third, by bringing them inhouse, expense items might well be converted into capitalized items on the balance sheet depending on what is most advantageous to your company at the moment. As a general comment, it is obvious that if the amount of work being done through a service bureau is low then the cost justification might not be there to warrant bringing the work inhouse. This is especially the case when it involves a complex application since one of the benefits of an outside computer service is that the fixed overhead for an unusual set of programs is spread among many users.

It is difficult to specify what the break-even point is since expenses, applications, and volumes vary widely among service bureaus. Computer costs and user companies also vary. Therefore, you need to define your company's own unique environment and its associated costs and options much as you would an application and be prepared to change your source of computing if the results indicate that you should.

Doing the necessary homework is not always a complex or time-consuming activity. The hardest step in gaining control over service bureau work is in first identifying how much your company uses and who the users are. Second, you must establish their costs and monitor these expenses over time. Costs may be hidden in budgets more because of how they are listed than through any devious attempt to hide numbers from DP managers. Often the terminals might be innocently listed as lab or test "equipment" and computing costs as "services" or "miscellaneous" expenses. Try to have them listed as service bureau expenses. Then ideally these should be reviewed collectively for the whole company in some formal fashion at least a couple of times each year. If the expense grows substantially then a study must be made as to whether or not to bring the work inhouse. Moreover, as the cost of computing declines and the availability of mini-computers and innumerable software packages increases, the need for some formal analysis of service bureau work becomes essential to good management of the DP cost.

## SELECTING A SERVICE BUREAU

Since it will always appear that some work through a service bureau might be justified, some ground rules should be established for selecting a firm to provide these services. Invariably, each department will do its own thing, make its own selection, contract for services independently of other departments, and often leave DP management out of the whole picture. Often users will make it a special point to leave data processing managers out of the decision-making precisely because they think DP would view a service bureau as a threat to them in their control over computing in the company or because DP cannot provide adequate services to a particular group of users. For whatever reason service bureaus become a preferred option, however, management as a whole should attempt to establish some procedures and guidelines for selecting such services. Next, have the user's selection approved by data processing managers (or at least reviewed by them for technical comments) or approved by some other designated central authority so that the company's overall best interests will be protected. Once a decision has been made to find a service bureau, certain steps should next be taken for the general welfare of the company.

1.    Define the application that is to be written or executed by a service bureau in specific terms. Try to avoid misunderstandings about the nature of the services to be provided and how often. This is especially important when some programming is to be done by the service bureau in meeting unique requirements of yours.

2.    Next determine how fast the turnaround time must be for a particular application. Does it have to be real-time via a terminal or can it be done overnight? The answer to such a question may carry with it various price tags.

3.    Negotiate with three to five service bureaus for the same work obtaining written proposals. The names of service bureaus can be obtained from DP departments, the yellow pages of the telephone book, or through advertisements in such technical publications as *Computer World*.

4.    Visit the service bureau that you are serious about using, to see whether they have the equipment you will be relying on. This will give you a feeling for the efficiency and organization of the data processing shop and the manner in which they deal with a client's applications and data.

5.    Research the financial condition of the service bureau. Someone in the financial department should be involved in obtaining a Dunn and Bradstreet report as a minimum. A financially weak service bureau could go out of business, thus interrupting service to your users. You might also find out how long the outfit has been in business as an indication of their financial health as a data processing company.

6.    Identify clearly the reliability of the services being provided. How long is turnaround time on applications? Do they deliver reports and how often? Do they pick up data and how often? What hardware are they using and do they have backup procedures and facilities? Can they do the work you want in a time acceptable to you? Are they near by? In large part these questions can be answered by simply asking the service bureau and in part by questioning references.

7.    Quality of the work being done is essential. Who pays for errors in data handling and in faulty reports? What procedures are in place to insure high quality without additional expense to you? You do not want

to do business with an organization with whom you will be fighting constantly because the amount of work being done will decline and always at your expense. You do not need the aggravation.

8.   Obtain a list of references from the service bureau of about three to five current users. Talk to them. To be sure, the service bureau will give you names of satisfied customers. There is no problem with this since these people will be able to tell you *why* they are happy with the service bureau. Ask them for advice in dealing with the service bureau, and find out how they feel about the data security being provided by the firm.

9.   The question of data security is absolutely critical. There must be written guarantees and no doubts on this point. You do not want your files seen by your competition. In visiting a service bureau, question their policies and note how free their personnel are in describing the services and data provided to other customers. Observe what facilities they have for the physical storage of cards, tapes, disk packs, and reports and what fire and flood prevention facilities are in place. What software protection exists for TP monitors and applications? Are there shredders and incinerators for old reports and cards?

10.   Before signing any contract have your company lawyer help negotiate it. It is amazing how few people perform this simple act. Lawyers will ask obvious and important questions that users never will. Examples: Can we buy the application code someday if we want to do the work inhouse? Who owns the data and/or the application code if it is especially developed for us? How can I terminate this contract and what penalty fees if any are involved? Specifically what are my obligations as well as yours? What provisions for data security and service are being offered and specified in writing? A lawyer will want a definition of liabilities for both parties, thus requiring some negotiations. Moreover, a lawyer will want the contract to cover in detail billing procedures, user-caused head crashes on disks, time for service provided, quality levels, and commitments for additional business. Many of these questions are simply not going to be asked by users such as engineers or financial analysts. So do your company and yourself a favor and give your lawyer some extra work. That is what he is there for.

11.   Periodically management must insist on a review of the costs and nature of the services provided. Can the same work be done less expensively inhouse? Is there another service bureau that can do the work less expensively? (Beware of the service bureau offering services too cheaply: it may be financially in trouble and thus trying to shore up its decaying situation by increasing its customer base too rapidly. Remember, you get what you pay for and too little may mean service for a short while with questionable workmanship.) In general, you should

keep in mind that any application may change in form and volume making it just good business practice to review what is being done through a service bureau.

## FACILITIES MANAGEMENT

Facilities management (FM) is a variation of the service bureau concept that has not had the same popularity and thus is not a widely used option in data processing. However, facilities management is common enough that its features should be understood in case this possibility should be presented to your company. As originally conceived, facilities management was the introduction of a team of data processing specialists and their managers into a company to run the DP center. They would work for another company using either your equipment and/or your software and applications. Variations came along later. For example, such a team might run a remote data processing site or might provide some of the manpower to use a service bureau's applications. In some turnkey instances, such people would come in and write an application, obtain the appropriate equipment and have it installed, and turn the whole thing over to you to run. In the case just described, facilities managers might be contracted to maintain the software for a number of specified years.

There are several reasons why facilities management has not proved to be as popular as service bureaus or inhouse computing. First, many of the early facilities management companies were financially unstable and therefore did not survive. Thus when such a company went out of business, all the data processing services offered to another company would be in jeopardy, and if you depended heavily on such work your firm could be in trouble and through no act of your own. Second, the providers of the services are in control of personnel, operate the equipment, and run the applications, thereby taking a large amount of control away from the customer who might want to make changes or object to certain policies. Thus the flexibility of managing a major portion of the business was being denied to the company paying for DP services. And as the dependency on data processing within a company has increased over the years, so has the reluctance to surrender control over its services and equipment to outside managers.

A third concern has been that facilities management groups have had to become extremely knowledgeable about their customer's operations. This has meant exposing company secrets to outside managers and constant retraining as FM personnel rotate in and out of accounts to whom they have no strong loyalty. Again the problem of control over DP is the issue. And closely related to the problem of control has been that of contractual restrictions. In such an environment, companies must develop highly specific contracts which in turn make change very difficult. Then ultimately there is the question of how does a firm sever its ties to an FM contract? Transition to your own DP staff, which now has to be developed, the documentation of applications requiring completion, and identification of data become a difficult and risky job at best, particularly if you had no DP personnel inhouse in the first place.

Yet in some form or another FM work is being done in a number of companies. The problems of managing DP departments are easily passed to a facilities management company by some executives. Another benefit is that the difficulty of training DP staffs and maintaining them, particularly at remote locations, is avoided. In regard to costs, they vary so widely that it becomes nearly impossible to judge whether or not it is cheaper to have your own staff along with all the responsibilities involved. Instinctively we know that an FM team, besides being paid their salaries, must also make a profit for their management, thereby increasing your overhead costs. Yet the FM option may provide the one exception in the DP industry to the old rule of thumb which says that flexibility costs you more. With FM, flexibility may cost you less money but requires more involvement in DP by your company's managers.

The key to a successful FM operation in your company lies in the contract. Do a poor job here and your troubles will be greater than in any other type of DP environment. This factor is so important that if you are contemplating using FM services you might consider hiring a DP consulting firm to help you define your needs, which in turn your company lawyer can have reflected in the contract. The concern is important because your contract becomes the basis for services rendered—and conversely for variations and deviations from the contract which result in additional expense to you and possibly unsatisfactory service.

### Checklist of Things to Do before Signing an FM Contract

(1)  Think of other alternatives to FM services since the loss of control over your operations can be extensive.

(2)  Define in minute detail what functions will be performed by FM and what are their and your liabilities. What levels of documentation of code (flowcharts and source programs) data security provisions, and terms and conditions for the acquisition of equipment and software will be provided?

(3)  Charges for services must be defined in great detail. Will there be a flat fee for running and maintaining existing applications? When and how do these charges change? What happens if more applications are added? If more FM people are joined to your company's DP operations by your request or FM management's, how does that influx change and influence your monthly ex-

penses? Are charges based on the level of experience or caliber of people or arrived at by some other method of calculation? The costs alone, you should by now realize, comprise a complex area of negotiations by themselves.

(4) Define in detail the process by which FM could be eliminated from your company down to the level of a tentative dismantling plan with phases all documented so that your people can come in and theirs leave without jeopardizing the provision of services to your company's users.

(5) Involve everyone in the negotiations. This means at least employing a company lawyer, very high-level executives (the higher the better, particularly if FM is to run a data center), and using finance and personnel managers. Obviously, management participation in such negotiations should increase with the degree of FM services being contemplated. If an FM organization is simply to write code and provide minis for some remote sites then the exposure for your company would not be as great as it would if you were negotiating for a group to run the main data center. But even with the simple case of a programmed mini-computer, questions about support and the significance of the application to the welfare of the company demand serious management attention.

If one general statement can be made about the things you should do in negotiating an FM arrangement, be thorough in the contract. Make sure that it spells out in detail costs, responsibilities, services, and liabilities. Moreover, some mechanism must also be incorporated for establishment of new costs for services periodically such as a statement as to how often increments in cost can come within a year and how much advance notice can and must be given. You also want to be able to tell FM that their services would no longer be needed if new cost rates could not be negotiated. Control over costs must never be lost by your becoming totally dependent on FM for the survival of your company's DP services. Along with the resolution of a good contract and cost policies, do the same things for FM companies as suggested for selecting and dealing with service bureaus. Check out their financial background and reputation carefully for the same reasons you would a service bureau.

## BUYING TIME FROM OTHER DP DEPARTMENTS

A third source of DP services—besides service bureaus and facilities management firms—is the data processing departments of other companies who are willing to sell computer time and services. Typically they are selling time in order to help offset partially the costs of their own operations.

This third option is a very attractive one particularly for intermediate-size companies that do not have multiple DP facilities where additional time and services can be obtained or used by others within the organization. Also there are companies that consider their data processing centers as profit points in the corporation which are expected to make money just like other parts of the organization. Companies that have more computer time than they are currently using may sell that extra time by the hour for use of the whole system, by the hour for whatever parts of a computer system are used, by a monthly rate for certain specified applications, or on a weekly or special job basis. The variety of arrangements is almost infinite.

Typically the times when someone might want to use another DP department's computer facilities are rare. If one DP department is undergoing a major software or hardware conversion, for example, and needs extra test time, it might make a special arrangement with another company in the area to use their facilities. Another common example is the company that wants to benchmark a particular piece of software or application on a specific computer model. Or, using a package of a certain brand, a company might make a similar arrangement with another firm in the neighborhood for testing or backup. The issue of backup is an important one resulting in numerous private arrangements among companies. Auditors and DP managers are always insecure without backup. This is needed for that rare catastrophe when, for example, the computer goes down just as paychecks are about to be printed. Having somewhere to go quickly to get the work done provides another example of how other DP departments may be used.

There is so much use of other department's computers that a whole subindustry of brokers has grown up. Their role is to find time on other compatible computers for those who cannot do either continuous or occasional work on their own equipment. Thus, for example, a company that adds a major batch application to its collection but cannot justify buying a bigger computer to run it and already existing work, might find it less expensive to have a broker find time on another company's machine to run the application. Then at some future date when justification exists for bringing that work inhouse—probably along with other applications—the broker's services would no longer be needed. Arrangements vary with each particular circumstance from a one-time need to use another department's people and equipment to a complex association with another company approaching the form and style of a service bureau. And as with anything else, there are some typical trade-offs involved.

## Advantages

Using someone else's DP department, usually in the same community, typically offers four advantages.

1. The arrangement may cost less than going to a service bureau since a company selling time, by not being in the service bureau business, may simply be willing to charge what it costs for overhead on unused computer time. Thus if a shop is paying $75 an hour 24 hours a day to keep a computer but has a partition which is unused during third shift, it might be happy to charge only about $25 an hour to someone who could use it.

2. Contractual arrangements can be kept quite simple—merely an exchange of letters or a handshake is common. Services if any are usually uncomplicated and few, thus making such an arrangement easy to implement and later eliminate. Typically a computer site operator might run jobs in the presence of another company's DP personnel while programming and systems services becomes a set of activities both companies share.

3. Some DP departments will even "rent" out programming services to help modify or convert applications for other shops that have bought time from them in the past. Usually this is done on an almost actual cost basis with little or no profit involved. It may also be done by individuals who might have some knowledge about the other company. The advantage to this is that there are controls on costs because you do not have to hire extra people on a permanent basis or use existing staff to make modifications of programs to run in another shop.

4. Often the arrangements for computer time are open-ended with no precise obligations to buy a specified amount of machine time over a period of months or years. You pay for only the services you use and when you need them. Thus minimum monthly fees do not have to be guaranteed. Typically you only have to make sure that your work gets scheduled just like any job being run by the host computer department would plan.

## Disadvantages

What can be a very useful and convenient source of additional computer time may have some drawbacks as well. The seriousness of these drawbacks always depends on your particular needs at the moment but they should be kept in mind.

1. As your source of computer power begins to fill up their machine with their own applications, the amount of computer time available to you will begin to decline. Ultimately this may mean that you will have to find another DP shop with which to do business. Therefore, before using another department, determine how fast they are adding volume of work on their equipment and what your projected workload will be. You may find that it pays to go to another shop for your work.

2.   Closely related is the fact that a computer shop has as its primary objective to do the work needed by its own company and not to sell you time. A service bureau, on the other hand, has as its primary mission to service you. Thus if you do work with another company remember that your jobs will be treated as secondary. It becomes an issue typically when year-end accounting and inventory control applications are run that require considerable machine time. Your jobs at this point could well be competing not too successfully for access to the machine.

3.   You may have less control over when your jobs will be run unless, of course, both companies have signed some contract which specifies availability in detail—hours, delivery time of data and reports.

4.   You do not have as much flexibility as to what applications, software packages, and hardware are available for your use as you would in a service bureau. Ordinarily this should not be a major problem since you would not be buying time if the facilities were inadequate.

5.   The question of data security and audit trails can be a serious point. Should you store your data at another company's DP department and use their software, particularly their application code, you must consider the procedures in place to protect your property, its accuracy and availability.

## Using Other DP Shops within Your Company

The same conditions just described regarding other computer departments outside your company apply if you are trying to find time and services within your own organization. Moreover, the environment may be complicated by budgetary considerations. If your company charges its users for services, funny dollars (budget numbers) may flow back and forth complicating the use of time. The charges to you might be more than going to the outside—which is another problem, more political than economic, to monitor. However, you eliminate the problem of having someone outside of your company handling sensitive data. In many cases, particularly for special one-time jobs, obtaining time on another computer within your company will present no problem regarding data security and could well cost you nothing. You then also have the added advantage of having personnel in the other shop working with procedures and possibly code with which they are familiar. More will be said about charge-out systems for services and their implications within a company in the next chapter. All that needs to be remembered is that the services one DP department offers another DP shop within the same organization have the same advantages and disadvantages faced by such other users of DP as accounting, engineering, or marketing.

## General Conclusions

In summary, to obtain the best return for the expense and effort spent on DP services obtained from other computer sites, service bureaus, and facilities management firms, the following guidelines are suggested:

(1) Insist that detailed statements of costs, liabilities, and availability of quality results be drawn up.

(2) Define in writing the time frames for which quoted prices will apply and make sure that you are given meaningful lead times before price changes go into effect so that you can plan for the added expenditures properly.

(3) Insure that you have established a mechanism for terminating your arrangement at some reasonable cost.

(4) In any complex arrangement, involve your company lawyer and if the money is significant enough, someone from finance.

(5) Retain for yourself as much control over the flow of data, reports, and quality control as possible to insure that the work you want is properly done.

More people should learn to
tell their dollars where to go
instead of asking them where
they went.

*Roger Babson*

*This is the meat of the book. All decisions, actions, and results are ulti-mately reflected in a data processing budget. This chapter shows what the role of a budget is, its variations, and how to develop one. Specific recommendations are made on what a budget should contain and next how to control it so that expenditures are planned and are advantageous to you. The budgeting process is treated as a control tool for utilizing money to the greatest advantage to the company and the department. The question of charging to other departments for services rendered is discussed and its significance to various groups within a company defined. The procedure to devise chargeout systems is explained in detail.*

# CHAPTER SEVEN

# Developing a Data Processing Budget and Controlling It

Budgets and cost control procedures in data processing are absolutely essential if companies are to maintain and improve their levels of profitability. These controls are critical since companies today spend anywhere from 1% to 5% of their operating dollars on data processing services. Also remember that the percentage of individuals within the organization dependent on DP to perform their own responsibilities is rising from an average of 30% today to an expected 70% by the mid- to late 1980s. Thus the kinds of controls which management imposes on manufacturing, sales, distribution, accounting, finance, and to corporate management itself, are being applied increasingly to data processing. Clearly the most useful and obvious tool for such control is the data processing budget.

## ROLE OF A DP BUDGET

A data processing budget must serve the same purposes as any other departmental budget. It must measure costs and allow expenses to be managed. The measurement must be by department and then by function or product within that department. Typically management requires certain characteristics to be reflected in a DP budget:

- Allocates planned and actual expenditures for all DP activities—whether in one or more departments—by people, applications, hardware, software, and housing or by other subgroupings as appropriate.

- Monitors actual expenditures against planned outlays on a continuous basis and reflects that activity in meaningful reports which allow management to understand the nature of costs and the company's performance against forecasted expenses.

- Allows for a realistic, equitable, and identifiable distribution of DP costs throughout the company either in one department's budget or in many, either by services rendered or costs generated.

- Creates a procedure for measuring the quality of management's plans against actuals so that experience can be put to use in drawing up better, more accurate budgets and cost plans in the future.

## TYPES OF BUDGETS

Budgets for data processing departments are fundamentally the same as for any other sector of the company. They are generated and used for the same reasons and typically have similar line items—for example, salaries, equipment, floor space, and paper supplies. Therefore, the use of budgetary accounting can and must be applied to DP. Fundamentally there are three types of budgets, each of which implies a certain management approach to spending money and controlling costs: ask, tell, and variable budgeting. Each of them allows management, first, to keep track of money allocated and spent, and, second, to understand and control various functions. Each of these budget types also serves two other purposes: to generate financial reports useful in providing data to stockholders, the government, and creditors; and to offer management accounting data which can help executives manage the business more effectively. Both require historical data on what has happened in the past and what is expected to be spent in the future.

## Ask Budgeting

In ask budgeting a manager determines what funds will be needed with which to operate the department over the next quarter or year. This is a particularly common approach taken by nonprofit organizations where cost controls are not as significant an issue as for a profit-motivated company. Typically in such an environment, the requested budget is subjected to less negotiation or alteration than in a regular company. One of the benefits of such a budgeting method is that managers can ask for what they reasonably want and obtain it without a great deal of effort being required to "sell" upper management on their numbers. The exceptions abound, of course, but that is due more to the nature of individual personalities than to the system. Another benefit is that the operational manager requesting the budget will have little excuse for failure if upper management gave that individual all that was requested.

The weaknesses of this type of budgeting are numerous, however. First, uncontrolled managers will always ask for more money than they really need, thus leading to poor use of funds and a decline in cost control measures. Second, upper management defers to lower levels the responsibility of determining how money will be spent, leading to competitive activities within the organization or to a less than total support for top management's objectives. But worst of all, this budgeting technique makes it very difficult for top management to control costs throughout the company and makes it hard to shift budget dollars from one department to another.

## Tell Budgeting

In tell budgeting, as its name implies, management assigns a budget to a particular department and often without the key operational manager's input. For example, a vice-president for finance to whom DP reports might draw up next year's budget, determining how much to spend on people, equipment, etc., without consulting DP management. Subsequently the numbers would be sent to data processing after they were approved by top executives. Tell budgeting is very widely used, particularly among companies under a billion dollars in sales and whose expenditures for data processing are small.

The benefit often cited for tell budgeting is that top management can tightly control the allocation of funds amongst many departments. Others claim that it eliminates all of the budget negotiations at various levels and the politics inherent in them. Yet tell budgeting is considered an unsatisfactory form of accounting by managers of highly profitable companies for a number of reasons. First, allocated budgets tend not to reflect the true needs of a department which may have changed since last year. Yet tell budgets are usually based on last year's performance and upper management's perception of needs. This is a major weakness in perspective. Take the example of the vice-president of finance who establishes a DP budget without discussing the numbers with the data processing manager. Odds are he will not know enough about the anticipated needs and problems within DP as would the lower-level departmental manager. So numbers are set and circumstances later in the year force the DP manager to go to his supervisor and ask for further allocation of funds, creating friction and even worse, extra unforecasted expenditures of funds.

Second, managers tend to spend all allocated funds whether necessary or not so there is hidden waste. As with ask budgeting, operational management will exaggerate the requirements of the department in anticipation of a decreased allocation. Therefore, managers' gamemanship is a common time-consuming feature of such an environment despite statements to the contrary. In either form of budgeting it would be very safe to say that overexpenditures of funds is at least 10%. And the reason for this is simple: the budget does not reflect the fine-tuned real needs of the department and company nor do they substantively support the important concerns and objectives of top management. They become artificial tools of control without responsibility, forms of cost without real effectiveness. Rigidity eliminates any advantages that could be gained from flexible management control of expenses.

## Variable Budgets

Probably the most common form of budgeting today, this approach represents a budget that evolves during the course of the year as needs and priorities change. Formal sets of numbers are still generated for the entire year and these are usually negotiated by various levels of management in order to insure a real reflection of departmental and company needs. Then the budget is used not only as a measure of how funds are spent but also as a management tool to guide the activities of the company in desirable directions. Thus, for example, if additional funds are required for personnel they are discussed and understood in some detail but then are allocated during the year over and above the original budget as required. Similarly, if terminals are no longer needed at, for example, a manufacturing center that is being closed down, then the allocation of money for those devices is then withdrawn from the budget effective the day the equipment is removed. Thus on the one hand the company spends when it is advantageous to do so and on the other saves when the opportunity exists.

The benefits of variable budgeting are numerous. First, budgets reflect current conditions more so than any other budgeting technique. Second, control over costs is continuous as new situations allow for beneficial changes. Third, since DP penetration of various sectors of the company with new applications is increasing, the need to support such activity with budget changes in various departments is easier than with ask or tell budgeting.

On the other side of the ledger, variable budgeting can lead to managers constantly coming back for more money which they should have forecasted and have reflected in the first budget document for the year. Second, variable budgeting requires management to participate more intensely in the control of costs to avoid undisciplined use of funds. The bottom line for many managers is, however, that variable budgeting is a tool which if properly used, allows the most effective use of DP dollars.

## ELEMENTS OF A DP BUDGET

Taking last year's budget and increasing the gross amount by, say, 9% to account for inflation, etc., to come up with this year's budget would be easy and many companies foolishly do this. One reason is that it becomes difficult to identify the various elements which have a cost and benefit attached to them that are quantifiable. Also, determining how best to spend money within a department is a time-consuming activity which a great number of managers cannot be bothered with. That is why in many companies DP budgets are unnecessarily high or why data processing cannot provide services which offer a very large return on investment. A little bit of hard work in determining what the various cost elements of a budget are and then controlling them will save a company a fortune. If a 10% savings could be obtained—and this is not an unreasonable amount if few controls were in place before—the dollar amounts will be high at no sacrifice in service. For example, a $1 million budget (which is not a lot for a DP department) could generate $100,000 savings continuously.

Identifying each element is admittedly not always easy. Costs can be categorized by center (for example, a DP shop and staff), by products produced (for example, reports), and by users (for example, departments using terminals and reports), and by elements of a DP budget (for example, salaries and equipment).

Cost centers should be identified from an accounting point of view in the same way as any subgroup on an organizational chart. For instance, if you have a data entry department where people are keying into terminals data from all over the company, this department generates costs for people and hardware and those expenses should be identified as part of a company's budget. Whether it is part of a larger department or is a stand-alone unit, some manager of that cost center who has responsibility for providing specific services to the company must also be held accountable for the way resources and money are used in that office. Thus even at a low operational level, cost control is tied to performance and is measured as actual against projected figures.

Budgets can be assigned by product, as for example, to an application. Suppose that the company hires a project leader and additional programmers to develop an online customer order servicing application that cuts across many departments. A budget for the project can be established (people, machine time, programs, etc.), and actual expenditures measured against plan. Thus again, performance and the use of company resources (for example, money and people) are tied to the individual responsible for using them, in this case, a project leader. If costs are coming under or over plan they can be discussed and corrective measures taken either to alter planned and assigned funds or bring costs under control again. And most obviously in project management, one can ask the simple question: "How much more has to be spent in order to complete the job?" The important point to keep in mind is that as many elements of the product have to be measured in quantifiable terms as possible. The costs of salaries, machines, cards, programs, travel, education, housing, consultants, etc., have to be identified and budgeted for independently if serious cost overruns are to be avoided.

Budgeting by users has its own set of requirements. If management wants to farm out the costs of data processing to users (charge-out systems will be discussed later), then within the DP budget there must be line items to reflect charges to various departments so that accounting can deduct these expenses from users and net them against DP's costs. The allocation of costs in this manner can be a gross number by function for the year that does not change or it may be subject to constant alteration depending on how much DP services were used in a month or quarter. An example of the first might be hardware or floor space cost while the latter might be terminal connect time to a computer.

The most common form of budgeting in DP is simply to establish a data processing budget (planned expenditures) and charge that budget for all computer work in the company. It is the simplest method currently being used. Keep in mind, however, that as the use of data processing by other departments continues to rise, so will the use of the budgeting allocation methods just described.

The typical budget for the data processing department will contain sections on personnel costs, hardware, software, teleprocessing communications (lines and telephones), paper, supplies, occupancy, education, transportation, and other minor items. A good budget should define as many of the cost elements as possible. Figure 7–1 lists headings which

*Key Elements in a DP Budget*

1.  Salaries and Personnel Expenses

    Salaries (by person, function, or sub-group, for example, systems analysist).
    Overtime (by the same groups as salaries).
    Benefits (taxes, insurance, education, vacations, other).
    Hiring, firing, and moving expenses.
    Education (for new software, programming, applications).

2.  Hardware Expenses

    DP equipment (by device type, computers, disk, tape, printers, terminals, control
    units) with line items for lease, purchased, depreciation, over-time charges,
    maintenance charges, insurance.

3.  Office Equipment Expenses

    Typewriters, copiers, office systems, telephones, with a breakdown for lease, pur-
    chased, depreciation, over-time charges, maintenance.

4.  Software Expenses

    Operating systems, telecommunication monitors, application and productivity
    packages (leased, depreciated, extra and over-time costs, maintenance expense).

5.  Supplies Expenses

    Tapes, disks, coding pads, printed forms, cards, stock printing paper, chemicals,
    films, binders, flowcharts, other office supplies.

6.  Telecommunication Expenses

    Line charges by line type or application or location, taxes, possibly equipment
    (for example, modems), consulting fees.

7.  Housing Expenses

    Office space rent, electricity, air conditioning, water, taxes, capital depreciation
    for buildings, cleaning, repairs, insurance, security, other.

8.  Other Expenses

    Travel, DP related education, postage, printing, office supplies, consulting fees,
    petty cash, telegraph, manuals, magazines (subscriptions), books, conventions,
    messenger services, dues, marketing of services, transportation of equipment,
    insurance.

**Figure 7-1**

normally should appear in a DP department's budget. Note that the
numerous items have different degrees of importance to each company
and that some subheadings might be rolled into larger ones. For example,
the various elements making up Social Security taxes, salaries, and benefits might be lumped into just one salary heading. The breakdown of

personnel costs might then take place for the entire division or company in the form of reports to management in the divisional or corporate personnel office.

## GENERATING COSTS FOR BUDGET LINE ITEMS

Once it has been established what the various line items will be in a DP budget, the next thing to do is to develop some numbers for each item by month and by year so that measurement against plan through actual expenditures is possible. This is a serious task that must be performed carefully since cost overruns can be so enormous that the actual profitability and financial strength of a company can be at stake.

### General Guidelines

1.  As a first step, identify what the DP department will be expected to do over the next year. Typically this involves running current applications (and understanding their volume growth), preparing plans for new applications, and appreciating what changes in equipment, software, and people will be made. Is a new computer to be brought in? Are we going to hire more programmers? These kinds of questions must be answered and a plan of action developed.

2.  Establish a set of assumptions regarding how a budget will be created and have those assumptions signed off by the manager ultimately approving the budget. Such premises might include: personnel costs will rise $x\%$ next year, that hardware expenditures will go up only 4%, that line costs will increase 12% due to plans to add $n$ more dedicated lines, that data entry expenses will decline by a certain amount due to distributive data entry by other departments. Then use these assumptions to generate various elements of the budget.

3.  Define the workload required to maintain existing and new applications. Typically 10% to 25% of an application's development cost can be expected to recur each year as a maintenance expense. So understand the costs of doing normal production work. This is also an opportunity to educate top management on the effort that is required to perform day-to-day operations.

4.  Show percent increases and decreases in cost along with actual money amounts. For example, if the costs of hardware maintenance are expected to rise 6%, show that, along with the steadily increased dollar amounts per month. Thus, if maintenance charges only climb at 4% or management says that the 6% assumption should be another figure, the dollar amounts can be altered accordingly in the budget.

5.   Factor into your personnel, education, travel, equipment, and software budget any conversion expenses you anticipate during the year as part of your normal day-to-day operating costs.

6.   Identify what costs can be eliminated from your budget and offloaded onto someone else's. For instance, insurance on equipment might in fact not have to be charged to your budget since the company may have a policy that covers all equipment (DP, manufacturing, cars, etc.). On the other hand, if accounting charges back to you certain expenses shared by the whole company, such as insurance, rent, and benefits per individual, understand those before generating any numbers for the DP budget.

7.   Write a report narrating not only the reasoning behind the numbers being submitted as your budget but also to explain all the benefits the company gained from their DP expenditures last year and what was actually accomplished. Thus if the numbers are high, top management can be persuaded to swallow the bitter pill. This is also an opportunity to highlight achievements and problems for political as well as budgetary purposes. For top management, such a report provides a perspective from which to assess the numbers which might otherwise have little meaning.

8.   Sell management on your budget by discussing various parts of it in advance of presenting the amounts to insure that there are no surprises, and also that those who will have to approve it will feel that many of the numbers were of their own making. This avoids problems with the executive who prejudicially feels that any budget that comes to him always has $x$ percent of fat which he cuts before even looking at the numbers. Closely related to this is checking the rumor mill as to what percent differences in budget will be allowed this year. Typically the word gets out that top management will only allow a predefined percent increase in the budget and so DP managers either miraculously develop a budget that just happens to come in at exactly that percent increase or take the other tact of making it even bigger knowing it will then be cut down to the rumored ceiling. All the best-laid plans and intentions are no good unless you appreciate the politics of budgeting and a large part of this lies in understanding the guidelines and the attitudes of the executives passing final judgment.

9.   Understand the budgeting practices and policies of your company before generating any numbers. These are technical points of accounting that are uniformly applied throughout the division or company. They involve how one allocates costs for operating budgets (revenues vs. expenses), cash budgets (dollars to be spent by checks written), and capital budgeting (showing the role of fixed assets and acquisitions).

Each is important to accounting. Operating budgets are what DP executives are primarily interested in: money allocated by function, by month, and by quarter on which departments are measured—allocated vs. actual. Cash budgeting is required so that the company will have sufficient money in its checking account to pay your bills when they come due. Capital budgeting becomes significant to finance, requiring data with which to determine its tax liability, and is responsible for developing income statements and controlling debt.

## Specific Guidelines

In defining the various entries in a data processing budget there are four factors which should be weighed whether the budget is for one DP department or for many within an organization. Those issues should be considered by line item within a budget and in the context of trends in data processing in general.

1. **Project Development Costs.**   Project budgets should look very much like departmental budgets, only with smaller amounts of money involved. Plans for the forthcoming year, and performance year-to-date should be kept in mind. Are projects on time? Are there typically cost overruns? The answer is usually yes to the latter question. So build a fudge factor into machine and personnel costs and identify what resources are being earmarked for project development and then for the new application's maintenance. Earlier in this chapter it was stated that each year maintenance costs should run 10% to 25% of original development costs depending on the project's size, its requirement for manpower, and the quality of its programming. Too often a new application's maintenance is overlooked in developing a budget, but this cost tends to become fixed for the life of that application, which can run over a decade in time.

2. **Personnel Costs.**   Currently personnel costs are rising faster than any other element in the DP budget, absorbing over 50% of all money allocated. These costs represent expenses and are not capitalized and therefore cannot be amortized over a number of years. On the average they are growing at a rate 11% to 12% yearly. The lack of sufficient numbers of experienced, well-trained technical people in the industrialized world has driven salaries upward for systems and programming personnel and their managers. (Hence the observable trend toward having users do more and more of their programming is also a phenomenon to watch.) But these technical people within data processing departments will still be needed and thus salary increases, perhaps out of proportion to the rest of the company, are predictable. Social Security taxes and other

costs for benefits as a percent of salaries are increasing in the industrialized world at well over 1% each year with no end in sight. Thus if
your benefits account for 25% of an employee's total compensation,
expect them to rise to 26%, 27%, etc., each year. The trend regarding
clerical and operational personnel (those who operate the hardware)
is toward stabilization of salary, rising only to reflect national inflation
rates. So keep national inflation rates in mind as a minimum or your
people will go to work for other companies.

Data processing personnel perceive that one of the benefits of their
job is the education in technical matters which a company offers them.
Companies typically offer education in order to have the necessary
technical experience and expertise inhouse ready for new applications,
hardware, or software. Employees, on the other hand, view education as
an enhancement of their professional development as either technicians
or managers, benefits which would help them obtain employment with
other companies or advancement within yours. Thus careful thought
should be given always to allocate some funds for education even if no
major project is in the works so that employee morale will remain high
and their productivity enhanced. In short, education is more than an
expense, its costs are typically an investment in personnel and although
a return on investment cannot always be pinpointed, it is high.

3.  **Hardware and Software Costs.**    As was shown in Chapter 1, the
unit cost of performing instructions in a computer is declining each year.
Some years the cost declines 10% and in others by as much as 30% to
40%. If your work load is increasing then you will probably not see a
decline in actual dollars spent on computing for hardware but you will
not see the cost rise as fast as the usage. Keep in mind for budgeting
purposes the cost trend in hardware. If you have a new computer coming
in, factor its cost into your budget now. Remember that terminals are
like rabbits, they multiply geometrically throughout the company. If
the cost is charged to data processing's budget, along with the expense
for lines, modems, control units, furniture, etc., allow for them in your
financial analysis. Disk and tape equipment tends to grow at lesser rates
but the requirement for storage (disk, mass, bubble, archival) is on the
rise although the cost per piece of data is declining. From a budget point
of view, however, one can expect that the number of dollars allocated
for storage devices will rise at better than 10% a year.

Software charges, both one-time and ongoing, and their maintenance
from the vendor or by your people, are increasing. Complex packages
and productivity tools designed to hold down the cost of personnel
nonetheless are up. It is too convenient not to have them. If you look
at what you spent over the last two or three years on software, that
percentage might prove as a useful guide to how much you will actually

spend next year. In that sense history is a useful guide. But remember, if you are planning some major project, unlike in the past, the cost of software may rise dramatically. For example, suppose you decide that this year data base will be used for the first time. You run out and buy a data base language package at $n$ dollars a month. Your costs are more, however, because after it is installed, you will want to go out and buy a data base dictionary, debug packages, and other DB productivity tools to keep your overall operating budget down. Thus dollars which might have been spent in other parts of the budget begin sliding into the section for software. Typically after a major piece of software is installed, such as a data base manager or a teleprocessing monitor, hang-on software begins to come in at anywhere from 10% to 25% more than was originally budgeted for the first package. There is nothing wrong with this trend since these are usually cost-justified programs but be aware that it will happen and thus affect the budget.

4.   **Teleprocessing Costs.**    After costs for personnel, the fastest rising element in the data processing budget is TP expenses. The number of terminals, modems, lines, printers, forms, clerks, etc., in this area is increasing sharply. By the late 1980s, most forecasters predict that the bulk of an equipment budget will be directly related to TP. And although satellite communications initially brings the expenses of transmission down near what telephone lines cost, their convenience and accuracy rate have a turnpiking effect in that more TP is used. This in turn drives the amount of money going for TP up and at a faster rate than for many other items in the budget. Therefore, when developing plans and budgets, consider the effect of turnpiking on the one hand and what the telephone company plans to do to you on the other. Since this area is expanding at a phenomenal rate, consider the following factors when determining next year's TP costs:

(1)   Line costs for each line and anticipated lines by length of distance from computer to terminal, baud speed, hours of use, the value of dial up lines vs. leased lines.

(2)   Cost, variety, and number of terminals, modems, printers, and furniture.

(3)   Transportation and travel expenses in setting up new equipment at remote locations. You will be surprised at the expanding cost involved.

(4)   Expense of new TP monitors, setup costs, and education.

(5)   Effect on computer utilization and demand for disk storage space.

(6)   If you have many lines and the overhead in maintaining them is

rising sharply, consider bringing inhouse a modeling program so that you can simulate other configurations of lines and terminals as a means of designing new networks to lower or slow down the rise in TP costs.

## DEVELOPING AND CONTROLLING A DP BUDGET

After you know all the elements that go into a DP budget, the next problem to solve is how to design the budget form and reflect the information on it in a useful manner. The organization of data thus is essential. There are several points to keep in mind at this stage. First, a budget is used by enlightened management not solely as an accounting method to keep track of dollars but as a tool with which to manage and control expenditures on data processing. Such budgets should be designed so that actual expenditures can be measured against plans and not simply to reflect what you were allotted and spent. The way you use a budget will determine how it is created and also the manner in which the data is presented.

Typically, budgets for data processing must employ the accounting guidelines established for the entire company. Thus the manner in which dollar amounts are generated for salaries, benefits, floor space, etc., and the form in which they are reported is by and large determined by accounting management and the laws and customs of the country. Beyond that, it is the attitude of management toward budgets which will determine how they are used and formulated. If it is employed as a contractual obligation and not as a planning tool, then the budget will reflect what has happened in the past and perhaps not even what is planned for the rest of the year. The rest of the ensuing discussion about budgets will assume that the budget reflects what expenditures have taken place and that it is a management tool for controlling data processing in an ongoing dynamic environment.

Figure 7–2 illustrates a mini-budget for a department. It shows expenditures year-to-date, planned expenditures year-to-date, percent over or under and identifies each major cost element. Moreover, it identifies in the planned last-year month, how much was spent in the same month last year. In each group a percentage has been given which shows the relationship between planned and actual expenditures so that a manager looking at the numbers could quickly see by how much under or over budget he was. The manager, seeing a significant difference (particularly if it happens over several months) can detect that something is not right and will have the opportunity to study the problem. The objective is always to come in under budget (under 100% where 100% equals what you were given to spend) and where additional funds are needed to

March 1979

| Item | Code | Planned | Actual | % | YTD Plan | YTD Actual | YTD% | Plan YTD Last Year | Actual YTD Last Year | % YTD Last Year | % Total Budget 1979 |
|---|---|---|---|---|---|---|---|---|---|---|---|
| Salaries | | 81,000 | 80,500 | 99% | 243,500 | 220,000 | 90% | 160,000 | 165,500 | 103% | 50 |
| Management | | 10,000 | 11,000 | 110% | 30,000 | 32,000 | 104% | 9,000 | 9,000 | 100% | 6.4 |
| Systems | | 20,000 | 20,000 | 100% | 60,000 | 60,000 | 100% | 18,000 | 18,000 | 100% | 12.2 |
| Programming | | 40,000 | 40,000 | 100% | 120,000 | 100,000 | 81% | 100,000 | 110,000 | 110% | 24.2 |
| Operations | | 10,000 | 8,000 | 80% | 30,000 | 24,000 | 80% | 25,000 | 20,000 | 80% | 6.3 |
| Overtime | | 1,000 | 1,500 | 150% | 3,500 | 4,000 | 114% | 8,000 | 8,500 | 94% | .9 |
| Hardware/Software | | | | | | | | | | | |
| Computer + I/O | | | | | | | | | | | |
| Terminals | | | | | | | | | | | |
| Software | | | | | | | | | | | |
| Lines | | | | | | | | | | | |
| Office Expenses | | | | | | | | | | | |
| Rent | | | | | | | | | | | |
| Supplies | | | | | | | | | | | |
| Travel | | | | | | | | | | | |
| Micellaneous | | | | | | | | | | | |
| Totals | | | | | | | | | | | 100% |

**Figure 7-2**  Sample operating budget (issued monthly).

| Date: Year | Jan. | Feb. | Mar. | ......... | | | | |
|---|---|---|---|---|---|---|---|---|
| Description | Actual Plan | Actual Plan | Actual Plan | ......... | YTD Budget YTD Actual | Cur. Monthly Variance YTD Variance | 12 Mo. Budget Last Year Actual | |
| | | | | | | | YTD | 12 months |
| Education | 587 440 | 300 450 | 400 451 | | 1,300 1,105 | 19— 193— | 5,200 | |
| | | | | | | | | 4 |
| | | | | ......... | | | | |
| | | | | ......... ......... ......... ......... | | | | |

**Figure 7–3**    Sample operating plan (budget).

put them into the budget before they are spent. In this way management can take resources from another part of the company where they are not currently needed and thus better manage the use of funds. Figure 7–3 shows another variation of a budget with different data on what is to be spent and likewise serves the purpose of showing plan vs. performance.

An annual budget, which is the document from which planned numbers by month are generated, would look similar to Figure 7–2 but show only planned expenditures. It should have these numbers by month, quarter, and year however. Figure 7–4 illustrates a sample budget form. Again the principle of showing expenditures by time period (month, quarter, and year) is followed and a percentage of what a particular item

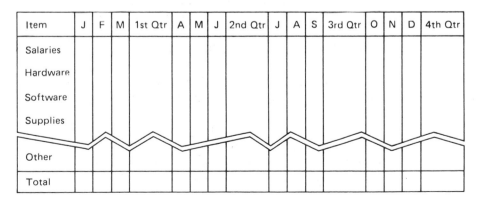

| Item | J | F | M | 1st Qtr | A | M | J | 2nd Qtr | J | A | S | 3rd Qtr | O | N | D | 4th Qtr |
|---|---|---|---|---|---|---|---|---|---|---|---|---|---|---|---|---|
| Salaries | | | | | | | | | | | | | | | | |
| Hardware | | | | | | | | | | | | | | | | |
| Software | | | | | | | | | | | | | | | | |
| Supplies | | | | | | | | | | | | | | | | |
| Other | | | | | | | | | | | | | | | | |
| Total | | | | | | | | | | | | | | | | |

**Figure 7–4**    Sample annual budget assigned.

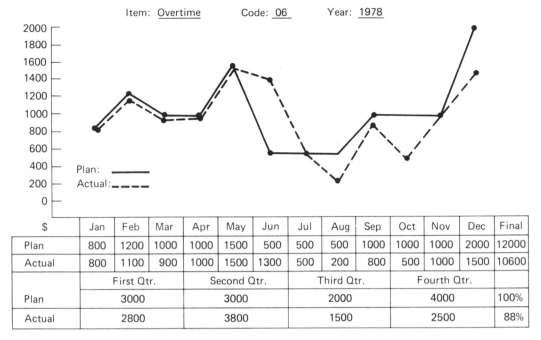

**Figure 7-5**    Budget performance analysis.

makes up in the total departmental budget can be generated. From the total numbers of such annual departmental reports a company-wide budget will be drawn. Conversely, as the year goes by, the actual performance budget report (in our case Figure 7-2) will be consolidated right up the line and will probably have a similar if not exactly the same format with the same types of entries. The only difference would be that the amounts of dollars would be higher as multiple DP budgets are consolidated into regional, divisional, or corporate level reports.

Looking at the numbers each month is usually adequate to determine if expenditures are exceeding or coming at or under plan. But the numbers themselves are not enough to define trends, which is essential to good cost control. A technique that works and which is widely used because of its simplicity is a graph of each major expenditure drawn as you go along through the year month by month. Figure 7-5 illustrates such a graph.

In the example illustrated in Figure 7-5, overtime salaries are being monitored. Each month the manager would fill in last month's actual expenditures and plot the graph of actual against currently planned outlays. In fact, in many companies this kind of report is computer-generated. If the graph lines do not run closely together several things could have happened. First, perhaps the planned expenditures were unrealistic and should be changed for the rest of the year or in next year's budget. Second, the demand for overtime or increased use is getting out of control. If there is a great deal of overtime being registered the manager here would find out why, then either reduce it or get his budget changed, or determine that it would be cheaper to hire other full-time personnel. The latter might be possible if, for example, he was below plan in salaries yet over plan on overtime. The point is, the manager could visually note how in one area of cost, his department was doing and could react quickly to a negative trend.

Looking at our example once again, we see that the manager was doing a great job in coming just under budget through May. In June, overtime expenditures exceeded plan and then came under plan substantially for the rest of the year with the exception of November. Obviously plan and actuals in the first half of the year were accurate but further along in time the opposite became true. In this case somewhere in the spring the plan should have been modified. The fact that total expenditures were under total budget on December 31 is not good enough because during the last few months the company had set aside $1500 which was not spent on overtime and could have been used productively elsewhere. So our DP manager here did a poor job in the second half of the year in controlling (managing) costs.

Using such a simple tool for each major measurement of a department whether it is budget, cost control, computer utilization, error rate in data entry, production run times, or whatever, is useful in managing the business. Upper management measuring the performance of a manager's department can use the same tool for the purpose of comparing performance of one group of employees against others. Most important, it points to problems early, giving management time to react and ultimately prevent unforecasted or uncontrolled expenses from driving up the cost of doing business. The same tool should be used for controlling the costs of projects in process.

Equally important as looking at past performance (year-to-date data) is to examine what lies ahead. If costs are to be controlled and accounting data to be used effectively, forecasting of costs and impact on budgets has to be done. You do not want to react to something that has already happened; you want instead to develop a plan of action for anticipated problems. Therefore, in many companies, departmental heads and their managers in turn, are requested to submit a budget forecast for the following month, quarter, or year so that the necessary negotiating, gamesmanship, and ultimately changes to existing budgets and company plans can take place. Figure 7–6 illustrates what a forecast might look like for data processing.

As with budgets in general, several principles should be observed. First, the items listed must be the same ones that appear on a budget

| Prepared by | Date | | | For yr. ending 19__ | | | | Reviewed by | Date | | |
|---|---|---|---|---|---|---|---|---|---|---|---|

| Items | 1 | 2 | 3 | 4 | Month 5 | 6 | 7 | 8 | 9 | 10 | 11 | 12 | 1 |
|---|---|---|---|---|---|---|---|---|---|---|---|---|---|
| Expenses | | | | | | | | | | | | | |
| Salaries | | | | | | | | | | | | | |
| Total | | | | | | | | | | | | | |
| Hardware | | | | | | | | | | | | | |
| Total | | | | | | | | | | | | | |
| Office | | | | | | | | | | | | | |
| Total | | | | | | | | | | | | | |
| Income | | | | | | | | | | | | | |
| Consulting | | | | | | | | | | | | | |
| Computer Time Sales | | | | | | | | | | | | | |
| Programming | | | | | | | | | | | | | |
| Total | | | | | | | | | | | | | |

| Net Totals | 1st Qtr | 2nd Qtr | 3rd Qtr | 4th Qtr |
|---|---|---|---|---|
| Expense | | | | |
| Income | | | | |
| Net Totals | | | | |

**Figure 7-6**

and occur in the same order for convenient comparison. Second, the data must be consolidated for each level of management upward in the same format. Thus if you have several DP departments within your company, they must all use the same report in order to produce the same consolidated summary. Ideally a similar format should be used throughout the company. Third, data has to be presented by month and quarter. Fourth, the form should be filled out every quarter and, if real problems exist, each month. This way the report becomes a useful tool in identifying what management at any given time feels will happen to the budget. Also the accuracy of a particular individual's forecasts can be measured—a consideration often overlooked but one that is essential in good managers.

How to forecast specific line items is difficult at best since no one can predict the future with any certainty. However, if you know your business and the department is under control, forecasting expenditures becomes easier, particularly since you have the ability to react to a problem if the correct data is available early enough. If overtime costs are rising then you know to look into the situation and determine if the expense can be reduced by stopping the work, shifting it to other people, or hiring others. But it is a decision you can make. The installation of equipment will have an impact on your budget as well. If you are spending more than planned, on-order equipment installation might have to be delayed, or instead of renting it, you could consider purchase to bring the monthly cash flow down. Again, understanding what is going on now by using budget data, a manager can control costs and manipulate them to the company's advantage.

A great deal of forecasting takes place with new application development. The kinds of control techniques illustrated in Chapters 2 and 3 are very useful. The principle is the same as in budgeting. Tasks are defined with their costs, and those that are left on the list to do are quantified and thus become measurable in dollars over time. This is all well and good; however, mistakes do take place. The most common occur in relating the number of tasks done correctly to the budgeted dollars. An illustration shows the problem involved.

Suppose you have a project budgeted at $200,000. As of today you have spent $130,000 or put in other terms, 65% of allocated funds. But what if only 25% of the work is completed? You have a problem. Because now that 25% of tasks completed have cost $130,000, based on the experience gained in this project, the rest of it will result in an expenditure of about $390,000 or nearly twice what you once thought. Now you know there is a crisis and that something had better be done about it right now.

The correct approach at this point runs as follows. You determine why it cost so much year-to-date to get the 25% of the work done and make up your mind about what it would take to finish the project. Based on that analysis management might say we will not continue with the project and simply write off the $130,000 already spent and fire you. This may be cheaper than pushing ahead either along the same old path or with new plans because the benefits to be realized may have been exceeded by the cost overrun to date (or anticipated). On the other hand, management might decide that with a new set of plans for the remaining work, the cost overrun might be reduced from its currently projected 100% to something far less and be willing to push forward. The point of this discussion is, we need to relate actual budget performance against the tasks to which it was assigned. Knowing what the rest of a job will require in money is thus more important than understanding what it cost before. That is real cost control in action.

## CHARGING FOR DP SERVICES: THE ISSUE

One of the most controversial issues in data processing management and cost accounting today is the question of charging for DP services within a company. Should a data center have a budget and provide services to the rest of the company free? Should those departments which use DP services pay for them? What are the effects of one approach vs. the other on DP costs, controls, and general efficiency of the company? Is it a control tool or a headache for management? Does it inhibit the use of data processing or encourage its wise application? There are no simple answers to these questions except to say that it depends on the circumstances existing independently in each company.

Yet there are patterns developing which may suggest an approach to these questions in your company. Typically when an organization begins to use data processing, the DP department is assigned a budget with which to provide services to the rest of the company. Management, typically just converted to the idea that DP can help make operation of the company more cost-effective and efficient, is motivated to create an environment where user departments will do more with computers. Thus few restraints are placed on them and simple forms of cost justification are accepted. Usually this is the period during which batch accounting applications are developed and afterwards converted to online in such areas as accounting, customer order servicing, distribution, sales, and ultimately manufacturing and financial modeling.

Then a company typically recognizes that its expenditures on data processing are rising faster than for most other departments. Management determines that some control measures are now necessary, regardless of whether or not the increased number of services are justified, in order to make sure that frivolous applications are not being developed. It is at this point that someone says, "We should charge the budgets of other departments for the amount of DP services used so that everyone will participate in cost control and in the development of optimal usage of data processing services." It is also at this juncture that user departments have enough of an understanding of what DP can do for them that they can participate in cost control. Thus user departments now take a hard look at what DP services they need and what they are willing to pay for them. Today the trend toward charging out for services is on the rise because more companies than ever have now acquired a large collection of applications and technical expertise in data processing usage with which to make some value judgments. When this situation exists throughout the organization it is easier to reach conclusions about the necessity of certain proposed applications along with existing ones and measure their possible impact on departmental budgets.

The perception that charge-out systems can be a management tool to insure that data processing is used effectively by everyone at all levels then becomes a hot issue and ultimately a way of life.

The challenge management faces when charge-out systems are discussed is to balance expenditures in DP against other areas in the most cost-effective manner. At the same time, existing resources have to be utilized in the most productive way yielding the greatest number of benefits to the organization. That is why the issue is complex, controversial, and uniquely different for each company. Tied to this concern are such questions as decentralization vs. centralization, data bases vs. corporate control, inhouse computing vs. service bureaus.

Charge-out systems should provide information to help control the ebb and flow of budget dollars within a company and also offer a pricing scheme by which to charge for the use of these services. There are several general arguments used for charge-outs which support these two ideas.

1.   DP and user managers are given incentives to use computer facilities most effectively and economically. While they enjoy its benefits they also incur its costs.

2.   Managers of user departments are forced to honor their statements of savings and benefits which they said would develop as a result of using data processing. If lower people costs were a savings forecasted for an application, then once it was used, that department's salary budget should decrease proportionately.

3.   Users of data processing are forced to become involved in application design, use, and cost, thereby encouraging the most effective use of computer technology department by department.

4.   Pressures increase on DP from users and upper management to use their resources and costs in a more businesslike manner. If they fail one of several things happens. Users do not come to DP for applications, or they go to a service bureau, or establish their own DP function.

The net result of a charge-out system is to provide for better use of DP resources, to balance demand for applications against available hardware and software, to weed out marginally beneficial uses of computers, and to provide management with data on DP. Moreover it generates a genuine dialogue between users and the data processing organization.

These four above-listed points, however, are difficult to put into action. There are problems in approaching charge-out systems as simple cost-allocation methods. Assigning costs for particular applications and hardware, as shared by various departments, is not easy, particularly since many fixed cots are hard to define (for example, the expense of unused computer power, or of mounting and dismounting a tape from a tape drive). Commitments to computers are for many years, so how do you factor the amortization of costs into daily charges for services? How do you establish the cost for specific uses of applications, files, software, and conversions? And there is always competition from service bureaus, other DP centers within the company, and stand-alone single-application mini-computers within a department.

One other danger spot exists to overcome. In charging for applications, many companies will want benefits to be returned in exchange. For example, in exchange for an application a department says it will save the cost of one dozen clerical personnel. The company rushes out and develops the application. Now try to get the department head to fire or transfer those dozen people. More than one DP executive has been heard to say that if his company fired all the people whose jobs were no longer needed due to computers there would be no one working for the company! And that would include all the programmers!

For such reasons data processing specialists and industry consultants are in general agreement that a perfect charge-out system that truly reflects costs and yet encourages the wisest use of services is nearly impossible to develop. They also believe that most current charge-out systems are incomprehensible to users because the systems measure activities from a technical point of view that has no meaning to nontechnical people. For examples, DP departments will charge by MIPs used (instructions executed), I/O read-writes (times the computer went to a file and got data or put some back), and time a printer meter ran. Thus in gathering minute details, departments are discouraged from using DP services effectively and even worse, from measuring and understanding how to control their own costs. Therefore, an objective should be that a charge-out system be reasonable in recovering costs and that the charges be in terms relevant to users.

So you decide that costs are escalating, that applications are complex, that pressure from users to control DP activities upon which they are increasingly dependent are characteristic of your company. Now what? You decide that a charge-out system must be put into place. Typically a combination of strategies is employed from a budgetary point of view. Departments will be given budget dollars which they then use to pay for services from their DP centers. This budget may be totally dedicated to paying for such services. A variation is to charge for some central site services (for example, computer time and file storage), but make the user departments pay directly for terminals and printers on their premises.

Usually these environments provide little incentive for a department to seek alternative DP services outside of their own data processing organization. Other companies, however, assign "real" dollars to a department's budget so that all alternatives can be weighed. Management in this case has to be careful to keep central site computing costs "competitive" with the outside world or all departments will begin to acquire mini- and microcomputers and therefore not take advantage of the economies of scale and possibly deny the organization the advantages of centralized control through company-wide applications.

## CHARGING FOR DP SERVICES: THE WAY IT IS DONE

Companies normally follow one of three general lines of action in developing charge-out systems. First, company or corporate management will want to encourage user departments to rely on DP for certain applications and thus will offer them services either at no charge or will subsidize them. These might include a company-wide budgeting application or order entry and include applications being developed for a particular department in which top management has a great deal of interest and wants to encourage.

Second, management might run out and buy a charge-out package which defines how many hours of computer time were used, along with disk and tape utilization, lines of printing created, line usage, etc., and assign billing locations for such use. Thus a department that made $x$ number of I/O calls would be billed for them. This is a very common although nearly meaningless form of charge-out. It is simple to implement, but it is one of the fastest ways of creating confusion and mistrust among users who now feel they have little control over their DP expenditures and entertain the sneaking suspicion that the data processing department has become a profit center at their expense.

The third, and the most rational business-like approach is to charge in terms relevant to users. Thus instead of billing for I/O calls one might charge a certain amount for each inquiry or update to a file by type of file for online applications. A flat fee for batch jobs based on the number of lines printed or data submitted is an alternative plan of action. Another form of charging in relevant terms might be for compilations of programs written by users, or the number of hours per month that a user's terminal was connected to the computer doing work. These charges are in laymen's terms and allow users to understand what they are paying for and also what functions they have to control. This makes it easier for them to predict expenditures into the future and to provide for such costs within their budgets. Also, this approach allows management to indicate to DP what future volumes of usage might be so that data processing can anticipate demand. Charges per function can be arrived at by data processing through some form of averaging which allows them to establish costing in a standard method common throughout the company.

This approach has several distinct benefits for the company as a whole. Users understand what they are being billed for and thus can appreciate and control these costs. The charges are fair and equitable throughout the organization so that no one party feels cheated. Stability in prices is possible with changes only coming when either absolutely necessary or long enough in advance to be reflected in the company's various budgets. The commonality of standard charges also allows for audit trails to be established which can show that if a given application were performed numerous times, the charges would be about the same. This becomes absolutely essential for managers in user departments who want to forecast their future DP expenses.

There are generally three clusters of charges which now have to be established. First, the costs of development work for an application is essential. Is it to be absorbed by corporate or departmental budgets? To be shared among departments implies one set of costs while charging them all to one department suggests another. Typically one of two methods is used: company management at the central site can absorb the charges or they are farmed out to various departments (or if for one department then to it) as they are incurred. There is a variation to these approaches whereby some companies will capitalize development costs and users are then charged against their capital budgets throughout the accounting life of the project much like a piece of machinery. Obviously the approach taken will depend on taxation and accounting methods in vogue at the time, the benefits of the application which are anticipated, and the cost of development.

Second, a company's accounting practices are married to a charge-out system to generate billing for production of an application and its usage. Use is measured by the amount of hardware, software, telecommunications lines, people, and specific applications utilized in any given period of time. Typically billing is either monthly or quarterly.

Third, expenses incurred for maintenance of applications, minor, and even major changes to programs requested by users can either be billed as they are incurred or capitalized. In some cases, the data processing center has a budget for such expenses, particularly if they are small.

Charging for the use of specific applications or hardware resources can be established in a common-sense way. Take computer usage as an example. If a computer costs the company in rental and operating personnel $30,000 a month and it estimates that this machine will be accessible for 400,000 seconds per month then the price would be

$30,000 divided by 400,000 seconds yielding a charge of 7½¢ per second. Another illustration: The DP department determines that every time an inquiry is made into a customer file the total cost in hardware, software, and manpower is 3¢. Then if a department makes 5000 inquiries in a month, their bill will be 5000 × 3¢ yielding 15,000¢ or $150. A third example: A particular application requires that two disk packs be available all day for accessing. The disk drive for these packs leases for $600/month and the packs each for $50/month. The constant billing for this availability would be $700/month not to mention other charges for rental of terminals and line usage, printing, or whatever else happens to be involved. The point is, the charges are straightforward and in laymen's language. Specialists in charge-out systems suggest that no more than ten variables (chargeable items) be used, otherwise user departments will find it difficult to keep track of expenses and control them.

Another variation in charge-out systems is that which is commonly used by service bureaus. Although complicated to devise, they are, however, easy for users to understand. The principle is that you charge only for inputs and outputs. There is a flat fee for each unit of data that the DP department or users input into the system, times the amount of data within a certain period of time (month, quarter) and there are fees per report generated, either measured by lines of data or number of characters printed. The intricate details of computer and line utilization, access of peripheral equipment, complex software, etc., are shielded from users. This method has proven very popular although it requires DP managers to devise accurate and sometimes complex programs to translate their costs into input and output charges—not an insurmountable task since some programming has to be done anyway for any charge-out system.

Yet another approach involves a flat annual or quarterly fee for services whether used or not. This provides for some security in developing user and DP budgets and allows for the maximum use of economies of scale in acquiring data processing equipment and software. This tactic will often be used in combination with some charges for specific services because it is easy for all concerned. Its negative point is that such a system is not very sensitive to the use of data processing and does not encourage the most cost-effective use from the point of view of user departments.

Beyond the methods described above there are some fine-tuning techniques that one must consider using if charge-out systems are to encourage optimal utilization of DP resources. Charge extra for rush jobs or unscheduled work. Give a discount for doing jobs during periods when DP resources are not fully utilized such as after midnight instead of 10 o'clock in the morning. Charge less for jobs which can be run at a lower priority than others. If these techniques are to be effective, the differences in prices, for example, between running a batch job in the morning or late at night must be over 100% or 200%. Put another way, discounts of over 50% often have to be employed in order to have work switched from one time slot or level of priority to another. And always charge for DP services to the lowest level in the company's organization where meaningful decisions can be made on whether or not to use an application, how much, and where efficiencies of operation can be employed.

Two leading commentators on the data processing industry, Dan Bernard and Richard L. Nolan, along with other co-authors wrote a book, *Charging for Computer Services: Principles and Guidelines* (New York: PBI Books, 1977), which provides the best detailed discussion of charge-out systems available as of this writing. In the last chapter these authors warn managers against installing charge-out systems without giving them any real thought as to how they might affect the organization. These writers state that "In our experience, charge-out systems are often less valuable than they might be because management has introduced charging as a 'good idea,' without ever clearly defining precisely what it wishes to achieve." (page 107). They correctly argue that charge-out systems should not be considered as merely an accounting method but instead as a tool for controlling the use and cost of data processing. This is the most relevant bottom-line statement that can be made about the use and design of charge-out systems. Take advantage of their experience and keep it in mind when establishing your own. And, as with any project, review it periodically so that you will understand its effect on the organization and can be sure that the assumptions underlying its form are still valid.

## HOW TO IMPLEMENT COST CONTROLS IN DATA PROCESSING

We can now summarize many of the points which have been stated or implied throughout this book and particularly in Chapter 7. These points reflect management concerns which transcend any particular department or company because they can be applied throughout any organization. They work and will save you money, lost time, and help you avoid wasted effort.

1.  Have operational managers develop a plan of action that is realistic, that they can live with, and which can be adjusted to conform to top management's own plans. Also monitor it carefully to make sure it is being carried out and changed if circumstances warrant.

2.  Quantify costs, performance, and benefits on an ongoing basis. Use budgets, requests for changes in applications, financial analysis of various acquisition options, and accounting reports which measure actual performance against plans.

3.   Periodically review current assumptions and plans. Is something needed? Why? Is the work being done on a timely basis and cost effectively? Is there a better way to do something? And give operational management time to ask for or develop answers to such questions within an encouraging environment. They should not feel that executives will avoid entertaining new ideas—no company can afford the luxury and cost of stagnation.

4.   Throughout the company encourage the use of exception reporting for all applications rather than the continued production of highly detailed voluminous reports. This will save in paper costs, printing and computer expense, and allow personnel to focus on the exceptional situations requiring attention now. To some readers this may sound patently obvious and to others merely a minor point. The name of the game, however, is to keep down the number of people and resources required to run a business and that means improving the productivity of what you already have. Exception reporting is a very specific way of doing that.

5.   Simplify work procedures and automate repetitive human functions. The more often a routine task is performed the greater the probability that computers can do it more accurately, faster, and less expensively.

6.   Always consider three or four options before approving any plan of action.

7.   Find out what other companies are doing, seek advice, ask questions. Your managers may be very experienced and talented, but they do not know everything. Key sources for information are data processing vendors, users of DP services within your company, DP classes and conventions, various industries' publications, and your data processing staff.

8.   Executives must encourage operational managers to look for new and better ways to use data processing. Incentives must be in place in the form of specific line items in performance plans, bonus programs, or other rewards such as increases in salary and promotions.

9.   Often overlooked is the fact that DP managers need just as many tools for managing their resources as do other department heads. Yet often they are the last to receive such necessary help. They too need reports on the utilization of hardware, files, software, people, services, data bases, TP, and can use very effectively monitors and simulation packages—not to mention programming productivity software and modular programming techniques. Because the question of DP tools is a detailed one requiring a book-length discussion of its own, the bibliography at the back of this volume lists useful publications in this field.

**To accept good advice is but
to increase one's own ability.**

*Goethe*

*Chapter 8 deals with the issue of how you can deal with salesmen, their support personnel, and consultants when it comes to data processing. Since ultimately you must buy or lease DP products and then use them, the issue of dealing with vendors is an important one. There is mistrust and concern at every bend in the road. This chapter will show you how to get the most out of these people, how to use them as assets, and how to control what they do within your company. First specific suggestions are made about salesmen and what they can do for you. Next, technical support people are examined to show you what they can do for you and how to control them to your advantage. Last the role of consultants in your company is defined and ways of utilizing their services to your maximum benefit are described.*

# CHAPTER EIGHT

# Dealing with Vendors and Consultants

As the volume of data processing services increases together with their related hardware, software, and personnel, so will contact with vendors and consultants within the DP industry. Field engineers will be maintaining hardware and software, systems engineers software and applications, salesmen selling equipment, software, and services, and consultants telling managers how best to use DP technology. Each one works within his or her own circle of priorities and concerns, some in conjunction with a customer and at other times in opposition. Always there are people coming in and out of the company on some data processing business. Yet some approach and philosophy on the part of a company's management as to how to deal with this ever-growing number of individuals is necessary, otherwise a great deal of everyone's time is wasted.

257

# SALESMEN AND MARKETING

Jokes and stories abound about salesmen. In data processing it is no different. DP personnel will kid about their white shirts and wingtips or at the other extreme, frown in mistrust. As with all industries, marketing representatives vary widely. Some push "iron," make the sale and then run away while at the other end of the spectrum are salesmen who view their role within a customer's company as that of consultants providing data processing as a means to solutions of problems. They vary in background from the highly experienced and knowledgeable individual to a "pitch" man who knows little about his product and could just as easily sell encyclopedias. But typically, because data processing is a complex field and the problems it attacks are large and expensive, marketing personnel are predominantly well-educated, knowledgeable about business and finance, and articulate in presenting their products. Theirs is a job where money can be made and influence used to really help or hurt a company, so many talented individuals are attracted to this calling.

There are two primary sets of vendors that a company will deal with over a period of time. The first represents the manufacturer who has the largest amount of products installed in a company, typically the main frame (computer) vendor since he or she has a computer and a large amount of software and peripherals involved. In this environment you may find a DP manager who sees his salesman once every eighteen months while down the street another vendor calls on his account every day. It is as much a question of a marketing representative's style as it is that of his employer.

A second set of vendors comprises the suppliers of specialized products such as forms, paper, tapes, terminals, cabling, and educational materials. Usually these individuals appear only on occasion and often when data processing operational management is asking for specific information or wishing to order some item constantly in use (such as preprinted forms). Typically these marketing individuals, unlike the general computer salesmen, will only specialize in one or a few items while the others will have knowledge of a broader product line from computers to terminals, operating systems to application programs. And how you deal with each type determines whether or not the marketing people are the enemy to whom you say "no" or are a source of help and information as well as products.

Everything depends on people and their situations of course. If you trust your salesman you will be inclined to think of him as a consultant and act accordingly. If the individual cannot be trusted then you think he is just pushing "boxes" at you regardless of how that person may view his or her role. But given the uniqueness of personalities and variability of company policies and one's DP needs, there are some general statements that can be made to help you optimize your relations with vendors.

## Salesmen as Sources of Information

Let us examine the vendor who is the prime supplier of products to your company's DP organization. Such an individual is reponsible for the main computers, their peripherals, and their hang-on software. Such a person should be a substantial source of information about his company's products and must be seen quite often, otherwise you are doing business with the wrong company. One of the reasons why you must see him or her frequently is that this person is a source of data about how other people are using his or her company's products and about what trends in product development are occurring within the vendor's company. For these reasons, such people should be treated as resources. If you are essentially a one-vendor shop (and most companies are) then it is important that your DP plans coincide with the product strategy of the vendor company you do business with so that your actions are supported by devices and software a vendor will maintain.

As sources of references, your contacts within the business community can be expanded, which will lead you to other people's experiences with, for example, a particular product or development of applications. This kind of help is extremely valuable when a major new step is contemplated and someone within the company is responsible for researching it out. The savings in time, people, and effort by learning from the experiences of others can be translated into thousands and thousands of dollars saved. The fastest way to get to people who have been down the same road you are planning to travel is a vendor since he or she has other accounts and contacts.

Often when managers are planning for new environments and applications the need exists simply to talk to other DP professionals about matters of concern which cannot be taken up with non-DP management within the company. In this sense the vendor can serve as consultant. Leaving aside for the moment any particular axes he or she may have to grind in giving data processing advice, being able to discuss DP strategies and plans with someone outside the organization can be of real benefit if for no other reason than to confirm or deny your own thoughts. And you can always put into your own perspective whatever a vendor says, editing it for possible prejudice.

Another type of assistance from the vendor is in the area of financial analysis. A vendor who works for a large computer company, a leasing concern, or brokerage firm dealing in computer equipment, probably has at least rudimentary knowledge about financial analysis while most salesmen are quite experienced in this field. These people understand how to cost-justify their products and can help you relate these numbers to your company. Their understanding of contractual terms, the applicability of the Investment Tax Credit to their products, and the possible impact of various depreciation methods is invaluable. So have them help with the financial analyses. Obviously they will build financial cases to make their products or desirable options look very attractive but you can control that easily. Define options and financial parameters. Often such vendors have cash-flow analyses programs at their offices which they can use in doing financial studies. So let them make the first cut on the numbers for a particular acquisition. Once you have zeroed in on an option and financial strategy that is desirable then let your own financial people finalize the numbers.

Vendors, in some cases, in their effort to sell products recognize that applications sell hardware. That is to say, if they can have you develop more applications then you will buy additional products. There is nothing wrong with this approach providing these applications are beneficial to your company and are cost-justified. However, in defining the applicability of some new way to use DP equipment and software someone has to do the necessary research and justification. Many vendors are willing to lend manpower to this effort since they see a sale in it for them. Furthermore they will identify areas of justification you might otherwise miss. Therefore, control the process but let a vendor help in application justification if the offer is made. You both can and will derive a benefit: he a sale and you a justified application.

Vendors can also be a source of education on data processing and management issues. Many will sponsor seminars and classes, free or for fee, on all aspects of data processing and on the use of this technology for those managers who have little or no understanding about computers. Managers who are resisting the introduction of computerized services are often won over in such classes which are routinely well presented throughout the industry. Technical people can take useful courses on managing the data processing environment and relating it to the business requirements of their companies. Data processing courses on specialized topics, such as distributed processing, or on specific products which you are considering installing or will install are also given. There are publications which vendors will sell or give away on every conceivable aspect of data processing products, services, applications, management, business in general—anything you can think of relating to computers. Today, in fact, the DP industry publishes more as a whole than any other industry in the world. The material and education is there; you have merely to use it when it is appropriate for your company. In well-run organizations, there is a continuous process of DP education going on because of its availability and also due to the constant changes in the industry.

## Salesmen as Sources of Concern

First, management will be nervous about contract negotiations. Vendors do this for a living, managers usually do not. In a prior chapter on contracts we considered how to neutralize this problem: simply involve your company lawyer and read contracts before signing them. There is nothing wrong with discussing the implications of a contractual arrangement with a vendor but if you do not understand its terms or significance to the operations then back off, think, study, get some advice, and use some common sense. Think of contractual obligations and their options much like you would various financial strategies. Weigh the pluses and minuses and select the way most advantageous to you. If the marketing person is good at his or her job and is ethical, that individual will have hit upon the same option as you because this is the fastest way to close a sale.

Vendor support and commitments offer a second source of potential problems. Again a great deal depends on your personal experience with the individual and the vendor's company. Yet sweet talk with no backup means empty promises. If you have prior experience with a vendor and understand what support can be offered then oral discussions may often well suffice. If the vendor is a new company or individual you will want to give serious thought to obtaining in writing specific statements of support. This is absolutely essential when establishing how much a vendor will do to support his software and to establish the quality of that support. Reputable vendors will have no problem in meeting these requests. But there are many new companies selling very specific products in the marketplace today and if you are to buy their wares without appreciating what is behind them trouble may lie ahead. Therefore, use your judgment about support and when in doubt obtain the commitment in writing.

Third, some managers will talk about pressure salesmanship. They may describe the vendor trying to make his numbers for the month practically promising the moon or arm-twisting to get an order. Unless there is a good business reason for you to order something immediately just say no. Is that so difficult? You bet it is. Therefore, if you feel uncomfortable then back off and think or obtain more information, or have the vendor send you a contract to study, or ask to see a reference account but satisfy yourself before committing. Many salesmen do not want to book an order that is bad business anyway, because someone will cancel it later. The point is, one can talk about salesmanship and its "tricks" but if a good business case is not built for a particular action and all reasonable objections (both technical and business) overcome, you should not agree to something. If you find that you are manipulated by a particular salesman the solution is simple—have someone else negotiate with the individual for you.

There is a cliché that goes something like this: "A glass of water is either half empty or half full." You either view an individual coming into your office as a potential ally with something useful for you or you see him as an enemy. The choice is yours. If the vendor is viewed as a source of information then you will be exposed to far more than if that person is only called in when you have something in mind. If treated as an enemy, that individual will not volunteer much information, or offer possibly useful suggestions, or do those little things which resolve small irritating problems within your company. And the two of you may overlook an application which can save your company a great deal of money. If treated as a resource, the person, being human, will react as other humans do in a positive manner. Common sense dictates that this is the usual case. What is amazing is how many managers dealing with vendors do not appreciate this simple fact. And so they miss so much in such cost control areas as new tax regulations regarding data processing developments, financial analyses, new cost-effective products, techniques, education, conventions, help with application design and justification. Remember, the vendor wants to make a dollar while you should want to run data processing better; working together conduces toward both objectives.

## TECHNICIANS AND SUPPORT

In the course of studying the possibility of using computers in new ways, in maintaining old applications, and in servicing software and hardware products, companies deal with technicians and support personnel from vendors. Maintenance contracts and marketing efforts are usually the two reasons for such people coming into a company. Their services are important adjuncts to a DP organization's activities. Because of this they can become assets to a company even though they are not on the payroll.

### The Role of Technicians

From the point of view of cost control, consulting individuals who maintain computer hardware is important. They can comment on the advisability of replacing equipment which might work better, have less downtime (thus less decline in productivity), use smaller amounts of electricity and throw out lower amounts of BTUs. Often they can offer suggestions about the optimization of hardware which can have real dollar savings attached to them. For example, if a company has a heavily utilized computer, a technician might suggest that its communications features be offloaded to a telecommunications control unit thereby restoring to the computer a certain amount of available horsepower— enough perhaps to delay the acquisition of another more expensive computer for a while. Tricks of this sort are often fully understood only by hardware technicians. So they should be cultivated as human resources of relevant data on how best to utilize hardware.

Software support people play much the same role. They obviously serve as consultants and trouble shooters when problems occur that your technical people cannot solve. Moreover, they understand what other software productivity tools exist to help which will reduce the cost to you of maintaining or adding new applications. For instance, using a telecommunications monitor, a technical support specialist might suggest that an existing program product which measures the TP monitor's utilization would be particularly useful here. It is installed and the DP department finds, as a result of using the productivity tool, that by fine-tuning its telecommunications monitor less computer power is used and response time is improved on the terminals.

Another example: a technical support person from a vendor company might suggest that an online debug package renting for $150 a month be used to do maintenance on existing programs. If current maintenance activities cost $2000 a month (one programmer in this case) and the tool allows one to do this work in 30% less time than before, $800 worth of programming time is freed up for other work. Netted against the $150 expense, the benefit derived is worth easily $650 a month. Packages of this kind are common and many varieties exist which often only a technical individual from a vendor's organization might fully understand and be able to relate to your organization.

Some vendors make available to their customers specialists on various types of applications and industries. Usually this vendor's customers will not be aware of who these individuals are and what they can do for them. Contact with various personnel of vendors (maintenance people, salesmen, etc.) often creates situations where the services of application or industry specialists can be brought in to help you. Typically they can help install a specific program product, advise on the quickest and most useful way to design a particular package, or play the role of consultants in defining a company's problems and possible data processing solutions. These people, although they work for vendors trying to sell products, usually view their services more from a consultative rather than a marketing viewpoint and thus will often come up with perspectives different from those of marketing people. Industry specialists can save you hundreds of thousands of dollars yearly no matter whom they work for but you have to be willing to consult with them.

## Technicians as Consultants

There are several general areas where technical people from a vendor can make significant contributions simply because they understand what other companies are doing (having helped them) and since they are aware of the latest technologies within their own organization's product line. The first useful area is in teleprocessing. With all kinds of new terminals and software appearing on the market, it becomes difficult to construct efficient networks and determine optimal line and equipment utilization and thereby control costs. Many vendors in this part of the DP marketplace can help you do these things with the aid of teleprocessing specialists. They will show you how to simulate networks, put together configurations, do line cost analyses, and evaluate the impact of software on users and teleprocessing. As the whole area of teleprocessing consumes a higher percentage of a data processing budget, these services become more important. Such guidance is worth billions of dollars within the American economy while down at your company's level at least tens of thousands of dollars in savings over just a few years.

A second area in which skilled personnel can be useful is in application design. A company that has batch processing and decides to go to online systems, for example, would benefit enormously from such individuals. The savings in using their advice about screen layouts, number of terminals and printers, and functions to be written within applications all mean thousands of dollars in savings. These consultations are usually easier to get to if you happen to be using software products of the technician's company. Therefore, when considering what products to use, remember that access to such individuals is worth a great deal to you in avoiding costly mistakes. So factor that availability of talent into your justification of one product against another. You will be surprised how many software packages then fall by the wayside because there is little consulting support behind them. In most cases, this is reflected in the price of the package. If it is more expensive there is probably a good reason for that and the cause is usually that there are people behind it to guide you in the development of new applications and the optimal use of the software in question.

A third area of help lies in the application study. Some vendors, in searching for new uses of computers within your company, will offer to help do surveys to justify additional applications. In the course of this work they can do two things. First, they can identify business problems and areas of justification for more computerized work which managers within a company were not aware of before. Second, they can export defenses of DP to other departments and give managers in various sectors of a company an understanding of the enormous effort data processing departments must go through to provide services. The political benefits of such a service are obvious. More important, users become educated as to what they must contribute in order to develop a cost-effective application—and to deliver it on time. As was emphasized in Chapter 2, without user involvement an application stands little chance of success, with the attendant enormous cost to the company.

On the negative side, as with any individual coming into your organization from outside, the technician may not always be fully aware of the intricate problems involved in attacking a situation. Moreover, he does not bear ultimate responsibility for what they suggest. And he does not spend as much time within the company as do your managers and users of data processing. Therefore, there are many times when the comments of a technical person must be treated carefully, netting them against what you perceive to be the realities of a situation. What these outside people do have, however, is the advantage of comparing your circumstances to those identified in other companies. This fact alone should give you courage to realize that your problems are not totally unique and that in one way or another they have been met and conquered by others.

## CONSULTANTS AND ADVICE

There are a number of good reasons why consultants are brought into a company. Consultants come in because they have specific expertise in a problem area. They may be hired because the company has no personnel resources to apply to a specific concern. They might be brought in to do a job for which management does not want to hire permanent people who would then represent a continuing overhead. And often consultants are introduced for political reasons to support the views of one faction over another. It is strange how people react to a consultant. If a manager within a company says to his boss that he has to spend $10,000 in a certain way there might be resistance. But bring in a consultant, pay him $5000 to say the same thing, and the chances are greater that management will spend the $10,000 the way their own manager originally suggested.

You enjoy the same benefits from a consultant as with a vendor's technical people when it comes to data processing. The difference is that most consulting firms do not owe an allegiance to a particular computer vendor. Sometimes, however, a consultant leans in the direction of favoring one so you should identify that characteristic in your consultant if it is there. As a rule, consultants are motivated differently than a DP vendor. Some are evaluated by their management by the number of dollars they save you each month your company uses the consultant's services. Others are judged by the length of time they "consult" and thus can bill you for their services. Yet others are brought in to do a specific job and thus are motivated to get it done and leave. Thus the first rule in working with consultants is to develop an understanding of what their motives are just as you would with a vendor.

## How to Pick and Use Consultants

The quality of consultants varies enormously since there are so many. Some specialize in auditing, others in application areas, still others in computers. They work by industry, by size of firms, or on any project. They vary thus in services provided and costs charged. So the question comes up how to pick a consultant. There are a number of proven ways companies do this. They check with other firms in their own industry group, with managers in their own company, with vendors of computer equipment and software, read advertisements in trade journals, and even consult previously used consultants.

Your objective should be to obtain the names of several consultants before selecting one. Then define the job you wish them to do in detail and ask for bids on getting the work done. Determine what costs will be and specifically what services are to be offered for those fees. Check their credit rating (a D & B report is enough) and some references. When in doubt, do business with a large consulting firm because this reduces the odds of working with an irresponsible organization. However, keep in mind that many small consulting firms can be quite inexpensive and excellent since they specialize in fewer areas and you do not pay for a fancy well-established name. Set up time frames for completing the work involved otherwise the consultant will begin to look like a permanent and expensive addition to your staff.

By doing these few things you will be able to hold down the costs of consulting. Now the next problem is to overcome a certain amount of hostility toward the consultant. Typically a departmental head will view such an individual as a threat coming in to expose all the problems and not to provide either a defense of the department or really useful solutions like extra people to get daily work done. Personnel have to spend time explaining how they do things and the consultant might never get the story right in the first place. Therefore, as with an application study for computers, management must say to lower-level personnel that the outsider is to be given time and attention, otherwise the company wastes a great deal of money on consultant's reports—dollars which can easily run into the hundreds of thousands—for something less than really useful.

If there is little confidence in the consultant's ability or willingness to protect politically sensitive data or competitive advantages, drop the consultant immediately. Get out of the contract. You will gain little advantage from keeping a consultant within your company doing risky intelligence gathering.

Once you commit to a consultant, however, make everyone in the company aware of his or her mission. Let the consultant know about the delicate, subtle factors involved in a problem as well as the obvious elements. This way a consultant can compare your situation to those seen in prior experiences and truly come closer to finding a solution to a problem than you can. After all, if you are going to spend a great deal of money, you might as well get a good return on it.

Consultants within the data processing environment have another relationship that you should be aware of when balancing them against vendors and internal DP staffs. Data processing managers and vendors are wary of consultants in general. There are occasional exceptions to this statement but not many. They are cautious because they never know what the consultant in the end will recommend to upper management. Seemingly innocent suggestions might become complex disruptive programs, particularly if mandated by executives who do not understand data processing. Therefore a common tactic is to cut the consultant off, destroy his credibility before final reports are generated, and even, in some cases, have the contract terminated early. Both DP managers and vendors are equally zealous in the use of this tactic. On the other hand, many DP managers and vendors of data processing products will view the consultant as another avenue to reach upper management with their views. They see the consultant as an asset, an extension of their own functions.

As a manager of your company you want to encourage vendors and lower-level management to view the consultant as an asset. Having vendors and all relevant personnel meet with the consultant is a beneficial move so that the final advice that comes in takes into account all the key points of view within the company. The consultant is motivated to present to upper management probably what it wants to hear and so the research into what the final report must have requires discussions among many groups. This must include major vendors if they are intimately involved in your day-to-day operations. Any reasonably intelligent consultant will realize that a vendor is a vendor and account for that fact in whatever data is received from salesmen and technical support personnel. But consultants also recognize that vendors often are quite knowledgeable about a company and have relevant and useful perspectives on the problems being studied. As a manager, the issue of vendor–consultant–departmental relations is one of managing effectively a number of resources whether they are on your payroll or not.

An area in which consultants have increasingly been useful to management in judging the performance of data processing is in auditing. Many auditing firms that study the financial and accounting books of the company also are properly staffed to measure the quality of work done by data processing. They specifically can comment on data security measures, audit trails within applications, effective use of quality software, and the manner in which data is presented (reports, terminal screens, cards). With audit controls and data security and its ability to be reproduced accurately becoming important legal and business concerns, consultants are increasingly more useful within DP.

A good policy for a company to follow would be to audit the data processing environment periodically either through the use of internal auditors or by relying on auditors brought in for that purpose. With companies relying almost 100% on data processing for accounting and financial data alone (not to mention other areas such as inventory control and customer order servicing), the need to measure the quality and security of data increases. Not to audit could cost you millions of dollars in faulty information. Lost profit due to faulty billing programs, and excess inventory because of inaccurate applications, are two common areas which should constantly be addressed. An audit consultant can be extremely useful in helping to control problems such as these.

When a consultants final report is presented, quite often a rebuttal (if it is deemed appropriate) is not offered by managers within a company. The only time a rebuttal is given is if it is an audit of some form. Yet rebuttals should be encouraged. When a vendor presents a proposal, if there is opposition to it, rebuttals are allowed. If not permitted for consultant's reports the situation becomes ridiculous. Consultants write about the same things that auditors and vendors do and so top management should have reaction to reports. Consultants are not perfect, and thus may have missed a major point or incorrectly defined a situation or solution. So it is to management's advantage to allow alternative points of view to be presented. In this fashion various plans of actions can be identified and their costs and benefits quantified. After such an exercise decisions can be made and action taken.

# Glossary of Accounting
# and Financial Terms

The terms presented in this glossary are primarily for the use of data processing management and are words and phrases used throughout this book. While by no means a complete list of financial terms, it contains the most important ones related to the general areas of cost control, budgeting, and justification.

**Accrual:**  Acquisition of unrecorded equity, revenue, or expense.

**Amortization:**  Periodic reduction in the value of a capital asset or reduction of a debt, used, for example, with computers.

**Asset:**  Anything owned by a company that has value and can be measured in monetary terms. It always appears on a balance sheet.

269

**Balance Sheet:**   A financial statement of what the company is worth and what it owes. Both numbers ultimately have the same value hence the term balance sheet.

**Bottom Line:**   The last line on a financial statement that shows what an expense or profit was after all the accounting has taken place.

**Break-even:**   The point where the cost of a project or product equals exactly the benefits gained, typically a point in time after which benefits or reduced cost dominate.

**Capital:**   In this book used to mean money or debt that can be used for investment purposes over a period of time.

**Capital Expenditures:**   Expenditures for items that a company will use for more than one year, such as computers and buildings and even programming.

**Capitalize:**   The task of raising funds and accounting for them as capital expenditures (e.g., computers and buildings) that will be amortized.

**Carrying Cost:**   The cost of capital, usually interest paid on a loan and the administrative expense of doing the necessary accounting.

**Depreciation:**   The annual reduction in the value of a capital item, charging it to expenses for the number of years that it has a useful life to the company. Various methods are used: the most common are straight-line, double-declining, and sum-of-the-years' digits.

**Discounted Cash Flow:**   A method of analyzing the value of money over time. Money is worth more now as a return on investment than it is later; thus accountants can establish the value of money at various points in the life of an investment. A comparison of investments would show which one returns the most purchasing power earliest.

**Double-Declining Balance Depreciation:**   A method of depreciation whereby the greatest amount of depreciation is taken early in the life of an asset. This is a popular form of depreciation for equipment which is expected to drop in value (computers for example) or for companies that need the greatest amount of depreciation now for tax reasons.

**Dunn and Bradstreet (D & B Reports):**   Oldest and highly respected firm providing credit ratings and analyses of a company's financial strength.

**Equity:**   The net worth of a company measured in monetary terms and includes all its possessions and earnings not given to the stockholders.

**Expense:**   Any cost that is charged to revenue during the period of time over which the revenue was made. For example, this years cost of doing business against this year's revenues is expensing.

**Factor:**   A banking measurement of the borrowing strength of a borrower. It determines the cost of a loan for a company and is based on a bank's assessment of the risk it has in lending your company money.

**Financial Statement:** One of a number of reports that defines the financial position of a company: earnings, debt, assets, and liabilities. Usually prepared quarterly and at least once each year.

**Income:** Another term for profit; the difference between cost and revenue.

**Internal Rate of Return (IRR):** A discount rate for present-value cash-flow analysis. It is a percentage that is used to measure the value of money over time saying what cash inflows have to be over time to give the company a certain percent return on the investment after taking into account taxation, cost of capital, etc.

**Investment Tax Credit (ITC):** It is a tax credit given to encourage a company to acquire new capital goods such as computers. You take a percent of the purchase price of the machine and deduct that amount from your tax bill providing you keep the equipment for a specified period of time. It is a major incentive for acquiring newly manufactured goods.

**Net Present Value (NPV):** The total amount of money coming in and going out as a result of an investment. Future sums are discounted in value and then represented in sums equal to the current value of money. This is done to show what the value of a particular investment would be over time. The discount rate is usually whatever the cost of capital is to the company.

**Overhead:** Also called **Burden,** it represents the fixed and variable costs of doing business, for example, salaries of permanent employees, maintenance charges on computer equipment.

**Payback:** Also know as **Payback Period,** is the amount of time necessary to recover an investment in some project. This time is measured in years and is a form of measuring the worthiness of an investment. In DP it is commonly used to determine if it is cheaper for $x$ number of years to lease or purchase an item and to determine at what point it would have become less expensive, for example, to have purchased from day one. Most companies establish what the maximum payback period can be for equipment expenditures.

**Present Value Factor:** A ratio that shows to what degree it is better to have a certain amount of cash today than later.

**Prime Rate:** The interest rate a bank charges its best customers for loans. Best is meant to be the safest credit risks.

**Principal:** The money being borrowed. You then add interest to arrive at the total amount that has to be paid back.

**Rate of Return:** A form of ROI, it is a percentage of an investment that a company recovers over a certain period of time, typically measured in units of a year.

**Return on Investment (ROI):** The income from an investment during a given period of time. Although various formulas exist for determining ROI, they all fundamentally divide the average annual income by the average or total investment in the project. The result is expressed as a percent and even with fixed money amounts. Most companies have a formula they use and a minimum ROI (also known as a **Hurdle Rate**) that must be achieved to be considered as a candidate for investment. This allows management to measure a DP investment's quality against, for example, a proposed manufacturing investment.

**Salvage Value:** The value of an investment that is recoverable at the end of its life. For example, if you sell your old computer for 10% of its original purchase price 7 years from now, that 10% of value (money you got for selling the box) is the salvage value.

**Straight-Line Depreciation:** A depreciation method that depreciates the value of an investment the same amount each year for the life of the project. Typically not used with computers since their market value declines faster than straight-line would show but is used for land and buildings whose market value may increase over the years.

**Sum-of-the-Years' Digits Depreciation:** Another method of depreciation of an asset in which the greatest amount of depreciation is done early in the life of the asset.

**Working Capital:** The amount of money a company has to invest in capital expenditures, such as computers. It can also mean cash available to meet operating expenses.

**Yield:** This is the return on an investment expressed in annual terms.

# Glossary
# of Data Processing Terms

The terms presented in this glossary are primarily for the use of nondata processing management and are words and phrases used throughout this book. While by no means a complete list of data processing terms, they are the most important ones related to the subject of this book.

**Analyst:**   A DP specialist who defines problems and their solutions in terms that will allow programmers to write programs to solve them.

**Application:**   A particular use of the computer, such as for order entry. It can also refer to a set of computer programs that make up a particular use of a computer.

**Batch Processing:**   Processing of data in groups or in a serial fashion according to some prearranged schedule. Usually one set of programs is run before another set is executed. This was the way computing was done before the development of real-time online systems.

**Byte:** A form of saying a character—numerical, letter, or symbol—in machine-readable form. DP personnel measure the size of records by bytes instead of number of characters.

**Code:** Programs, or lines of computer language within a program.

**Computer:** A machine that can process, analyze, and control data in a manner defined by programs.

**Conversion:** The process of changing from one method of processing data to another. This usually will involve changing languages or variations in programming languages and the set of programs that runs a computer (operating systems). This is typically a major and costly effort that periodically is done to take advantage of developments in programming technology.

**Core:** Another word for computer memory; that is, the portion of a computer where the data is brought for processing. Think of it like a football field where the various players play out their game.

**CPU:** Another name for computer, it is where all the processing of data takes place. It includes the memory and the machinery to process data.

**CRT:** Cathode ray tube, just another name for the terminal that looks like a television set with a typewriter in front of it. It is the most commonly used terminal for online data processing.

**DASD:** Direct access storage devices for storage of data. Data is stored on cards, tape, or disk (much like on phonograph records in stacks). It is the most commonly used device for online systems because data can be reached directly without having to read all the data before the desired one as in tape.

**Data Base:** A set of data usually separate and apart from programs that thus can be shared by a number of applications. Think of data in a data base as the settlers in a circle of wagons and the application code as the Indians coming at them from all directions.

**Flowchart:** A set of diagrams that illustrates the flow of a program's logic from one step through another. It is drawn up by an analyst prior to a programmer writing programs.

**Generation:** Each wave of new technological developments in data processing are called generations. The terms used are first, second, third, fourth, etc., generation to refer to specific levels of development or evolution in, for example, computers.

**Host Computer:** The main computer to which data cames from remote locations for processing and which drives a teleprocessing network by controlling it.

**Input/Output:** Also called I/O; refers to those devices that either accept data to go into the computer or spit it out (a printer for example).

**Keypunch:** As a verb, it is the process of entering data into a computer system by an individual; as a noun it is a device for punching holes in computer cards with data that can then be read by an input device (reader) for the computer.

**Mainframe:** Another way of calling a computer a computer.

**Mass Storage:** A device that allows for the storage of large quantities of data.

**Modem:** Little devices at either end of a telephone line that control and even out the flow of data from one end to the other.

**Operating System:** A collection of programs that controls the execution of programs written by a DP department for its computer. Think of it as a traffic policeman in a computer.

**Partition:** A section of a computer that has a set of programs in it.

**Peripheral Equipment:** Machines which are directly connected to a computer by way of cables. They include input/output devices such as card readers and printers, and storage units such as disk drives and tape drives. It may also include equipment relevant but not attached to the computer, such as keypunch machines.

**Process:** The act of using a program in a computer and running data through the program.

**Program:** A collection of commands specifying to the computer what to do. It is often called a routine.

**Programmer:** A person who writes programs or sets of instructions that the computer will understand.

**Real Time:** Processing almost instantaneously at the command of a user at a terminal. Real time is also like having a conversation with a computer at a terminal.

**Remote Job Entry (RJE):** The submission of work to a computer from a distant point, like another city, through a terminal and a telephone line.

**Resource:** Aggregate of hardware, software, and personnel that defines the capabilities of a system. Something your data processing people always complain they never have enough of.

**SNA:** Abbreviation for systems network architecture which is a collection of standards, discipline, products, and programs to control teleprocessing networks.

**Structured Programming:** A method of organizing programs that is based on the idea of breaking pieces of programs into modules collected together in hierarchies with the most important being written first.

**System:** A collection of machines, programs, and equipment and methods of running a data processing shop or department. It usually refers to a set of machines and programs.

**System Programmer:** The individual who installs and maintains the set of programs that runs a computer. This is also a person who will design applications and might even write some of the programs for them.

**Telecommunications Network:** Also called TP network, it is made up of telephone lines, terminals, and control units.

**Terminal:** A device from which data is either entered or received by a person. These can include CRTs or hardcopy devices (like typewriters) connected to a computer system by cables or telephone lines.

**Turnaround Time:** The period of time from when you asked data processing to run a program (job) for you and the time you get it back completed. The reduction of turnaround time through online systems has always been a classic source of cost justification for real-time systems since it eliminates people waiting around for computer results before continuing their work.

# Select Bibliography

In order to keep up with current publications and trends within the data processing industry, periodical literature is the easiest to consult. The leading publications are *Datapro* literature, *Infosystems, Datamation,* and *Computer World* which last is a weekly newspaper. The other source would be various publications produced by DP vendors.

## Chapter 1: Computer Technology

Davis, John J. "Economic Effects on DP Departments," *Data Management,* 14, No. 10 (October, 1976): 41–43.

Diebold Research Program. *Trends in Systems Software: 1980, 1985, 1990.* New York: Diebold Inc., 1975.

Dolotta, T. A. et al. *Data Processing in 1980–1985. A Study of Potential Limitations to Progress.* New York: John Wiley & Sons, 1976.

## Chapter 2: Project Planning and Data Processing

Ditri, Arnold E., John C. Shaw, and William Atkins. *Managing the EDP Function.* New York: McGraw Hill, 1971.

Gildersleeve, T. R. *Data Processing Project Management.* Princeton, N.J.: Van Nos Reinhold, 1974.

Rubin, Martin L., ed. "Data Processing Administration." *Handbook of Data Processing Management,* vol. 6, pp. 387–432. Princeton, N.J.: Van Nos Reinhold, 1971.

Soden, John V. and George M. Crandell, Jr. "Practical Guidelines for EDP Long-Range Planning." In AFIPS *Conference Proceedings: 1975 National Computer Conference,* vol. 44:675–79. Montvale, N.J., 1975.

## Chapter 3: Application Justification

Gorry, G. Anthony, and Michael S. Scott Morton, "A Framework for Management Information Systems." *Sloan Management Review,* 13 No. 1 (Fall, 1971): 55–70.

Krauss, Leonard. *Administering and Controlling the Company Data Processing Function.* Englewood Cliffs, N.J.: Prentice-Hall, Inc., 1969.

Metzger, Philip W. *Managing a Programming Project.* Englewood Cliffs, N.J.: Prentice-Hall, Inc., 1973.

Prentice-Hall Editorial Staff. *Handbook of Successful Operating Systems and Procedures, with Forms.* Englewood Cliffs, N.J.: Prentice-Hall, Inc., 1964.

Seth, Ray, et al. "Information Resource Management Cost Justification Methods." Guide International *Proceedings 45* vol. 1, Atlanta, Ga., October 30–November 4, 1977: 183–196.

## Chapter 4: Hardware Justification

Financial Accounting Standards Board. *Statement of Financial Accounting Standards No. 13, Accounting for Leases, November, 1976.* Stamford, Conn., 1976.

First Chicago Leasing Corporation. *Leveraged Leasing.* Chicago, 1973.

Gravitt, Charles A. "The Truth About Investment Tax Credit." *Computer Decisions* (July, 1978): 44–48.

Joslin, Edward O. *Computer Selection: An Augmented Edition.* Fairfax Station, Va.: The Author, 1977.

Roenfeldt, Rodney L., and Robert A. Fleck, Jr. "How Much Does a Computer Really Cost?" *Computer Decisions* (November, 1976): 77–78.


## Chapter 5: Contracts

Bigelow, Robert B. "Contract Caveats." *Datamation,* **16** (September 15, 1970): 41–44.

Coffin, Royce A. *The Negotiator.* New York: American Management, 1973.

Data Processing Management Association. Management Reference Series, No. 1 *Understanding Computer Contracts.* Park Ridge, Ill., 1974.

Freed, Roy N. "Computers and the Work of Lawyers." *Case and Comment,* No. 76 (July–August, 1971): 46–50.

Technical Staff of Auerbach Corporation. "Computer Rental Contracts and Proposals." Philadelphia: Auerbach Corporation and Auerbach Info. Inc., 1967.


## Chapter 6: Service Bureaus and Facilities Management

Avedon, Don M. "Selecting a Service Bureau." *The Journal of Micrographics,* **10** No. 1 (September–October, 1976): 3–8.

Ruder, Brian, et al. *Data Processing Audit Practices Report Systems Auditability and Control Study. Prepared for the Institute of Internal Auditors, Inc.,* Altamonte Springs, Fla., 1977.

Russell, Susan H., et al. *Data Processing Control Practices Report Systems Auditability and Control Study. Prepared for the Institute of Internal Auditors, Inc.,* Altamonte Springs, Fla., 1977.


## Chapter 7: Data Processing Budgets and Control

Bahr, D. "Capacity Planning for EDP Systems." In *Proceedings SEAS Anniversary Meeting 1973, Leuven, Belgium, 11–14 September 1973,* pp. 303–12.

Bernard, Dan, et al. *Charging for Computer Services. Principles and Guidelines.* New York: PBI Books, 1977.

Gladney, H. M., et al. "Computer Installation Accounting." *IBM Systems Journal,* No. 4 (1975): 314–39.

Hand, A. B., and William L. Rives. "Constructing a Data Processing Cost Accounting System." *Magazine of Bank Administration* (April, 1974): 34–44.

IBM Corporation. *Managing the Data Processing Organization.* Lidingö, Sweden, 1976.

Martin, Donald D. "Data Processing Managers Need to Know Accounting." *Data Management* (Park Ridge, Ill.), **13** No. 11 (November, 1975): 26–28.

Nolan, Richard L. *Management Accounting and Control of Data Processing.* National Association of Accountants, June 1977.

Norton, David P. and Kenneth G. Rau, *A Guide to EDP Performance Management.* Wellesley, Mass.: Q. E. D. Information Sciences, 1978.

Smidt, S. "The Use of Hard and Soft Money Budgets and Prices to Limit Demand for a Centralized Computer Facility." *Proceedings AFIPS Fall Joint Computer Conference, 1968:* 499–509.

Statland, N., et al. "Guidelines for Cost Accounting Practices for Data Processing." *Data Base,* **8** No. 3 (Winter, 1977), supplement.

Wuchina, Stephen W. "Application of Industrial Engineering Techniques to the EFP Center." In *Proceedings of the 22nd Annual Conference, The American Institute of Industrial Engineers, Boston, Mass., May 12-15, 1971:* 67–80.

## Chapter 8: Vendors and Consultants

There is no adequate literature as of this writing on the subject of vendor-consultant relations with their customers. On occasion trade publications carry articles on the subject.

One final note: items listed under one chapter heading often apply just as well under another. Titles were not listed more than once; therefore, if you are looking for additional material on a subject, consult various chapter bibliographies.

# Index